T0277662

BEDE AND THE THEORY OF EVERYTHING

Covering one of the most fascinating yet misunderstood periods in history, the MEDIEVAL LIVES series presents medieval people, concepts and events, drawing on political and social history, philosophy, material culture (art, architecture and archaeology) and the history of science. These books are global and wide-ranging in scope, encompassing both Western and non-Western subjects, and span the fifth to the fifteenth centuries, tracing significant developments from the collapse of the Roman Empire onwards.

SERIES EDITOR: Deirdre Jackson

Albertus Magnus and the World of Nature *Irven M. Resnick and Kenneth F. Kitchell Jr*

Alle Thyng Hath Tyme: Time and Medieval Life *Gillian Adler and Paul Strohm*

Andrey Rublev: The Artist and His World *Robin Milner-Gulland*

The Art of Anatomy in Medieval Europe *Taylor McCall*

Bede and the Theory of Everything *Michelle P. Brown*

Christine de Pizan: Life, Work, Legacy *Charlotte Cooper-Davis*

Francis of Assisi: His Life, Vision and Companions *Michael F. Cusato*

Margery Kempe: A Mixed Life *Anthony Bale*

BEDE AND THE THEORY OF EVERYTHING

MICHELLE P. BROWN

REAKTION BOOKS

For Bede and in fond and grateful memory of Bedan friends, gone before

St Cuthbert, Benedict Biscop, Ceolfrith, Eadfrith

Gerald Bonner, Julian Brown, Malcolm Parkes, David Farmer, Paul Meyvaert, Jennifer O'Reilly, George Hardin Brown, Roger Norris and Rosemary Cramps

Published by Reaktion Books Ltd
Unit 32, Waterside
44–48 Wharf Road
London N1 7UX, UK

www.reaktionbooks.co.uk

First published 2023

Printed and bound in India by Replika Press Pvt. Ltd

A catalogue record for this book is available from the British Library

ISBN 978 1 78914 788 9

CONTENTS

When you read this book, and in pious recollection of that holy father, lift up your souls with ardour in aspiration for the heavenly kingdom, do not forget to entreat the Divine clemency in favour of my littleness, in as far as I may deserve both at present with singleness of mind to long for and hereafter in perfect happiness to behold the goodness of our Lord in the land of the living. But also, when I am defunct, pray ye for the redemption of my soul, for I was your friend and faithful servant.

BEDE, *Prose Life of St Cuthbert*, Preface

Introduction

'My chief delight has always been in study, teaching and writing': so wrote Bede (Baeda in Old English), an Anglo-Saxon who was born in northeast England in 672/3 and died there in 735, having lived as a priest and monk of the Northumbrian twin monastery of Wearmouth-Jarrow. He wrote those words in the autobiographical note with which he concluded his most famous work, the *Ecclesiastical History of the English People* (*Historia ecclesiastica gentis anglorum*),[1] which he completed in 731, according to the unified dating system from the birth of Christ which he established in popular use in the West. His life of service through scholarship earned him the title 'Venerable', for he was declared a Doctor of the Church in 1899 by Pope Leo XIII – a rare acknowledgement that these little islands on the edge of the then known world had produced a Church Father and one of the most influential thinkers of the post-Roman world. He is acknowledged as a saint in the Orthodox, Catholic and Anglican traditions, and his feast day originally fell on 26 May, the anniversary of his death in his monastic cell at Jarrow. Fittingly, in the year of his death it was also the feast of the Ascension, calculated to fall forty days after the moveable Easter date that Bede had worked so hard to establish.

Yet Bede was more than a religious figure and a historian. In my view, his reputation is so great because of his remarkably joined-up thinking and his ability to see the bigger picture, his studies embracing diverse areas in pursuit of a 'theory of everything' in which the arts, sciences and faith were integrated.

A theory of everything (TOE) is a theoretical framework that seeks to explain all known physical phenomena throughout the universe or multiverse. Researchers have searched for such a model ever since Albert Einstein's theory of relativity was advanced in the early twentieth century and since quantum mechanics began to be theorized. But so far quantum mechanics and relativity both fail when applied to each other's subject-matter, with an overarching theory of everything continuing to elude scientists. Some continue to pursue it through quantum gravity theory or string theory.

'I want to know how God created this world,' Einstein told a young physics student named Esther Salaman in 1925. 'I'm not interested in this or that phenomenon, in the spectrum of this or that element. I want to know His thoughts; the rest are just details.' In his *A Brief History of Time* (1988), physicist Stephen Hawking expressed his desire to help create a theory of everything, but later said, 'I'm now glad that our search for understanding will never come to an end and that we will always have the challenge of new discovery . . . Without it, we would stagnate.'[12]

Science was in its early stages in Bede's time, but he applied himself to explore the nature of things and their physicality, even penetrating something of the mystery of gravity. For him, however, time, human history, the workings of the human brain and heart and the inner life of the spirit were as important as materiality in understanding the nature of eternity and the mind of God. The how was one part of it, the why was another, and the reconciliation and unity of Creation and Creator was the ultimate conclusion. His theory of everything was as valid as those that are proposed today, even if the parameters of knowledge were more limited – Bede sought to expand them.

How did a seven-year-old boy who entered a newfangled monastery a mere generation after his people, the Anglo-Saxons of Northumbria, had begun the long process of conversion to Christianity, and who is known to have travelled only within a radius of some 130 kilometres (80 mi.) during the whole of his life, come to be the greatest Western scholar of the post-Roman world?

Bede was born on land (tradition favours Monkton as the site – the place name suggesting monastic ownership) belonging to the twin monastery of Sts Peter and Paul, comprising two monastic houses located at Monkwearmouth and Jarrow, strategically situated near the mouths of the rivers Tyne and Wear, which were founded by Benedict Biscop in 674 and 682 respectively. Bede tells us that when he was seven his kinsfolk entrusted him to the monastery to be educated and he remained there for the rest of his 62 years, becoming a monk, a deacon and a priest. He is thought to have visited the monastery of Lindisfarne on Holy Island, some 103 kilometres (64 mi.) further north on the Northumbrian coast, and other ecclesiastical centres in that prominent Anglo-Saxon kingdom, but ventured no further. Nonetheless, his guide to the holy sites of the Near East was still being used as a practical travel guide in the nineteenth century and by the time of his death he was already being acknowledged as a foremost intellectual and as a Church Father. The demand for copies of his works, notably his *Ecclesiastical History of the English People*, led to a publishing drive by the Wearmouth-Jarrow scriptorium and eventually earned him the popular sobriquet 'the father of English history'.

That we know any of this is in itself a tribute to Bede's rigour as a historian. His autobiographical details are given in the *Ecclesiastical History* v.24 and in a note at the end of the work that takes the form of a brief biography and bibliography, establishing the author's credentials, rather like a cv.[3] He also effectively invented footnotes and the practice of highlighting quotes from other authors.

The very system of dating from the incarnation of Christ (AD – 'anno domini', the year of the Lord) was popularized by Bede and it is largely thanks to him that we use the terms BC and AD, or BCE and CE.[4] The gargantuan computistical task of converting the various dating practices of his sources – imperial and papal indictions and the like – to create a unified chronology was enough to warrant his sobriquet 'the father of English history', but he also perceived cause and effect, the interconnectedness of things. Knowledge, during Bede's age, was very different to our own, but in the face of the losses of much classical learning and the limited nature of existing scientific and historical research, Bede sought rigorously to reconcile tradition and innovation and to test his sources. His studies also embraced diverse areas in pursuit of an understanding of the Cosmic Logos and the Creator's masterplan for Creation, as played out through the natural world and human history – the why as well as the how, the how as well as the why.

1 The coffin of St Cuthbert (Durham Cathedral), Lindisfarne, 698, carved with images of the Virgin and Child, the evangelists and their symbols and angels, which would have been painted, recalling early Christian parallels from Coptic Egypt.

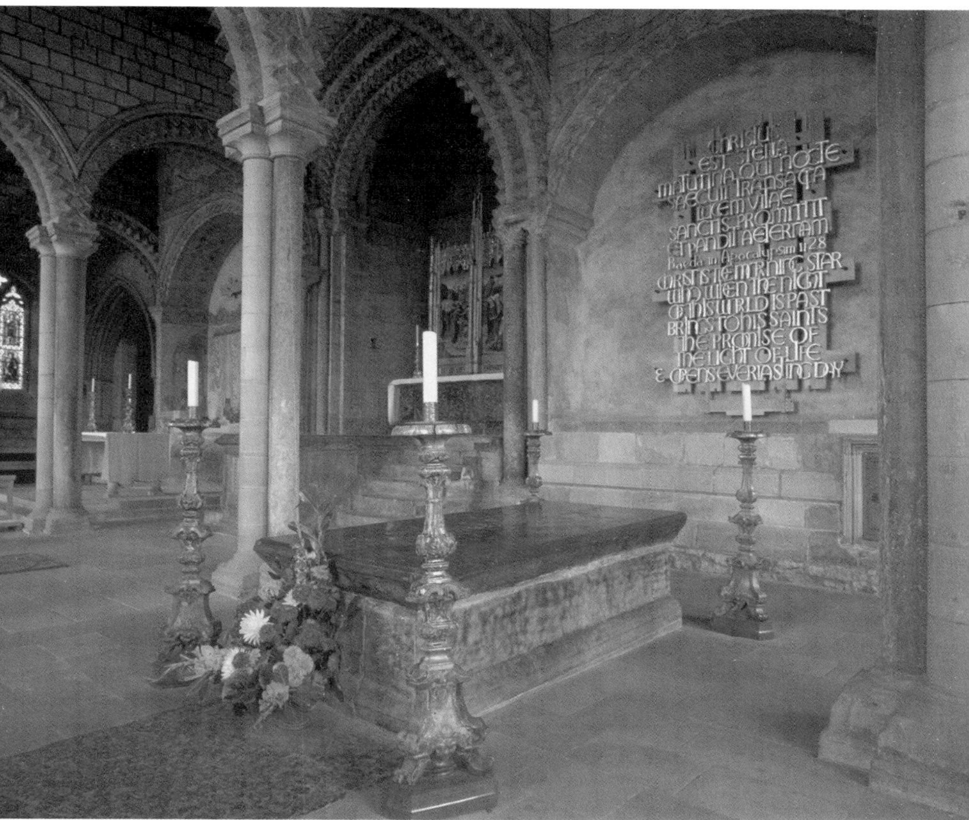

2 Bede's shrine in the Galilee Chapel at the West end of Durham Cathedral, where he has lain since 1370.

The *Ecclesiastical History* was only one of some 33 works that Bede lists and some forty works are securely attributed to him from a total of sixty that have been ascribed to him. His works of biblical exegesis are among the most nuanced, multivalent early Christian commentaries, siting his own people in a perpetual biblical landscape, while his *On the Holy Places* (*De locis sanctis*) extended his temporal vision eastwards. Within his own region, he struck up a relationship with Bishop Eadfrith that would lead to the construction of the cult of St Cuthbert (on whom he composed both a prose and a verse Life) and the making of the Lindisfarne Gospels.

Bede's own work as what he terms a 'scribe of Scripture', the Christian equivalent of the Jewish *sofer* (a priestly calling), would have led to his scholarly – and probably physical – contribution to the production of the great Ceolfrith Bibles, which perpetuated the publishing legacy of late antiquity via the models of Jerome, Cassiodorus and the Vivarium. This would in turn shape the Carolingian biblical publishing endeavour of Alcuin of York and the Tours scriptorium, resulting in an edition that would form the basis of the medieval university syllabus and which would feed into the creation of the first printed editions of the Bible.

Bede also made a major contribution to the study of science, to the extent that its various branches were then known. He wrote *On the Nature of Things*, building on the encyclopaedic natural history of Pliny and Isidore of Seville, and works such as *On Times* and *On the Reckoning of Time*. Bede knew the configuration of the solar system, even if, as was generally thought until Copernicus, he thought it all revolved around us rather than the Sun, and his work on lunar observation led him to think about the gravitational pull of the Moon and to construct the first tide-tables – a crucial contribution to a maritime people such as those on the Northumbrian coast. Couple all of this with a fine Latin literary style, a love of poetry and song (both of which he wrote on) and a pioneering attitude towards the written vernacular and you have not only the father of English history, a committed transmitter and liver of 'the Word', a creative scientific thinker and a deep-thinking exegete and hagiographer, but a pioneer of the English language and a rare authorial desktop publisher, physically penning his own compositions (a highly unusual act during Antiquity and much of the Middle Ages). He was also, as we shall see, something of a radical reformer, concerned by the abuse of power in both Church and State and an admirer and advocate of the service and asceticism of the desert fathers, especially as interpreted by Sts Aidan and Cuthbert at Lindisfarne.

The sobriquet 'the Venerable Bede', first used of him from the ninth century, was formalized in 1899. By the 780s Bede's relics were considered miracle-working by Alcuin. They were collected by York, Fulda and Glastonbury and in the mid-eleventh century were obtained from Jarrow by the acquisitive keeper of St Cuthbert's shrine at Durham, Alfred Westow, joining Cuthbert in his coffin. In 1370 they were translated to the Galilee Chapel in Durham Cathedral, where pilgrims were received and to which women visitors were restricted. There Bede lies still, doorkeeper of this symbolic focus of Northumbria's identity, just as his *Ecclesiastical History* serves as the portal to its origins.

ONE

Boyhood and Background

What do we know of Bede's family background and of the society of which they formed a part? The names 'Biscop' and 'Beda' both appear in a list of the kings of Lindsey from around 800, suggesting that Bede may have come from a noble family. Bede's name reflects the West Saxon Bīeda (Northumbrian Bǣda, Anglian Bēda),[1] an Anglo-Saxon short name formed on the root of *bēodan*, 'to bid, command'. The name also occurs in the Anglo-Saxon Chronicle, under the year 501, which identifies a Bieda as one of the sons of the Saxon founder of Portsmouth. The use of a 'king-worthy' name often indicates descent from that lineage, however distant. The *Liber vitae* of Durham Cathedral, the ninth-century benefactor's book of the Lindisfarne monastery, names two priests named Bede, one of whom is presumably ours. Some manuscripts of the Life of St Cuthbert, one of Bede's works, mention that Cuthbert's own priest was named Bede. Since Cuthbert died in 687, when our Bede was around fourteen, this priest, who was effectively Bishop Cuthbert's chaplain, may be the other one remembered in the *Liber vitae*. Perhaps Bede had some family connection to him or to Benedict Biscop, the founder of the Wearmouth-Jarrow monasteries.[2]

Bede's writings proclaim the nature of his educational background. He was steeped in the learning of the monastic schoolroom, as remodelled in late seventh-century England by

Archbishop Theodore of Tarsus (in Asia Minor) and Abbot Hadrian, a North African Berber, latterly from Naples. In the school that they established at Canterbury, where Biscop presided over St Augustine's Abbey for two years after their arrival, having accompanied them from Rome to Britain, Bede says that they taught Latin, Greek, theology, exegesis, computistics, astronomy, medicine, poetry and Gregorian chant; Aldhelm, one of their most famous pupils and an early English author, adds that he studied Roman law there too, under Abbot Hadrian.[3] Instruction by structured question-and-answer sessions and by testing and proofs would have joined the traditional learning by rote and memory-training exercises of the late Roman Empire.

In his autobiographical note Bede reveals that he was an Angle, born in Northumbria; his scholarly output and his writing agendas reveal, however, a deep-rooted respect for the earlier Irish learning and traditions of religious life – and social justice – that at its best it enshrined. Bede, like Northumbria (and the rest of early Anglo-Saxon England for that matter) was a mongrel product of mixed cultural influences – and was all the stronger for it.

A figure who featured in the religious and secular life of Anglo-Saxon England at this time was Wilfrid of York (c. 633–709/710), some of whose deeds Bede relates and with whose politics and methods he would come to find himself at odds. It is all too easy, in view of the controversies of Wilfrid, to forget that he too was an educator and that Ripon, where he served as one of its first abbots and which he subsequently aggrandized with impressive building projects, trained many key figures in the Northumbrian Church, including Bede's own beloved abbot at Wearmouth-Jarrow, Ceolfrith. Having himself started his religious career on Holy Island, Wilfrid obtained the community's permission to travel in Gaul and Italy, heading for Rome, where he conceived a profound desire to shape the English Church in its image. Unfortunately, he imported the politics of the papal curia – and some rather ruthless methods of achieving his aims – with it. The ousting of humbler prelates such as Chad from offices that he himself aspired to and the conversion of the Isle of Wight by the sword were not his finest moments, although he received many blows and setbacks in a career that began so spectacularly, with his eloquent defence of the universal Church winning the day at Whitby, and determinedly fought his way back. Both he and Chad are commemorated as saints for their achievements that helped to form a Church. Following Wilfrid's death, Stephen of Ripon (formerly known as Eddius Stephanus) wrote a Life of St Wilfrid and the crypt at Ripon became the focus of his cult. I have suggested that this may have contributed to the move to escalate the stature of the cult of St Cuthbert at Lindisfarne and to make the Lindisfarne Gospels. The major implications of all this for Bede will become apparent throughout much of this work. It is as well to encounter it now.

Like Biscop, Wilfrid was a Northumbrian nobleman. He liked fine living, kept a good table and travelled with a large retinue. (Ceolfrith also took eighty men with him to Rome in 716 and many would have been needed to help transport home the books, paintings and devotional objects that he obtained there.) He claimed to have been the first to introduce the Benedictine Rule to Britain and invested in extensive building projects at Ripon and Hexham, with their crypts based on the concept of the Holy Sepulchre (and physically, one suspects, on the early churches of Rome), and their displays of the relics of the saints and martyrs, images and sculptures (those at Hexham are particularly indebted to the classical sculpture that adorned Corbridge and other places in the frontier orbit of Hadrian's Wall). Work was underway on Ripon's crypt in 672 and at Hexham in 675. Biscop's first building project at Monkwearmouth in 674 was perhaps related to them.

When the new monastery at Ripon was founded by Alchfrith, king of Deira (the southern part of Northumbria, focused on York), Cuthbert became its guest master under Eata, but when Wilfrid became its abbot, Eata and Cuthbert returned to the monastery of Melrose, now in the Scottish borders. On Bishop Cuthbert's death in 687 the monastery at Lindisfarne was placed under Wilfrid's rule for a short time – a period that Bede can barely bring himself to speak of and which appears to have caused great dissension in the long term, to judge from the 'friendly fire', aimed both at the Lindisfarne community and at Bede, as a result of his support for it, elicited from Wilfrid's supporters after his death. Wilfrid may have been intent upon radically reforming or perhaps even closing the Irish foundation of Lindisfarne monastery on its Holy Island.

To return to the background of Bede and the twin monasteries (which were essentially one, but spread across two locations, like some modern university campuses) in which he spent his life, Monkwearmouth was founded by Benedict Biscop in 674 and Jarrow followed in 682; it is usually assumed that Bede's birthplace lay near the former in Sunderland (although some traditions favour nearby Monkton). Bede relates that his kinsmen, a term which has been taken by some to indicate that he may have been orphaned or that his parents may have seemed less personal to him by the time of writing, had entrusted him to abbots Biscop and Ceolfrith, successively, to be educated. Although we know nothing of his social background, we may assume that he was of free birth and that his kin were Christians who aspired to learning and to religious devotion and who were wealthy enough – and sufficiently blessed with other heirs – to be able to spare the boy. The practice of placing children in monasteries as oblates, to be given an education and either to remain in church life or to return with literate skills to secular life, was a relatively common practice in early Irish Christianity. The ancient Celtic practice of placing children in foster homes to consolidate the ties across kinship groups and tribes would have provided a familiar context for this in Britain. The children of the wealthy would often be raised by relatives or allies, while their parents would raise the offspring of others in return, forming an interlaced web of relationships. The Irish component in the conversion of the Germanic settlers of Northumbria, with many early monasteries such as Lindisfarne (founded in 635 as a daughter-house of Iona) having been founded as part of the Irish mission initially led by St Columba (who died in 597 on Iona, which he had founded in 563), may have led to the practice also becoming a feature of early English monasticism.

Whatever their motivation, in personal or logistical terms, the decision to place the boy Bede in a radical new monastic context, so different in many ways (not least its communal coenobitic Benedictine emphasis and its innovative grand masonry buildings, under the leadership of a prominent nobleman, Biscop) from the tutelage of the much-respected eremitic Hiberno-Northumbrian tradition that centres such as Lindisfarne, Melrose, Whitby and Hartlepool represented, was a bold and telling choice on the part of his guardian kinsfolk. Topographical convenience may have been a factor, as he was locally born, but Monkwearmouth was only six years old and in the infancy of its reputation. Bede took to it with the alacrity of the most agile fish in the monastic pool of Cassiodorus' Vivarium (the Latin name of which means 'the place of the living things' or 'fishpond').

Being presented in this way, as an oblate, and studying in the monastic schoolroom did not necessarily mean that pupils would embrace religious life, but one can imagine the boy Bede's omnivorous love of knowledge and his delight in the regularity of the monastic life rendering him an eager novice. Bede relates the story of a little boy, Aesica, who was similarly placed at Barking Abbey and that of Ælfled, the daughter of King Oswy, who was dedicated to the religious life by her father before she was a year old. These stories may have had a particular resonance for Bede and it is poignant that he describes the boy's transfer of affection to a maternal nun who is even permitted to accompany him to heaven. His writings show that Bede considered children to possess innocence, wisdom and receptiveness. He himself seems to have felt a particular bond to Abbot Ceolfrith, to whose care he was entrusted at an early age:

> How a little boy, dying in the same monastery, called upon a virgin that was to follow him; and how another nun, at the point of leaving her body, saw some small part of the future glory.
>
> There was, in the same monastery, a boy, not above three years old, called Aesica; who, by reason of his tender age, was being brought up among the virgins dedicated to God, there to learn his lessons. This child being seized by the aforesaid pestilence, when his last hour was come, called three times upon one of the virgins consecrated to Christ, speaking to her by her own name, as if she had been present, Eadgyth! Eadgyth! Eadgyth! and thus ending his temporal life, entered into that which is eternal. The virgin, to whom he called, as he was dying, was immediately seized, where she was, with the same sickness, and departing this life the same day on which she had been summoned, followed him that called her into the heavenly kingdom.
>
> (*Ecclesiastical History*, IV.8)

Of Ælfled's dedication to God, Bede writes that before the Battle of Winwaed in 655 King Oswy vowed that, should he be granted victory against the pagans, he would give his baby daughter and parcels of land each capable of supporting ten families to the Church to found monasteries upon. These included

Hartlepool and Whitby (of which Ælfled later became abbess) and eventually also Monkwearmouth and Jarrow.

Bede spent the rest of his life at the unusual bilocational monastic foundation of Wearmouth-Jarrow (a shortened form, denoting their combined nature, with Monkwearmouth being the full title of the first of the foundations), devoting himself 'entirely to the study of Scripture', teaching and observing the Benedictine-style communal rule of monastic life and singing the offices daily. Bede moved at its opening to the newly established second house, Jarrow, and was entrusted to the care of its abbot, Ceolfrith, who, along with Benedict Biscop, exerted a formative influence upon him, which he later viewed fondly. He probably moved to Jarrow when he was nearly ten, when the building work commenced following Biscop's foundation in 682, or when the monastery was consecrated in 684 – an event recorded in the dedication inscription that survives there still and which Bede may have watched being carved, For the consecration occurred two years after the new monastery was first occupied, with building work continuing.

3 Ceolfrith's dedication inscription for St Paul's Church, Jarrow, 681, modelled upon Roman inscriptions.

Work on the first of Biscop's constructions, the church at Monkwearmouth dedicated to St Peter, may have begun in 674, but its story began in 653 when the young nobleman Biscop Baducing left Northumbria to visit the original St Peter's, in Rome. His travelling companion for part of the trip was a young man who would become the powerful and contentious Bishop Wilfrid of York. They were both as smitten with the early Christian culture they encountered there and in other ancient Roman cities they passed through as any English traveller undertaking the Grand Tour in the eighteenth century and conceived a desire to rebuild Rome in Northumbria. Biscop spent eleven years in monasteries in Italy and Gaul and joined the monastic community at Lérins, on an island lying off the southern coast of France, where he became a monk, taking the name Benedict. On his third visit to Rome, in 667, he was appointed as interpreter and guide to Theodore of Tarsus on his journey to England to become Archbishop of Canterbury. Upon his return, Biscop became abbot of St Peter's and St Paul's Abbey in Canterbury for a short time and would have been party to Theodore's programme of diocesan and parish organization. He would also have witnessed the start of Theodore's moves to ensure that the nascent English and neighbouring Celtic churches did not embrace the monothelete heresy that was causing such a rift in the Eastern churches and would have been privy to his plans to establish an important early Christian school of learning at Canterbury, which would help form the English scholars Bede and Aldhelm.

In 671 Biscop made a fourth trip to Rome to collect books, manuscripts, icons, panel paintings and relics. On his return, King Ecgfrith of Northumbria gave him land on which to found Monkwearmouth. Biscop made a fifth trip to Rome in 678–9 and another in the 680s. I have suggested elsewhere that the unusual twinning of the double foundation may have been intended as a symbolic statement of the conformity of the

English Church to the findings of the sixth Ecumenical Council held in Constantinople in 681 and the pre-council convened by Archbishop Theodore at Hatfield, just north of London, in 679.[4] They resolved the thorny question of how Christ could be both human and divine by proclaiming that he had two wills but that the human will was obedient to the divine will in accepting birth as a human and death on the Cross. Images of the Virgin and Child and the Crucifixion abound from this point onwards, not least in Anglo-Saxon England. The concept of two places with but one will, as Bede puts it, would have been a tangible representation and affirmation of this belief. Benedict Biscop died in 689; by 716 Wearmouth-Jarrow had six hundred monks and was one of the foremost centres of learning in the West – a truly remarkable achievement.

Bede would have met Biscop between 680, when the boy joined Monkwearmouth, and 682, when the abbot left for his final trip to Rome and Bede made ready to join his new foundation at Jarrow. He tells us that Biscop imported masons and glaziers from Gaul to build his monasteries 'more romanum', in the Roman technique of dressed masonry with glazed windows to keep out the winds and chilly drafts. This would have been an exciting new feature of the English landscape – like the first modernist skyscrapers. For all the rigours and constraints of monastic life, they would have represented a massive advance in standards of living, with their communal refectories, kitchens, dormitories, facilities for washing and ablutions, abbatial lodgings, separate areas for study and writing and for burial and, most importantly, for worship. They would also have had gardens, attached farms and areas where industrial and agricultural activities took place, with lay brothers, travellers and pilgrims making the site a busy, buzzy place. With their strategic riverine locations these monasteries would also have had busy quays where boats landed supplies, trade goods and visitors. The excavations of both sites directed by Rosemary Cramp from 1963 to 1978 and again in 1984 have given us an unprecedented insight into this influential monastic landscape.[5]

The west wall of the original main church's nave and the lower part of the tower and open porch still survive at St Peter's and show that the nave had two storeys, with the library and scriptorium perhaps occupying the upper floor. The foundations of other monastic remains revealed to the south of the church during excavation are marked by stone paving in the surrounding parkland. There was an underlying earlier Christian cemetery and some timber structures, palimpsested in stone by the Gaulish masons and glaziers imported by Biscop.

The Historic England listing for the site records that the early buildings on the site included a covered walkway with glass windows (like a partial cloister?), at least 32 metres (105 ft) long and running between the church and the southern edge of the site.[6] This separated two cemeteries, that to the east being for the monks and that to the west being for lay burials of men, women and children. A round-ended shrine 3.66 × 3.2 metres (12 × 10.4 ft) was found in the monastic cemetery, with a floor of fine white concrete sunk 1 metre below the level of the Saxon ground surface (about 2 metres below the present ground surface). This had a wattle and plaster superstructure which may have housed some of the relics of the saints brought back from the Continent, or perhaps those of Biscop and other key members of the Monkwearmouth community. The Anglo-Saxon monastery is also known to have included a chapel of St Mary, porticus chapels on the sides of the church nave, a refectory (dining area) and *cubiculae* (private chambers) for the abbot, prior and senior members of the community. It was abandoned after Viking raids around 874, with evidence of burning. However, around the year 1000 upper storeys were added to the tower and further burials occurred. In 1072 Alwine, Prior of Winchcombe, revived the

4 Porch with Style II beasts and baluster columns, St Peter's Church.

5 Nave and tower of St Peter's Church, Monkwearmouth (lower three levels, with later Anglo-Saxon upper stages), late 7th century, with the markers of excavated outlines of monastic buildings and cemeteries to the right of it.

monastery, which after 1083 continued as a cell of Durham Cathedral until the Dissolution of the Monasteries in 1540.

Biscop's use of Gaulish masons and glaziers to revive the art of masonry buildings in post-Roman Britain makes sense, for there was greater continuity in such matters on the Continent. However, there is a deeper significance that Bede is pointing to when he mentions this, which is that Solomon had employed gentile craftsmen – foreigners – in the building of the Temple.

For Bede, the parallels with the building of Monkwearmouth and Jarrow signalled the aspiration of the Anglo-Saxons as the new children of Israel, a chosen people recently arrived in the Promised Land, to emulate them in building the kingdom of God.[7]

Such verbal images and their visual counterparts played an important role in Bede's life, just as they had for his ancestors. The future of art in the West was determined when it was accorded the freedom to explore relationships between word and image, at a time when iconoclasm was rife in the Byzantine Empire and Judaism and Islam had proscribed the use of images in sacred texts on grounds of idolatry. This freedom was established by Bede's hero Pope Gregory the Great in a letter that he wrote around 600 to Bishop Serenus of Marseille, censuring his destruction of images on the basis that

> It is one thing to adore a picture, another to learn what is to be adored through the history told by the picture. What Scripture presents to readers, a picture presents to the gaze of the unlearned. For in it even the ignorant see what they ought to follow, in it the illiterate read.[8]

Biscop fully embraced this approach when adorning his monasteries with treasures from his six pilgrimages to Rome, for, as Bede relates,

> he brought back many holy pictures of the saints to adorn the church of St Peter he had built: a painting of the Mother of God, the Blessed Mary Ever-Virgin, and one of each of the twelve apostles which he fixed round the central arch on a wooden entablature reaching from wall to wall; pictures of incidents in the gospels with which he decorated the south wall, and scenes from St John's vision

of the apocalypse for the north wall. Thus all who entered the church, even those who could not read, were able, whichever way they looked, to contemplate the dear face of Christ and His saints, even if only in a picture, to put themselves more firmly in mind of the Lord's Incarnation and, as they saw the decisive moment of the Last Judgement before their very eyes be brought to examine their conscience with all due severity. (*Lives of the Abbots of Wearmouth and Jarrow*, ch. 6)

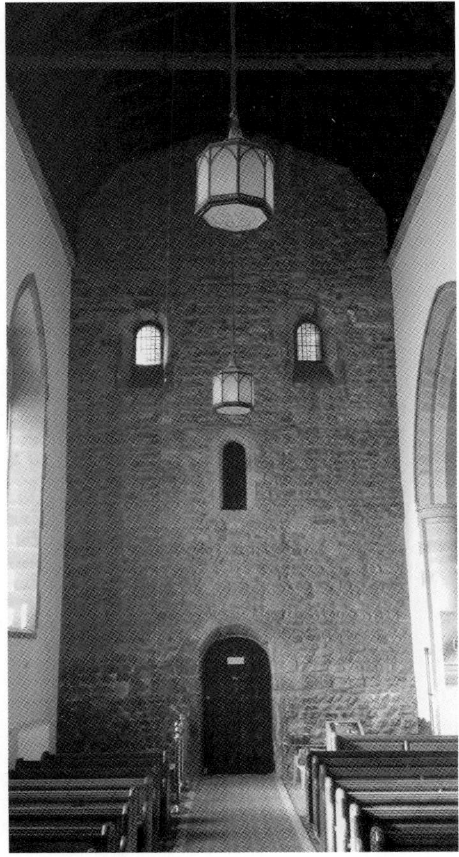

6 Two-storey nave, St Peter's Church, Monkwearmouth, late 7th century.

On his sixth journey to Rome, in the 680s, Biscop returned with

> a large supply of sacred books and no less a stock of sacred pictures than on previous journeys. He brought back paintings of the life of Our Lord for the chapel of the Holy Mother of God which he had built within the main monastery, setting them, as its crowning glory, all the way round the walls. His treasures included a set of pictures for the monastery and church of the blessed apostle Paul, consisting of scenes, very skillfully arranged, to show how the Old Testament foreshadowed the New. In one set, for instance, the picture of Isaac carrying the wood on which he was to be burnt as a sacrifice was placed immediately below that of Christ carrying the cross on which He was about to suffer. Similarly, the Son of Man up on the Cross was paired with the serpent raised up by Moses in the desert. (*Lives of the Abbots*, ch. 9)

The images adorning Biscop's churches therefore served as visual summaries of Scripture and of the relationship between Old and New Testaments, illustrated by means of didactic typology in which Old Testament figures were presented in teaching as precursors of New Testament episodes and of Christ – devices also employed by Bede. Recollections of such images may be preserved in the Christ in Majesty miniature in the Codex Amiatinus and in the Valenciennes Apocalypse (Bibliothèque municipale de Valenciennes, MS 99), a Carolingian copy made around 800 of a Wearmouth-Jarrow book that contains illustrations perhaps modelled on the panel paintings that Biscop brought back from Rome to hang upon the North wall of the nave of St Peter's Monkwearmouth.

Opposite: 7 Christ in Majesty at the Second Coming, from the Codex Amiatinus (Biblioteca Medicea Laurenziana, Florence, MS Amiato 1, f. 796v), Wearmouth-Jarrow, early 8th century.

Above: 8 Valenciennes Apocalypse, the opening of the Abyss, from a Carolingian copy of a Wearmouth-Jarrow manuscript, *c*. 800 (Bibliothèque municipale de Valenciennes, MS 99, f. 18r). These images may recall the panel paintings of the Apocalypse that were among those which Biscop and Ceolfrith brought back from Rome to hang on the walls of the churches at Monkwearmouth and Jarrow.

Bede's work was made possible by access to the greatest library of its day, assembled by Biscop and Ceolfrith. On a trip to Rome, circa 671, Bede writes of Biscop:

> He brought back a large number of books on all branches of sacred knowledge, some bought at a favourable price, others the gift of well-wishers. At Vienne on the journey home he picked up the books he had left there in the care of his friends. (Bede, *Lives of the Abbots*, ch. 4)[9]

Bede also writes that upon assuming the abbacy of both foundations in 689, Ceolfrith, who had accompanied Biscop once to Rome and was commissioned by him to found Jarrow:

> doubled the number of books in the libraries of both monasteries with an ardour equal to that which Benedict had shown in founding them. He added three copies of the new translation of the Bible to the one copy of the old translation which he had brought back from Rome. One of these he took with him as a present when he went back to Rome in his old age, and the other two he bequeathed to his monasteries. For eight hides of land by the River Fresca he exchanged with King Aldfrid, who was very learned in the scriptures, the magnificently worked copy of the Cosmographers which Benedict had bought in Rome. (Bede, *Lives of the Abbots*, ch. 15)[10]

This valuable riverside site would have supported at least eight families. By 716 Wearmouth-Jarrow owned 150 hides of land – worth nineteen such books in a library thought to have contained over three hundred volumes. The library was the community's most valuable financial, spiritual and intellectual asset. Ceolfrith's three Bibles, formed of some 1,550 calfskins each, represented a massive investment of resources, much of them undoubtedly donated.

The beauty of worship and ritual, and the sacred spaces in which they were performed, were important to Bede. As a boy, he would have observed the Frankish masons and glaziers imported by Biscop building Monkwearmouth and Jarrow and seen the stained glass and sculptures in classical Roman and early Christian style that remain there still. Classical balusters and the scrolling tendrils of the True Vine of the Eucharist (that is, Christ), inhabited by humans and other creatures, co-existed with the interlacing forms of Germanic animal art within splendid churches and monastic buildings, built 'more romanum' of finely dressed stone in an otherwise timber and mud world. Passages in Bede's *On the Reckoning of Time* afford us glimpses of his mind meandering in meditation while in church, leading him to contemplate optical illusions of light and shadow and their scientific and spiritual interpretation. His commentaries *On the Temple* and *On the Tabernacle*, and their plans in the Codex Amiatinus, also reveal the parallels he drew between the symbolic proportions, fittings and implements of the Holy of Holies of the Israelites and those of the churches of the Holy Land, of Rome – and of England.

Substantial parts of the Wearmouth-Jarrow churches remain standing (see illus. 4, 5, 6, 9, 10). Both sites have been excavated and although more remains to be discovered, we have a picture of gracious stone buildings – pairs of 'gemini' churches in an east–west alignment, a smaller one for the monks at the eastern end and a larger one to accommodate the people to the west, together with abbatial lodgings, communal refectories, cloisters and monks' cells. Bede's cell, described in the priest Cuthbert's account of his death, was inhabited by him alone and, although small, had an area railed off for worship. At Monkwearmouth the scriptorium was upstairs in the tall two-storey nave of the church,

9 Original stained glass depicting an evangelist holding a Gospel book, *c.* 681, St Paul's Church, Jarrow.

10 Latin inscription in Anglo-Saxon capitals, *c.* 681, St Paul's Church, Jarrow: ((INHO)) // ((CSI.- GVLA // R((- BOVI // TAR((E.- DITVR // MVN((DO- restored to IN HOC SINGULARI SIGNO VITA REDDITUR MUNDO ('In this unique sign life is restored to the world', recalling the Dream of the Rood, Constantine's triumph in the sign of the Cross and that of King Oswald at Heavenfield). There are also traces of a Roman inscription as this late 7th-century carving reuses Roman stones.

while at Jarrow it probably lay within the abbot's lodging. Both sites lay on tributaries of major rivers – Wear and Tyne – and were bustling harbours situated near earlier Roman sites, receiving and distributing trade goods and welcoming visitors from far and wide. The vellum upon which Bede's works were written was prepared on these riverbanks, amid a flurry of agricultural and industrial activities – metalworking, carpentry, stone-carving, pottery and the like. At the centre of all this physical activity, however, lay the *nemeton*, the sacred space of burial, study and worship, the community's pulsing spiritual heart.

The material culture of Bede's home therefore combines with archaeological, artistic and written sources to help us to reconstruct a resplendent image of his well-illuminated age. Among these sources shines brightly the beacon of Brother Bede's writings.

At Jarrow, evidence for writing in the form of a metal styli and a whetstone for sharpening pen-knives have been found in a building thought to have been used as the abbot's lodging, measuring 18 × 8 metres (60 × 26 ft), with a refectory block adjacent. It may have included a teaching and/or writing area, perhaps even Bede's schoolroom. The main room measures 13 × 6.5 metres (43 × 21 ft) and adjacent is a southern room of 3.3 × 4.3 metres (11 × 14 ft), with a wash basin, and a smaller northern room with an altar, measuring 3.3 × 2.1 metres (11 × 7 ft). It has been speculated that this latter room might be Bede's own

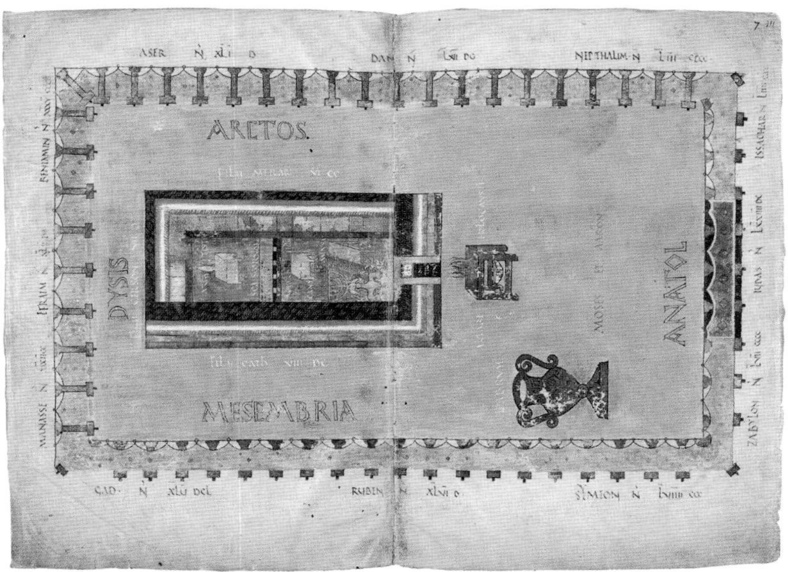

11 Plan of the Temple and Tabernacle in Jerusalem, probably based on a diagram by Cassiodorus, from the Codex Amiatinus (Biblioteca Medicea Laurenziana, Florence, MS Amiato 1, ff. 2v–3r), early 8th century.

12 The central part of the Anglo-Saxon monastery of Jarrow as it may have appeared in the 8th century, with the two churches in the background and the monks' communal building and the abbot's lodging/schoolroom in the mid-ground, model reconstruction by Rosemary Cramp.

cell, where he undertook his last works and sang his last praises, sitting on the floor with his head in the hands of his young assistant, Wilberht, in 735. Might this area also have been the schoolroom where one of Bede's own teachers, T(r)umberht, gave him a firm foundation of biblical and patristic learning, or where Ceolfrith taught him Scripture-study techniques? Monkwearmouth also had a suite of such rooms, thought to be reserved for the use of the abbot and senior personnel. Or was this the scriptorium, partnering with that at Monkwearmouth (although there it was housed upstairs in the main church, which at Jarrow has since been replaced by the later medieval nave of the current St Paul's Church)?

There were around three hundred monks at the twin monastery in Biscop's day and Ceolfrith doubled that number. The excavated remains seem quite limited to accommodate that many people, but more may yet be revealed. The Jarrow building would have been very small if it accommodated Jarrow's scriptorium needs, but it might make sense as teaching rooms. The young, oblates and novices, would be taught by a *magister*, but like women in double monasteries of the period, it is likely that the areas they habitually frequented were kept somewhat separate from those of the monks, who shared communal eating, washing and sleeping accommodations.

The young Bede would have learned to write initially with a pointed metal stylus, like those excavated at Jarrow and Whitby, on wax tablets. The end of the stylus would be expanded into a triangle, giving a broad surface with which to smooth out the wax when making corrections or preparing it for reuse. He would then have graduated to a quill pen and vellum (prepared calfskin, particularly good for pigment adherence and illuminated manuscripts) or parchment (sheep or goatskin). These materials were either given to abbeys as pious gifts or came from their own farming estates. They would be used to make the manuscripts written in the scriptoria and published wider afield. The quill would be the flight feather of a goose or swan, or perhaps that of a crow for tiny minuscule (lower-case) script such as that used for glosses or Irish portable pocket gospels.

The nearby Jarrow Slake, a marshy river estuary, like the River Wear at Monkwearmouth, would have provided a convenient place to make leather and vellum or parchment. Waterfowl from them would have supplied the flight feathers from their wings that were made into quill pens for writing manuscripts. Galls hanging from oak trees in nearby woods, formed as protection when an insect – the marble gall wasp – stung the tree to lay its eggs, would have been used to make the ink, along with carbon or iron salts to give the clear gall its colour. Woad, grown in the gardens perhaps, gave a blue dye used as a pigment (but, as an all-growth feeder, left land exhausted for two centuries after growing in it – so perhaps the garden was not the place for it);

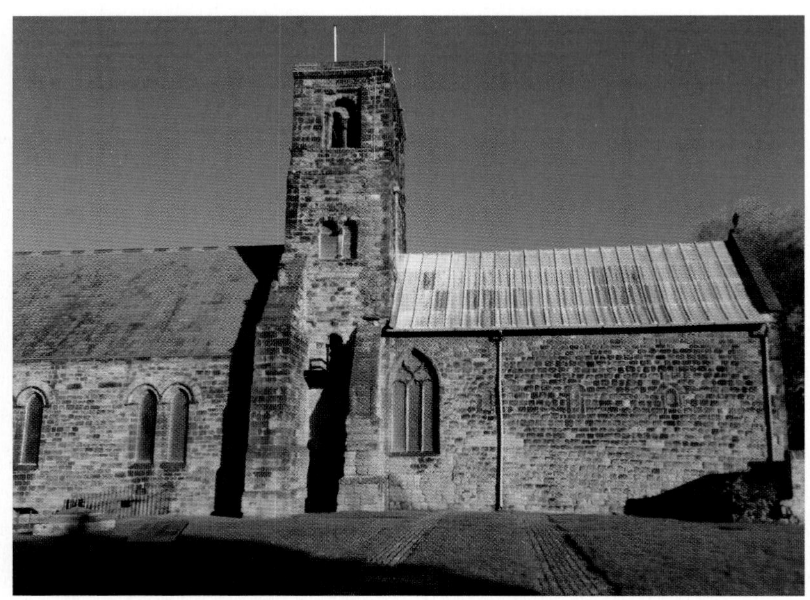

13 St Paul's Church, Jarrow, showing the easternmost of the two 7th-century churches (now the chancel), with a later Anglo-Saxon tower inserted and later medieval nave replacing the original western church. This photo was taken from the spot in the cell where Bede may have died, next to the schoolroom.

lumps of copper were suspended over cups of vinegar or wine to form a green corrosion which, when scraped off and mixed in a shell with beaten egg white (glair or *clarea*) from the monastic hens gave a green pigment, or alternatively, green malachite and blue azurite were extracted from ores; yellow pigment was made from trisulphide of arsenic (a by-product of Cornish tin mining) or from earth-based yellow ochre; black was made from soot; white from ground shell chalk or white lead, which when toasted also yielded a yellow and an orange/red; cinnabar (mercury-based) from Iberia gave an exotic red; organic purples could be extracted from lichen or turnsole (*Chrozophora tinctoria*); crushed insects, kermes, gave a bright fuschia pink. Lead, perhaps mined in Weardale, could also be used as an alloy in making the pointed metal styli for preliminary or pragmatic writing and for drawing on wax tablets, ruling writing lines and pricking holes to be used as guides in the membrane pages of books – the use of one such in the laying out of the Lindisfarne Gospels led its maker to go a step further and invent the lead-point, the forerunner of the lead pencil. Oak or elm trees provided the wood for said tablets and for binding boards for books. Mead from the monastery's bees sustained the scribes and illuminators, as well as helping to form gum.

The rivers would have brought goods, including books, from far afield, as would the network of Roman roads that had served the military and trading network of this important border area. The eastern end of Hadrian's Wall terminated a mere 2 kilometres (1¼ mi.) away from Jarrow at Wallsend (Segedunum fort) on the opposite, northern bank of the River Tyne. The monumental sculpture and inscriptions of Roman Britain would have been visible still in places and served as a source of inspiration, along with more recent imports from Rome itself, Gaul, Iberia and the East, coupled with the rich cultural traditions of the peoples of northwest Europe.

The dressed stone, glazed and weatherproof edifices, with their militaristic communal arrangement suited to the style of coenobitic monasticism advocated by St Martin of Tours and St Benedict and revived by Benedict Biscop and Ceolfrith, with Archbishop Theodore's encouragement, were very different from those of the monasteries established in the 'Celtic' tradition of figures such as St Columba.[11] These tended to consist of a circular enclosure (known as a rath in Ireland and Scotland and as a llan or lan in Wales, Cornwall and Brittany), or inner and outer enclosures, surrounded by earthen or stone wall(s), perhaps surmounted by wooden stockades. The inner rath was the *nemeton*, the sacred space housing the church/oratory chapel, monks' or nuns' cells in the form of individual huts and a burial ground. The outer rath housed the huts that accommodated non-monastic laity and visitors and any associated industrial, agricultural and domestic activities. There might be crosses demarcating parts of the enclosure, as well as gravemarkers. Bede describes their timber construction as 'more scottorum' (in the manner of the Irish/Scotti). In areas where wood was scarce it was replaced by drystone walls with corbelled beehive-shaped huts and perhaps a rectangular church or one shaped like an upturned corbelled stone boat (a *curragh* or long hide-covered boat of the sort still used in the Aran Isles – the 'boat with no oars'). A fully preserved, if small, complete example intended as a hermitage is on the island of Inishmurray, Co. Sligo, off the coast of western Ireland.[12] This was a wilderness (Old Irish *diseart*) into which to retreat, a watery desert paralleling those frequented by the early desert fathers of the East. Larger monasteries, such as Glendalough, would have many such enclaves and might house over a thousand people.

Earlier Irish foundations in Northumbria would have been in this Irish tradition, arranged on the eremitic model of the Eastern desert fathers, in which individuals living the monastic life had their own accommodations for their spiritual and study life and came together for worship, working out of their hub to do the work of mission and ministry in the world and to work the little gardens that supported them, fish or gather resources. Some would also retreat to more isolated hermitages for times of spiritual testing and renewal. Such was the Lindisfarne of St Aidan, but by Bede's day it had been reordered along more 'Roman' lines, following Archbishop Theodore's visit, with stone churches capable of serving both the monastic community and the pilgrims who increasingly flocked to St Cuthbert's shrine.

In 678 Theodore, having visited Northumbria, decided to divide the huge diocese of York along the lines of its two ancient kingdoms, Bernicia in the north and Deira to the south (focusing on York). Eata, a pupil of St Aidan, became bishop of Hexham and when that was again divided into the two dioceses of Lindisfarne and Hexham he became the fifth bishop of Lindisfarne in 681. But when Cuthbert was asked to be bishop of Hexham and was unwilling to do so, Eata humbly transferred to Hexham and Cuthbert became Bishop of Lindisfarne instead from 685 until 687. He was appointed bishop by King Ecgfrith (who died in battle against the Picts, against Cuthbert's advice, in 685) and then served the part-Irish king Aldfrith (d. 705), who trained on Iona and who frequently opposed the agendas of Wilfrid of York. In 687 Cuthbert died alone in his hermitage on Inner Farne island, within sight of the Bernician royal fortress of Bamburgh, having modelled the living-out of the Gospels and spoken truth to power.

Having his life transformed on his entry into the recently constructed monastery of St Peter's, Monkwearmouth, and a few years later seeing all this innovation grow up again from scratch at St Paul's, Jarrow, at the same time as he himself was growing, must have been exciting and memorable for the teenage Bede. We can picture him gazing at the painted images that Biscop had hung on the walls of St Peter's Church (illus. 7) and watching as more of them were hoisted onto the walls of St Paul's. We can hear him asking his elders – perhaps Biscop of Ceolfrith themselves – what their meaning was and being introduced to iconographic mysteries and exegetical techniques such as allegory and typology when he was told that King David was the Old Testament 'type' (prefiguration) of Christ or that Moses raising the brazen serpent aloft in the Sinai desert was a 'type' of Christ raised up on the Cross. Bede had a wonderful imagination and we can think of him learning building construction and masonry and carving techniques and watching molten glass being worked, just as children do today in the National Glass Centre in Sunderland, a five-minute walk from St Peter's,

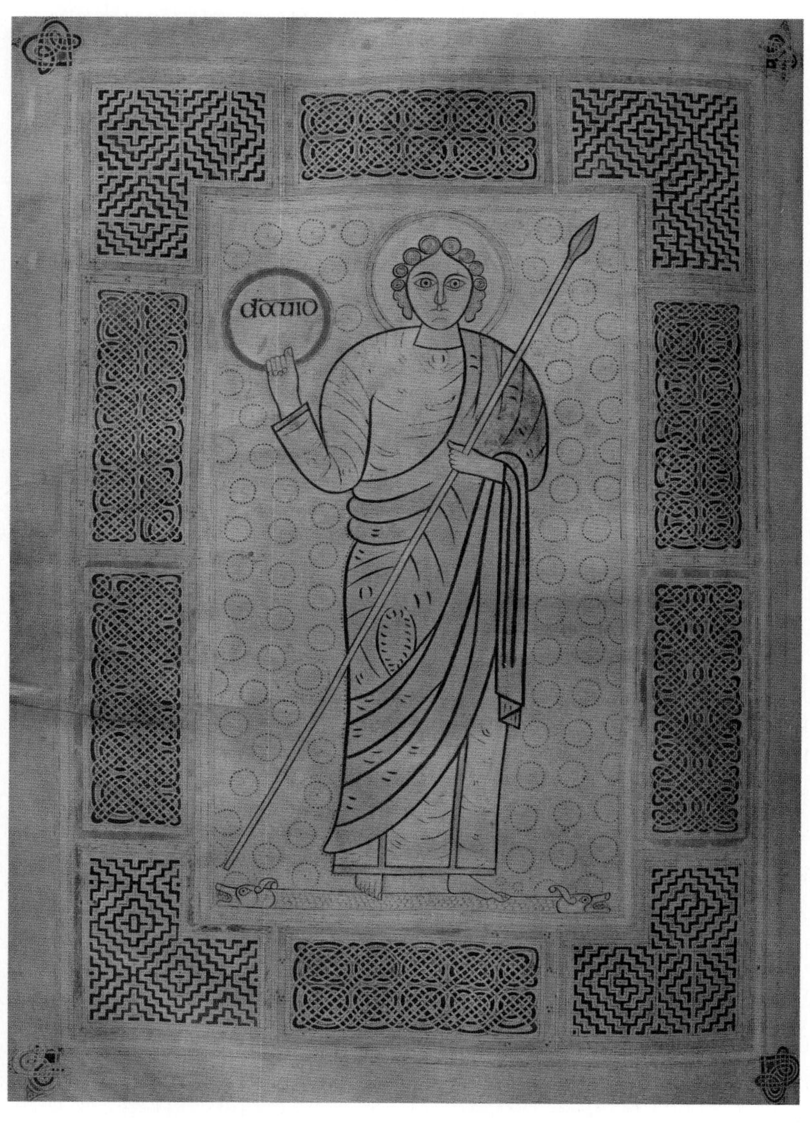

14 King David, Old Testament Type of Christ, trampling the beasts (Psalm 91:13: 'You will tread on the lion and the adder; the young lion and the serpent you will trample underfoot') in the Durham Cassiodorus, an early 8th-century Wearmouth-Jarrow copy of Cassiodorus' *Commentary on the Psalms* (Durham Cathedral Library, MS B.II.30, f. 172v).

15 Reconstruction of an early Anglo-Saxon house, Jarrow Hall Museum.

Monkwearmouth. The original glass, along with masonry, sculpture, tiling (including *opus signinum*) and plasterwork, can still be seen in its church and at St Paul's and the adjacent Jarrow Hall Museum, where there is also a reconstruction of a seventh-century Anglo-Saxon village, farm buildings and practices of the period, set up initially as part of 'Bede's World'. All of this helped shaped Bede's interest in the symbolic meaning of the Temple in Jerusalem and other holy places, and its application to the contemporary Anglo-Saxon environment and people, which is evident in his writings.

Bede may well have had a recollection of such farmyards and timber structures from his childhood – a world of shadowy, smoke-blackened, fire-flickering timber and thatch interiors, muddy yards, flowering meadows, heather-bloom moors, horses, dogs, cats, livestock, fowl, babies, byres and kinsfolk. Then he entered the brand new and no doubt mind-blowing stone edifices of Monkwearmouth – the 'work of giants', as a later Anglo-Saxon poet would describe the ruins of Roman Britain that were still to be seen around the year 1000 in the Old English poem *The Ruin*, made anew and peopled primarily by sober older men. Memories of the smoke-filled timber hall where he ate, slept and listened to tales told and songs sung around the central hearth – as well as the sounds of relationships enacted in the dark of communal spaces – would have faded in the well-ordered stone structures which resonated to the chant of plainsong, but his early love of epic verse and storytelling evidently remained and served him, and us, in good stead in his later creative life.

It may seem harsh to us for a child to be separated from family and consigned to perpetual institutionalization, and in many respects it would have been. Yet this was perhaps not so different from the experience of many university dons, progressing from prep and boarding school, through university, to the regime of college fellows, enjoying a communal life of teaching and research in a safe and comfortable environment, with an excellent library and artworks attached. Bede would likewise have been cushioned from front-line experience of many of the trials and tribulations of his day, with its virulent warfare and competition for limited resources hard-won from trade and the land – and as plunder and war booty – although he became its chronicler. Bede would nonetheless have had to undertake hard manual labour, to demonstrate monastic humility, and would have relinquished personal property and the joys, pains and distractions of relationships with wife and family. In exchange, he gained security, the fellowship of the monastic *familia* and the eternal communion of saints – and fame, if only posthumous. Perhaps most significant for his contribution to Western culture was that by embracing the contemplative life he gained the time, space, techniques, resources and stimulus in which to be and to think deeply.

The library, where Bede must have spent so much of his time, was shared between the two locations, some 11 kilometres (7 mi.) apart. It is likely that Bede worked in both and the same may be true of the scriptorium or writing office. This spectacular resource – the heir to the libraries of the late antique and early Christian worlds – made Bede's achievement possible, along with his research and networking skills, which opened up source material to him from near and far. Together, these resources enabled Bede to remain put and for the world to come to him; in this respect his work was a precursor of modern Internet-based research.

Yet religious life was not always peaceful and safe. The author of the *Life of Ceolfrith* writes that the Jarrow community was decimated by plague in 686, when Bede was about thirteen. It was one of the worst years ever for pestilence and famine in Northumbria. Only Ceolfrith and a boy (presumably Bede) remained to sing the office in the church, which still survives as St Paul Jarrow's chancel. It is moving to stand in that nearly complete seventh-century structure with its tiny original stained-glass windows (illus. 9) – the earliest to survive in the West – contemplate the boy and his abbot keeping the flickering flame of faith alive in prayer and sung psalmody.

They would have learned how to conduct the liturgy in accordance with practices in Rome and how to chant from John, the pope's own archcantor, who returned to England from Rome with Benedict Biscop in the 680s to teach singing and to assist in their plans to bring the nascent Church there into line with international orthodox practices. Music was not written down until the ninth century, when neumatic notation was introduced by the Carolingians, and had to be taught *viva voce*.

This is how Bede related John's mission to England, in the *Ecclesiastical History of the English People*:

Book 4, chap. 18. Of John, the precentor of the Apostolic see, who came into Britain to teach. [680]

Among those who were present at this synod, and confirmed the decrees of the Catholic faith, was the venerable John, archchanter of the church of the holy Apostle Peter, and abbot of the monastery of the blessed Martin, who had come lately from Rome, by order of Pope Agatho, together with the most reverend Abbot Biscop, surnamed Benedict, of whom mention has been made above. For the said Benedict, having built a monastery in Britain, in honour of the most blessed chief of the Apostles, at the mouth of the river Wear, went to Rome with Ceolfrid, his companion and fellow-labourer in that work, who was after him abbot of the same monastery; he had been several times before at Rome, and was now honourably received by Pope Agatho of blessed memory; from whom he also asked and obtained, in order to secure the immunities of the monastery which he had founded, a letter of privilege confirmed by apostolic authority, according to what he knew to be the will and grant of King Egfrid, by whose consent and gift of land he had built that monastery.

He was also allowed to take the aforesaid Abbot John with him into Britain, that he might teach in his monastery the system of singing throughout the year, as it was practised at St. Peter's at Rome. The Abbot John did as he had been commanded by the Pope, teaching the singers of the said monastery the order and manner of singing and reading aloud, and committing to writing all that was requisite throughout the whole course of the year for the celebration of festivals; and these writings are still preserved in that monastery, and have been copied

> by many others elsewhere. The said John not only taught the brothers of that monastery, but such as had skill in singing resorted from almost all the monasteries of the same province to hear him, and many invited him to teach in other places.
>
> Besides his task of singing and reading, he had also received a commission from the Apostolic Pope, carefully to inform himself concerning the faith of the English Church, and to give an account thereof on his return to Rome. For he also brought with him the decision of the synod of the blessed Pope Martin, held not long before at Rome, with the consent of one hundred and five bishops, chiefly to refute those who taught that there is but one operation and will in Christ, and he gave it to be transcribed in the aforesaid monastery of the most religious Abbot Benedict. The men who followed such opinion greatly perplexed the faith of the Church of Constantinople at that time; but by the help of God they were then discovered and overcome. Wherefore, Pope Agatho, being desirous to be informed concerning the state of the Church in Britain, as well as in other provinces, and to what extent it was clear from the contagion of heretics, gave this matter in charge to the most reverend Abbot John, then appointed to go to Britain. The synod we have spoken of having been called for this purpose in Britain, the Catholic faith was found untainted in all, and a report of the proceedings of the same was given him to carry to Rome.

Bede would have encountered other important visitors to the monasteries, however briefly, and would certainly have listened wide-eyed as those around him discussed them and the reasons for their visits. They would have included kings and nobles, bishops and archbishops (probably including Theodore of Tarsus himself), envoys, reeves, thegns and merchants. Travelling women and children and pilgrims might also have been offered hospitality in the guest quarters, including some of the influential abbesses of the day. He would have mixed with lay brothers, agricultural workers, blacksmiths, cooks, craftspeople, cart-drivers and sailors. His brethren would have included those with skills in the infirmary, kitchen, the gardens and apiary as well as the library and scriptorium and together they would have performed the divine office eight times in each 24 hours, rising at roughly three-hourly intervals in the night and breaking in the day's activities to intone prayers and sing psalms in one or other of the two churches on the site. In these they would also celebrate the mass (each priest had to perform a mass each day, hence the frequent inclusion of many altars in early churches), celebrate the saints' feast days and high holy-days, and exhibit prized relics to visiting pilgrims and dignitaries.

Bede tells us that at nineteen (*c.* 691–2) he became deacon, responsible for reading the Gospel during the liturgy, and at thirty (*c.* 702–3), the age at which Christ began his ministry, he was ordained a priest. Most monks did not take priestly orders, but Bede was evidently called to both vocations. He speaks of his obedience to the bonds of monastic humility, and his appreciation of being a priest subject to monastic authority and a rule of common life may have helped shape his sympathetic attitude to the contribution of the Irish-style bishop-abbots and of earlier monasteries of that tradition, such as Lindisfarne.

His commentary *On First Samuel* reveals Bede's personal affinity with this prophet-priest, who anointed Saul and David and established the sacral role of kingship mediated through, and regulated by, the priesthood.[13] Samuel was promised to the service of Yahweh, by a mother desperate to conceive, and entrusted to the care of the high priest Eli in the temple of Shiloh.

> Wherefore it came to pass, when the time was come about after Hannah had conceived, that she bore a son, and called his name Samuel, saying, Because I have asked him of the LORD.
>
> And the man Elkanah, and all his house, went up to offer unto the LORD the yearly sacrifice, and his vow.
>
> But Hannah went not up; for she said unto her husband, I will not go up until the child be weaned, and then I will bring him, that he may appear before the LORD, and there abide for ever.
>
> And Elkanah her husband said unto her, Do what seemeth thee good; tarry until thou have weaned him; only the LORD establish his word. So the woman abode, and gave her son suck until she weaned him.
>
> And when she had weaned him, she took him up with her, with three bullocks, and one ephah of flour, and a bottle of wine, and brought him unto the house of the LORD in Shiloh: and the child was young.
>
> And they slew a bullock, and brought the child to Eli.
>
> And she said, Oh my lord, as thy soul liveth, my lord, I am the woman that stood by thee here, praying unto the LORD.
>
> For this child I prayed; and the LORD hath given me my petition which I asked of him: Therefore also I have lent him to the LORD; as long as he liveth he shall be lent to the LORD. And he worshipped the LORD there. (1 Samuel 1.20–28, King James Version)

Bede identified with this, casting his own father figure, Ceolfrith, in the role of Eli. Ceolfrith's decision to travel to Rome in 716, to spend his last days among the tombs of the apostles, caused Bede such severe sorrow that his work temporarily suffered. In the preface to Book IV Bede shares his trauma and expresses his hopes for his community under Ceolfrith's successor, Hwaetbert, whom he calls 'Eusebius'. His fourth-century namesake, Bishop Eusebius of Caesarea, had chronicled and legitimatized Emperor Constantine and the early Church – a service performed by Samuel for the early kings of the Israelites – and had prepared the first full copies of Christian Scripture at the behest of Constantine, along with the canon tables, which compared the witnesses of the four canonical Gospels. In labouring to produce the best possible copies of Scripture and in composing his own *Ecclesiastical History*, in emulation of Eusebius, under abbots Ceolfrith/Eli and Hwaetbert/Eusebius, Bede fulfilled the prophetic role in respect of his own people, a task to which he evidently felt himself to have been dedicated in the womb.

TWO

Bede the Monk and Priest

Not all inhabitants of monasteries took the tonsure and their oaths of obedience to its rule of life and not all of the monks who did were priests, but Bede was both. He was not ambitious within church and court life, preferring the cloistered existence of the prophetic scholar/teacher/scribe.[1] He did not lack political astuteness, however. In his *Letter to Bishop Ecgbert* of 735 he recommends solutions to the ills diminishing Northumbria's power. Its spiritual life, learning and religious integrity were crucial (as Alfred of Wessex would also later recognize in the face of Viking attacks). Bede therefore suggests reforms, laments the hypocrisy of those who founded monasteries on their land for temporal benefits (the equivalent of modern tax breaks) and fears for the defence of the kingdom should too many youths follow his path into the cloister. Nor was he without his prejudices, especially against those he considered enemies of Northumbria, and pagans, heretics and schismatics, especially those of the ancient British Church, which he presents (exaggeratedly) as refusing to engage in debate and even contact.

The Northumbria of Bede's day was a complex landscape of monasteries, nunneries, double monasteries of men and women living life in parallel, hermitages (some in caves and on islands, emulating the wilderness experience of the desert fathers), chapels, shrines, wayside and preaching crosses and ancient holy wells. The wooden and drystone buildings of monasteries and churches were being joined by edifices of dressed stone in modern monasteries such as Wearmouth-Jarrow and Wilfrid's Hexham and Ripon, with their crypts emulating the Holy Sepulchre and filled with the relics of saints from far away – which were supplemented by a growing body of local figures whose sanctity was affirmed by popular acclaim and miracles. Archbishop Theodore's arrival also stimulated the reactivation of papal plans for a diocesan organization of bishops' seats – cathedrals (so named for the bishop's throne, the *cathedra*), missionary minsters and parish churches. Augustine's Canterbury had reintroduced this master plan along late Roman lines, established following the empire's adoption of Christianity as its state religion in the 380s. It became the archbishopric because it was the powerbase of King Ethelbert of Kent, the most powerful of the new Germanic rulers, and his Christian Frankish bride, Bertha. St Augustine's Abbey and St Martin's church, outside the old Roman city walls, and other early churches such as Bradwell-on-Sea in Essex, reused Roman masonry in their sites and structures. London had been the earlier Roman primatial seat but it lay in hostile East Saxon territory. St Paul's Cathedral was established by Augustine's follower Mellitus in 604 and he wrote to Pope Gregory informing him that the people had their own religions and requesting advice, to which Gregory wisely replied that if there was a place where folk traditionally brought their hopes and fears and times of year when they celebrated, then the missionaries should embrace them, providing no evil was being practised. Hence the major Christian festival of Easter was named after a Germanic goddess, Eostre, and the church at Rudston in Yorkshire stands beside an enormous prehistoric standing stone. Nonetheless, Mellitus was soon ousted as the mission hit the first of several setbacks in Essex and East Anglia. Bede tells us of the price paid for sponsoring the mission by several convert rulers:

Ecclesiastical History of the English People, Book 2, chap. 18. Of the life and death of the religious King Sigbert. [c. 631]

At this time, the kingdom of the East Angles, after the death of Earpwald, the successor of Redwald, was governed by his brother Sigbert, a good and religious man, who some time before had been baptized in Gaul, while he lived in banishment, a fugitive from the enmity of Redwald. When he returned home, as soon as he ascended the throne, being desirous to imitate the good institutions which he had seen in Gaul, he founded a school wherein boys should be taught letters, and was assisted therein by Bishop Felix, who came to him from Kent, and who furnished them with masters and teachers after the manner of the people of Kent.

This king became so great a lover of the heavenly kingdom, that at last, quitting the affairs of his kingdom, and committing them to his kinsman Ecgric, who before had a share in that kingdom, he entered a monastery, which he had built for himself, and having received the tonsure, applied himself rather to do battle for a heavenly throne. A long time after this, it happened that the nation of the Mercians, under King Penda, made war on the East Angles, who finding themselves no match for their enemy, entreated Sigbert to go with them to battle, to encourage the soldiers. He was unwilling and refused, upon which they drew him against his will out of the monastery, and carried him to the army, hoping that the soldiers would be less afraid and less disposed to flee in the presence of one who had formerly been an active and distinguished commander. But he, still mindful of his profession, surrounded, as he was, by a royal army, would

> carry nothing in his hand but a wand, and was killed with King Ecgric; and the pagans pressing on, all their army was either slaughtered or dispersed.

Sigbert may have lost the battle, but he won the war in bringing his people more fully to the new faith. However, the threat from paganism and apostasy still loomed large.

Monasteries played a key role as part of this infrastructure. They were not all closed cloistered communities and were each governed by the rule of common life adopted by their founders. These might be of their own devising or might draw upon those of important monastic founders such as St Augustine, Martin of Tours, John Cassian, Basil and Pachomius, and were often inspired by the example of the eremitic desert fathers Paul and Anthony. These last also informed the rules devised by Irish founders such as Sts Brigid, Columba and Columbanus and were adopted or adapted throughout houses in their monastic federations. The Penitential of Columbanus gives us a glimpse of just how demanding such rules could be. One that would become even more influential, in the long term, was the Rule of St Benedict, upon which Biscop and Ceolfrith based that of Wearmouth-Jarrow.

Around the year 500, Benedict of Nursia (*c.* 480–547) had left Rome, appalled by its immorality, to become an ascetic living as a hermit in a cave near Subiaco. His example drew disciples and from his first community at Subiaco he wrote his Rule in 516 and founded the monastery of Monte Cassino in 529. Compared to others, Benedict's 'Little Rule for Beginners' trod a path between individual and institutional spiritual growth, manual labour, service, study, worship and prayer, whose followers lived in a community in obedience to the governance of a spiritual father and developed personal and collective vocations. The monastic day and night were punctuated by prayer, biblical readings and the singing of psalms and hymns at eight intervals, known as the Divine Office (Matins, Lauds, Prime, Terce, Sext, Nones, Vespers and Compline). Priested monks would perform the eucharistic mass for the brethren. The growing popularity of Benedictinism with the Carolingian Empire from the late eighth century onwards would in turn foster a monastic reform movement in tenth-century England in which the Benedictine Rule became the norm.

In the prologue and first chapter of his Rule, St Benedict of Nursia cut to the core of the monastic vocation and outlined regular and irregular patterns of observance:

Prologue to St Benedict of Nursia's 'Little Rule for Beginners'

Now, brethren, that we have asked the Lord who it is that shall dwell in His tabernacle, we have heard the conditions for dwelling there; and if we fulfil the duties of tenants, we shall be heirs of the kingdom of heaven. Our hearts and our bodies must, therefore, be ready to do battle under the biddings of holy obedience; and let us ask the Lord that He supply by the help of His grace what is impossible to us by nature. And if, flying from the pains of hell, we desire to reach life everlasting, then, while there is yet time, and we are still in the flesh, and are able during the present life to fulfil all these things, we must make haste to do now what will profit us forever.

. . . We are, therefore, about to found a school of the Lord's service, in which we hope to introduce nothing harsh or burdensome. But even if, to correct vices or to preserve charity, sound reason dictateth anything that turneth out somewhat stringent, do not at once fly in dismay from the way of salvation, the beginning of which cannot but be narrow. But as we advance in the religious life and faith, we shall run the way of God's commandments with expanded hearts and unspeakable sweetness of love; so that never departing from His guidance and persevering in the monastery in His doctrine till death, we may by patience share in the sufferings of Christ and be found worthy to be coheirs with Him of His kingdom.

CHAPTER I: Of the Kinds or the Life of Monks

It is well known that there are four kinds of monks. The first kind is that of Cenobites, that is, the monastic, who live under a rule and an Abbot.

The second kind is that of Anchorites, or Hermits, that is, of those who, no longer in the first fervor of their conversion, but taught by long monastic practice and the help of many brethren, have already learned to fight against the devil; and going forth from the rank of their brethren well trained for single combat in the desert, they are able, with the help of God, to cope single-handed without the help of others, against the vices of the flesh and evil thoughts.

But a third and most vile class of monks is that of Sarabaites, who have been tried by no rule under the hand of a master, as gold is tried in the fire (cf Prov 27:21); but, soft as lead, and still keeping faith with the world by their works, they are known to belie God by their tonsure. Living in twos and threes, or even singly, without a shepherd, enclosed, not in the Lord's sheepfold, but in their own, the gratification of their desires is law unto them; because what they choose to do they call holy, but what they dislike they hold to be unlawful.

But the fourth class of monks is that called Landlopers, who keep going their whole life long from one province to another, staying three or four days at a time in different cells as guests. Always roving and never settled, they

> indulge their passions and the cravings of their appetite and are in every way worse than the Sarabaites. It is better to pass all these over in silence than to speak of their most wretched life.
>
> Therefore, passing these over, let us go on with the help of God to lay down a rule for that most valiant kind of monks, the Cenobites.

Towards the end of the eighth century, Emperor Charlemagne would take measures to limit the activities of what he termed 'gyrovagues', seemingly itinerant Irish monks not subject to a stable rule of life and transcending the territorial bounds of imperial and local authority. Benedict's concerns in respect to eremitic monasticism and religious who, unlike hermits and anchorites, did not owe obedience to a monastic house may well have coloured Bede's view of the British and 'Celtic' Irish/Scots churches. His personal admiration for role models such as the saints Columba, Aidan and Cuthbert, fostered no doubt by his close relations with Lindisfarne and its bishop, Eadfrith, led him to adopt a very different approach to their work, as opposed to that of the British churches. This stance would also have been shaped by an acute awareness that much of the Columban Church and its Cuthbertine reformed offshoot had conformed to the international orthodoxy of Chalcedon in its practices (as interpreted by the Orthodox mainstream by this time) following the Synod of Whitby in 664, with Iona being the last house to enter into conformity and unity in 715. The British, however, had not and were probably viewed askance both by Bede and the international Church community as schismatic.

Bede was ordained a deacon in 692 and was priested in 702. His authorial career began the year before when he penned his first work, *De arte metrica et de schematicus et tropis*, a book of the art of poetry and a little book of tropes and figures used in Scripture, designed to be used in the monastic schoolroom to teach the art of poetry. His last extant work is a letter to Ecgbert, Bishop of York, one of his former students, dating from 734 and expressing his concerns at lapses in the Christian commitment of both ecclesiastical and secular society and urging episcopal leadership. He was still dictating on his deathbed a year later, concluding a writing life of 34 years during which he produced some forty works.

The curious 'red herring' of Bede's marital status remains to be dealt with. In two of his works, the *Commentary on the Seven Catholic Epistles* and *Commentary on Luke*, he mentions having a wife, writing in the first person. This has led to some discussion concerning whether priests could marry. Until measures were introduced by Pope Innocent III at the end of the twelfth century they could, but celibacy was considered the ideal and was certainly the theoretical norm for monks and nuns, unless in a house where irregular practices prevailed, such as those censured by St Cuthbert at the double (dual-sex) monastery of Coldingham. It would certainly not have been tolerated at Wearmouth-Jarrow, male houses governed by a rule based on that of St Benedict. Bede's bride, like Christ's, was the Church (characterized in feminine form), and it is probably she to whom he alludes metaphorically.[2]

Nevertheless, some scholars would argue that Bede never specifically says he was a monk, whereas he does say he was a priest. There could be untonsured brethren at contemporary monasteries and therefore he might have been married. But Bede's references to evincing monastic humility, singing the monastic offices and to his cell and the evidently large proportion of his time devoted to *lectio divina* (reading of sacred texts) and study would all strongly suggest that he was a monastic brother, subject to the rule of common life at Wearmouth-Jarrow.

In the *Commentary on the Seven Catholic Epistles*, he writes: 'Prayers are hindered by the conjugal duty because as often as I perform what is due to my wife I am not able to pray.' A passage in the *Commentary on Luke* likewise talks of a wife: 'Formerly I possessed a wife in the lustful passion of desire and now I possess her in honourable sanctification and true love of Christ.' If Bede is speaking rhetorically, the distraction of the other duties associated with monastic life, as dictated by the Church, could be what he means (manual labour, domestic duties and even study and writing time), while the desire of a former time might express his ardour to attain his vocation and the possession of it honourably would then refer to his fully ordained role as a priest and as a mature scholar and scribe of Scripture. One cannot but feel that Bede's only other mistress was another female personification, Lady Learning.

If, as seems likely, Bede was a celibate, his writings show that he was no misogynist. Women people the pages of the *Ecclesiastical History* and the lives of St Cuthbert, many of them as heroic to him in their service of God and community as their male counterparts. That he valued their intellectual abilities too is demonstrated by his reliance in places upon research provided by the nuns of Barking Abbey in Essex, to whom Aldhelm's *De virginitate* (In Praise of Virginity), with its complex Latin hermeneutics, was addressed.

When Bede entered Monkwearmouth monastery it was just over fifty years since Christianity had been introduced into Anglo-Saxon Northumbria; or, rather, reintroduced, as it had been the state religion of the Roman Empire from the 380s and the area had an earlier Romano-British Christian tradition which endured in many of the fragmented British territories. He relates the first hearing given to Paulinus, who had been sent North by the mission of St Augustine in Canterbury, with the characteristic panache of the accomplished storyteller and preacher, in an endearing, memorable and highly visual allegory.

Ecclesiastical History of the English People, Book 2, chap. 13

He [King Edwin of Northumbria] summoned a council of the wise men and asked each in turn his opinion of this strange doctrine [Christianity] and this new way of worshipping the godhead that was being proclaimed to them.

Coifi, the chief Priest, replied without hesitation: 'Your Majesty, let us give careful consideration to this new teaching.'

'For I frankly admit that, in my experience, the religion that we have hitherto professed seems valueless and powerless. None of your subjects has been more devoted to the service of our gods than myself; yet there are many to whom you show greater favour, who receive greater honours, and who are more successful in all their undertakings. Now, if the gods had any power, they would surely have favoured myself, who have been more zealous in their service. Therefore, if on examination you perceive that these new teachings are better and more effectual, let us not hesitate to accept them.'

Another of the king's chief men signified his agreement with this prudent argument, and went on to say: 'Your Majesty, when we compare the present life of man on earth with that time of which we have no knowledge, it seems to me like the swift flight of a single sparrow through the banqueting hall where you are sitting at dinner on a winter's day with your thegns and counsellors. In the midst there is a comforting fire to warm the hall; outside, the storms of winter rain or snow are raging. This sparrow flies swiftly in through one door of the hall, and out through another. While he is inside, he is safe from

> the winter storms; but after a few moments of comfort, he vanishes from sight into the wintry world from which he came. Even so, man appears on earth for a little while; but of what went before this life or of what follows, we know nothing. Therefore, if this new teaching has brought any more certain knowledge, it seems only right that we should follow it.' The other elders and counsellors of the king, under God's guidance, gave similar advice.

Recognition of transferable professional skills among the priesthoods of both the pre-Christian Germanic and Celtic peoples, leading some of them to convert and become Christian religious personnel, can be traced in the work of Bede and other sources. Others actively resisted conversion and ordinary folk were not always eager to relinquish the old ways either. Bede tells a sorry tale to illustrate how apostasy could lurk beneath the surface, relating how some Northumbrian monks were using rafts to transport wood along the Tyne when a storm swept them out to sea. Their fellow monks wept and prayed on the shore, but peasants watching nearby jeered and called for them to be drowned, 'for they have robbed people of their old ways of worship, and how the new worship is to be conducted, nobody knows.'

Bede tells us how this lack of knowledge was addressed. He is not uncritical of the means, praising King Ethelbert of Kent for never compelling conversion by the sword and relating with great reserve Bishop Wilfrid's role in the conversion of Sussex and his part in King Caedwalla of Wessex's bloody conquest of the Isle of Wight, the final bastion of paganism in Anglo-Saxon England, in 686.

Paulinus is credited by Bede with commencing the conversion of the English in Northumbria. He was part of the reinforcement band of missionaries despatched from Rome which reached Kent in 604. He had accompanied the Kentish princess Æthelburh on a diplomatic marriage to King Edwin of Northumbria soon after the accession of her brother, Eadbald, to the Kentish throne in 625. Despite initial success in high-level court conversion, the Kentish party had to withdraw rapidly homewards following Edwin's death in battle against the Mercians at the Battle of Hatfield Chase near Doncaster. This had pitted the Northumbrians against an alliance of Gwynedd and Mercia. The Northumbrians were led by Edwin and the alliance of Gwynedd and Mercia was led by the Welsh Christian ruler Cadwallon ap Cadfan and the pagan Penda. To Bede, this represented a heinous, unholy alliance of schismatic Christian Britons with a self-appointed champion of Germanic paganism, intent on resisting the expansion of Northumbrian power and the tide of conversion. It is but one of a number of instances that Bede relates to demonstrate the errors of the Britons and their churches, although he is inclined to gloss over the Northumbrian territorial expansionism that fostered such alliances to resist it.

The *Ecclesiastical History* is in many respects an account of the conversion to Christianity of the Germanic settlers in post-Roman Britain and the role of the faith in helping them to establish successor states. Their internecine wars and alliances are charted, with the process of big fish eating little fish and good governmental decisions along with sponsorship of the nascent Church leading to the emergence of a quasi high-kingship in the role of bretwalda (or 'top dog'), as Bede puts it. The formation and conversion of Bede's own people in the kingdom of Northumbria and its rise to a golden age under kings such as Edwin (616–32), Oswald (634–42) and Oswy (642–54) features, but so does its decline latterly under rulers such as Ecgfrith (670–85), whom he treats critically in the *Ecclesiastical History* and his lives of St Cuthbert for his aggression towards fellow Christian peoples, notably the Picts, and his treatment of his wife, the saintly Æthelthryth, in resisting her desire to become a nun, which she successfully achieved as founder abbess of Ely. Bede's concerns extend to the time of writing and the reign of King Ceolwulf (729–37; temporarily deposed in 731), who found it expedient to abdicate and join the monastery of Lindisfarne. He dedicated the *Ecclesiastical History* to Ceolwulf and visited him on Holy Island. Bede also wrote, towards the end of his life, a letter urging Archbishop Ecgbert of York (whose brother, Eadred, was king of Northumbrian Deira) and the episcopate to exert more influence for the good. Bede's concern with social stability, justice and ethics mark him out as a reformer.

The translation of St Cuthbert's relics to the high altar at Lindisfarne in 698 marked the start of the creation of his cult, which Eadfrith constructed after his accession as bishop that same year. He may have commissioned a Life of St Cuthbert from an anonymous Lindisfarne monk and then a reworking by Bede, who initially produced an epic verse version and then a prose Life which he completed around 721 and, significantly, dedicated to Eadfrith. Lindisfarne was apparently actively collaborating with Wearmouth-Jarrow and may have borrowed a prized Italian gospel book, or a copy of it made there, from their library as a text model. Bede's influence can be detected in the symbolic imagery of the evangelist miniatures and the Lindisfarne Gospels' harmonious blending of cultures would fit the image promoted by those working together to create a new collaborative Christian identity for these islands, such as Eadfrith, Bede and Abbot Adomnán of Iona.

Bede's narrative understandably favours his own people and the traditions of Wearmouth-Jarrow, with its coenobitic Benedictine-style monasticism and their internationally orientated adherence to the Church in Rome and its continental orbit. But his horizons were wider. There is a tendency for the papacy at this period to be viewed as representative of a high medieval 'Roman Catholicism', but, prior to the split between East and

West as a result of the schisms in the ninth and tenth centuries, the pope was the westernmost of the Eastern patriarchs and authority focused upon the Byzantine capital, Constantinople (now Istanbul). During the seventh and early eighth centuries many of Rome's popes were Syrian and part of a large Syriac expat community there. Archbishop Theodore of Tarsus, one of the most erudite churchmen of the Near East, was primate of the new English Church when Bede entered Monkwearmouth and his colleague Hadrian, Abbot of St Augustine's Canterbury, was a Berber from North Africa and latterly an abbot in Naples. Biscop, the founder figure, had studied at Lèrins in a monastery established off the southern coast of Gaul by John Cassian, an Eastern desert father. And my current research at St Catherine's Monastery at the foot of Mount Sinai in Egypt is pointing to the presence there of at least two English scribes writing hands influenced by Northumbrian script later in the eighth century.[3]

The ancient prehistoric trade routes that linked the East and the Mediterranean world to the peoples of the Atlantic seaboard also continued to function in the aftermath of the western Roman Empire's collapse. Continued trade fostered cultural and religious connections, leading to a markedly Eastern eremitic strand in what is often called 'Celtic' Christianity. As early as AD 431 Pope Celestine had sent Palladius as bishop to those in Ireland who already followed Christ and early Christian Roman practices would have been known, but some of the monastic federations that emerged in Ireland as founder saints proliferated embraced early practices from the East that came to be seen as outdated elsewhere in Europe. The most influential of these was the monastic family established by St Columba, a prince of the powerful Uí Néill (O'Neill) dynasty. He died at his most famous foundation, Iona, in 597, the year that Augustine arrived in Canterbury, and he and his followers formed an extensive federation of monasteries that included Derry, Durrow, Kells, Melrose, Jedburgh,

Coldingham, Lindisfarne, Hartlepool, Lastingham, Lichfield, Bradwell-on-Sea and Tilbury on the Thames.

Many other Irish missions and seeded churches also flourished in Scotland, for the Scotti were expats from northeast Ireland who had carved out the kingdom of Dalriada in western Scotland (Argyll) and the Inner Hebrides and who, by the mid-ninth century, gained primacy over the earlier Pictish inhabitants. Likewise, Wales, Cornwall and Brittany all witnessed Irish missions and participated themselves in extended monastic networks that transcended regional borders and authorities.

By the middle of the seventh century it was becoming apparent that there were various Christian traditions and teachings in these islands. Bede's *Ecclesiastical History* is our primary historical source for a synopsis of the competition and conflicts that ensued. These were manifold but crystallized into a focal point – the crucial debate that took place at the Synod of Whitby in 664. Bede highlights the central issues, which focused upon divergence in practices relating to the visible enactment of faith, namely the celebration of the most important liturgical feast of the Christian year – Easter – and the physical appearance and identifier of priests: the style of their tonsure.

This has been presented, historically, as a struggle for authority between the 'Roman' and 'Celtic' churches, but I have contended that this is an over-simplification and misprision of the wider situation. The practices that were disputed were those of the tradition established by St Columba and observed throughout the network of houses established by him and his followers, rather than those current in many other foundations in Ireland and abroad. Columban personnel had their foreheads shaved from ear to ear, with a mane of hair flowing behind (in a manner that some would attribute to earlier druidic fashion), while elsewhere in the West they wore the *corona* tonsure, a bald pate recollecting the crown of thorns that Christ wore at the Passion.

The different datings of Easter stemmed from the Columban Church adhering to the lunar-based calculations favoured in the Judaic rabbinic tradition and the teaching of St John. Modifications made to accommodate the Roman solar calendar led to different calculations being observed throughout what had been the late Roman Empire, which remained current throughout Christendom. There would undoubtedly have been a plethora of other variant practices, and the British and Columban churches were not intentionally non-Nicene but followed calculus that had become outmoded in the Mediterranean, but the bigger picture was one of international disputes within the Christian faith. The fear of the pattern of heresies and schisms that had been threatening the cohesion of the faith in the East spreading to the new churches of the West was a controlling factor. This was not Celt versus Roman Catholic: it was the dignity of the Columban Church versus the unity of international orthodoxy, as defined by adherence to the findings of the Council of Chalcedon (as interpreted by the Orthodox Church by the seventh century) – that is, 'catholic' with a small 'c', even if it did turn out to be a key moment in establishing the primacy of the Apostolic See and inaugurated 'Catholic' with a capital 'C' in Rome.

This is such an important episode that it will be well to read some parts of Bede's own account of proceedings in the *Ecclesiastical History*:

Book 3, chap. 25. How the question arose about the due time of keeping Easter, with those that came out of Scotland. [664]

. . . Bishop Aidan being taken away from this life, Finan, who was ordained and sent by the Scots, succeeded him in the bishopric, and built a church in the Isle of Lindisfarne, fit for the episcopal see; nevertheless, after the manner of the Scots, he made it, not of stone, but entirely of hewn oak, and covered it with reeds; and it was afterwards dedicated in honour of the blessed Peter the Apostle, by the most reverend Archbishop Theodore. Eadbert, also bishop of that place, took off the thatch, and caused it to be covered entirely, both roof and walls, with plates of lead.

At this time, a great and frequently debated question arose about the observance of Easter; those that came from Kent or Gaul affirming, that the Scots celebrated Easter Sunday contrary to the custom of the universal Church. Among them was a most zealous defender of the true Easter, whose name was Ronan, a Scot by nation, but instructed in the rule of ecclesiastical truth in Gaul or Italy . . . Queen Eanfled and her followers also observed it as she had seen it practised in Kent, having with her a Kentish priest who followed the Catholic observance, whose name was Romanus. Thus it is said to have sometimes happened in those times that Easter was twice celebrated in one year; and that when the king, having ended his fast, was keeping Easter, the queen and her followers were still fasting, and celebrating Palm Sunday. While Aidan lived, this difference about the observance of Easter was patiently tolerated by all men, for they well knew, that though he could not keep Easter contrary to the custom of those who had sent him, yet he industriously laboured to practise the works of faith, piety, and love, according to the custom of all holy men; for which reason he was deservedly beloved by all, even by those who differed in opinion concerning Easter . . .

But after the death of Finan, who succeeded him, when Colman, who was also sent from Scotland, came to be bishop, a greater controversy arose about the observance of Easter, and other rules of ecclesiastical life . . . it was arranged, that a synod should be held in the monastery of Streanaeshalch [Whitby], which signifies the Bay of the Lighthouse, where the Abbess Hilda, a woman devoted to the service of God, then ruled . . .

King Oswy first made an opening speech, in which he said that it behoved those who served one God to observe one rule of life; and as they all expected the same kingdom in heaven, so they ought not to differ in the celebration of the heavenly mysteries; but rather to inquire which was the truer tradition, that it might be followed by all in common; he then commanded his bishop, Colman, first to declare what the custom was which he observed, and whence it derived its origin. Then Colman said, 'The Easter which I keep, I received from my elders, who sent me hither as bishop; all our forefathers, men beloved of God, are known to have celebrated it after the same manner; and that it may not seem to any contemptible and worthy to be rejected, it is the same which the blessed John the Evangelist, the disciple specially beloved of our Lord, with all the churches over which he presided, is recorded to have celebrated.' . . .

Then Wilfrid, being ordered by the king to speak, began thus: 'The Easter which we keep, we saw celebrated by all at Rome, where the blessed Apostles, Peter and Paul, lived, taught, suffered, and were buried; we saw the same done by all in Italy and in Gaul, when we travelled through those countries for the purpose of study and prayer. We found it observed in Africa, Asia, Egypt, Greece, and all the world, wherever the Church of Christ is spread abroad, among divers nations and tongues, at one and the same time; save only among these and their accomplices in obstinacy, I mean the Picts and the Britons, who foolishly, in these two remote islands of the ocean, and only in part even of them, strive to oppose all the rest of the world.'

Wilfrid went on to answer Colman's protestations of the validity and earlier authority for the Columban calculation of the date of Easter . . .

'But as for you and your companions, you certainly sin, if, having heard the decrees of the Apostolic see, nay, of the universal Church, confirmed, as they are, by Holy Scripture, you scorn to follow them; for, though your fathers were holy, do you think that those few men, in a corner of the remotest island, are to be preferred before the universal Church of Christ throughout the world? And if that Columba of yours, (and, I may say, ours also, if he was Christ's servant,) was a holy man and powerful in miracles, yet could he be preferred before the most blessed chief of the Apostles, to whom our Lord said, 'Thou art Peter, and upon this rock I will build my Church, and the gates of hell shall not prevail against it, and I will give unto thee the keys of the kingdom of Heaven?'

When Wilfrid had ended thus, the king said, 'Is it true, Colman, that these words were spoken to Peter by our Lord?' He answered, 'It is true, O king!' Then said he, 'Can you show any such power given to your Columba?' Colman answered, 'None.' Then again the king asked, 'Do you both agree in this, without any controversy, that these words were said above all to Peter, and that the keys of the kingdom of Heaven were given to him by our Lord?' They both answered, 'Yes.' Then the king concluded, 'And I also say unto you, that he is the door-keeper, and I will not gainsay him, but I desire, as far as I know and am able, in all things to obey his laws, lest haply when I come to the gates of the kingdom of Heaven, there should be none to open them, he being my adversary who is proved to have the keys.' The king having said this, all who were seated there or standing by, both great

> and small, gave their assent, and renouncing the less perfect custom, hastened to conform to that which they had found to be better.

Colman and many of his followers subsequently left for Ireland, leaving Abbot Eata of Melrose to lead Lindisfarne. Bede speaks of what they left behind them:

> . . . The place which they governed shows how frugal and temperate he and his predecessors were, for there were very few houses besides the church found at their departure; indeed, no more than were barely sufficient to make civilized life possible; they had also no money, but only cattle; for if they received any money from rich persons, they immediately gave it to the poor; there being no need to gather money, or provide houses for the entertainment of the great men of the world; for such never resorted to the church, except to pray and hear the Word of God. The king himself, when occasion required, came only with five or six servants, and having performed his devotions in the church, departed. But if they happened to take a repast there, they were satisfied with the plain, daily food of the brethren, and required no more. For the whole care of those teachers was to serve God, not the world – to feed the soul, and not the belly.
>
> For this reason the religious habit was at that time held in great veneration; so that wheresoever any clerk or monk went, he was joyfully received by all men, as God's servant; and even if they chanced to meet him upon the way, they ran to him, and with bowed head, were glad to be signed with the cross by his hand, or blessed by his lips. Great attention was also paid to their exhortations; and on Sundays they flocked eagerly to the church, or the

> monasteries, not to feed their bodies, but to hear the Word of God; and if any priest happened to come into a village, the inhabitants came together and asked of him the Word of life; for the priests and clerks went to the villages for no other reason than to preach, baptise, visit the sick, and, in a word, to take care of souls; and they were so purified from all taint of avarice, that none of them received lands and possessions for building monasteries, unless they were compelled to do so by the temporal authorities; which custom was for some time after universally observed in the churches of the Northumbrians.

The influence of the Irish continued to be felt in Northumbria and throughout England:

> ***Chap. 27. How Egbert, a holy man of the English nation, led a monastic life in Ireland. [664]***
>
> In the same year of our Lord 664, there happened an eclipse of the sun, on the third day of May, about the tenth hour of the day. In the same year, a sudden pestilence depopulated first the southern parts of Britain, and afterwards attacking the province of the Northumbrians, ravaged the country far and near, and destroyed a great multitude of men. By this plague the aforesaid priest of the Lord, Tuda, was carried off, and was honourably buried in the monastery called Paegnalaech [Finchale?]. Moreover, this plague prevailed no less disastrously in the island of Ireland. Many of the nobility, and of the lower ranks of the English nation, were there at that time, who, in the days of the Bishops Finan and Colman, forsaking their native island, retired thither, either for the sake of sacred studies, or of a more ascetic life; and some of them presently devoted themselves faithfully to a monastic life,

> others chose rather to apply themselves to study, going about from one master's cell to another. The Scots willingly received them all and took care to supply them with daily food without cost, as also to furnish them with books for their studies and teaching free of charge.

From the foregoing it is possible immediately to gauge Bede's absorption with the role of computistics and calendrical calculation – and his mastery of its complexities and of its local and international political ramifications. His personal concern was that of the scholar and professional religious, but the historian cannot help indicating the underlying secular preoccupations of the king: that his people should not be part of an isolated, idiosyncratic political and ecclesiastical alignment at the rocky edges of the then known world, but should turn from looking westwards – the traditional prehistoric nexus of Atlantic-borne trade – and turn eastwards towards Europe, the Mediterranean world and the Holy Land itself. King Oswy, like certain other of the Anglo-Saxon kings, wished to be a player on a much larger stage.

Yet Bede could not conceal his profound admiration for those from the Columban Church who had played such an important role in the conversion of his people. In this respect, his treatment of figures such as Columba, Aidan, Hild, Cuthbert and their followers is very different to that of the British Church, which gets short shrift in terms of historical coverage and which Bede criticizes for its failure to evangelize the pagan Germanic incomers, for its backing of armed resistance to their land-grab and the ongoing British resistance to further expansion by the new Anglo-Saxon kingdoms – even to the extent of allying with pagan Germanic rulers against Christian ones.

The British, in turn, felt an enmity towards their Germanic conquerors and it is not surprising that they resisted Anglo-Saxon expansionism into the remaining British kingdoms.

Given that some of their churches may have had an unbroken continuity since the late Roman period and that many others had been founded during the fifth and sixth centuries by missionaries from Ireland and south Wales, before the Columban and Augustinian missions got under way, it is not surprising that they did not accord Augustine the precedence that he felt his papally sanctioned office as Archbishop of Canterbury demanded. Bede, in the *Ecclesiastical History*, relates the defining moment in relations with the British churches when he writes:

Book 2, chap. 2. How Augustine admonished the bishops of the Britons on behalf of Catholic peace, and to that end wrought a heavenly miracle in their presence; and of the vengeance that pursued them for their contempt. [c. 603]

In the meantime, Augustine, with the help of King Ethelbert, drew together to a conference the bishops and doctors of the nearest province of the Britons, at a place which is to this day called, in the English language, Augustine's Ác, that is, Augustine's Oak [Aust?], on the borders of the Hwiccas and West Saxons; and began by brotherly admonitions to persuade them to preserve Catholic peace with him, and undertake the common labour of preaching the Gospel to the heathen for the Lord's sake. For they did not keep Easter Sunday at the proper time, but from the fourteenth to the twentieth moon; which computation is contained in a cycle of eighty-four years. Besides, they did many other things which were opposed to the unity of the church. When, after a long disputation, they did not comply with the entreaties, exhortations, or rebukes of Augustine and his companions, but preferred their own traditions before all the Churches which are united in Christ throughout the world, the holy father, Augustine, put an end to this troublesome and tedious contention, saying, 'Let us entreat God, who maketh men to be of one mind in His Father's house, to vouchsafe, by signs from Heaven, to declare to us which tradition is to be followed; and by what path we are to strive to enter His kingdom. Let some sick man be brought, and let the faith and practice of him, by whose prayers he shall be healed, be looked upon as hallowed in God's sight and such as should be adopted by all.' His adversaries unwillingly consenting, a blind man of the English race was brought, who having been presented to the British bishops, found no benefit or healing from their ministry; at length, Augustine, compelled by strict necessity, bowed his knees to the Father of our Lord Jesus Christ, praying that He would restore his lost sight to the blind man, and by the bodily enlightenment of one kindle the grace of spiritual light in the hearts of many of the faithful. Immediately the blind man received sight, and Augustine was proclaimed by all to be a true herald of the light from Heaven. The Britons then confessed that they perceived that it was the true way of righteousness which Augustine taught; but that they could not depart from their ancient customs without the consent and sanction of their people. They therefore desired that a second time a synod might be appointed, at which more of their number should be present . . . and it happened, that as they approached, Augustine was sitting on a chair. When they perceived it, they were angry, and charging him with pride, set themselves to contradict all he said. He said to them, 'Many things ye do which are contrary to our custom, or rather the custom of the universal Church, and yet, if you will comply with me in these three matters, to wit, to keep Easter at the due time; to fulfil the ministry of

Baptism, by which we are born again to God, according to the custom of the holy Roman Apostolic Church; and to join with us in preaching the Word of God to the English nation, we will gladly suffer all the other things you do, though contrary to our customs.' They answered that they would do none of those things, nor receive him as their archbishop; for they said among themselves, 'if he would not rise up to us now, how much more will he despise us, as of no account, if we begin to be under his subjection?' Then the man of God, Augustine, is said to have threatened them, that if they would not accept peace with their brethren, they should have war from their enemies; and, if they would not preach the way of life to the English nation, they should suffer at their hands the vengeance of death. All which, through the dispensation of the Divine judgement, fell out exactly as he had predicted.

For afterwards the warlike king of the English, Ethelfrid, of whom we have spoken, having raised a mighty army, made a very great slaughter of that heretical nation, at the city of Legions, which by the English is called Legacaestir, but by the Britons more rightly Carlegion [Caerleon]. Being about to give battle, he observed their priests, who were come together to offer up their prayers to God for the combatants, standing apart in a place of greater safety; he inquired who they were, and what they came together to do in that place. Most of them were of the monastery of Bangor, in which, it is said, there was so great a number of monks, that the monastery being divided into seven parts, with a superior set over each, none of those parts contained less than three hundred men, who all lived by the labour of their hands. Many of these, having observed a fast of three days, had come together along with others to pray at the aforesaid battle, having one Brocmail for their protector, to defend them, while they were intent upon their prayers, against the swords of the barbarians. King Ethelfrid being informed of the occasion of their coming, said, 'If then they cry to their God against us, in truth, though they do not bear arms, yet they fight against us, because they assail us with their curses.' He, therefore, commanded them to be attacked first, and then destroyed the rest of the impious army, not without great loss of his own forces. About twelve hundred of those that came to pray are said to have been killed, and only fifty to have escaped by flight.

Unhappily, Bede does not condemn the slaughter of these fellow religious, for he viewed them as schismatics, intent upon destroying the unity of Christendom that he and his brethren were working towards, and as enemies of his people and their aggressors in prayer, which he considered potentially even more effective than arms. There is, however, a note of empathy with them in the face of Augustine's autocratic behaviour.

Bede also abhorred the Pelagian heresy – the teachings of a Briton, Pelagius, which particularly emphasized free will and were more popular on the Continent – which Bishop Germanus had travelled from Gaul to combat in 429. Indeed, some of the 'Roman' party in the Easter controversy would accuse the Columban and British churches of Pelagianism for celebrating Easter during the Jewish Passover and thereby denying the crucial importance of the Resurrection.[4] Intervention from Gaul would continue with the Frank Agilbert (*fl. c.* 650–80), who became the second Bishop of Wessex (and subsequently Bishop of Paris, after the king of Wessex replaced him as he had not learned to speak Old English; see *Ecclesiastical History* I ch. 7), and another Frank, Felix of Dunwich (d. 647), who became Bishop of East Anglia.

THREE

Bede the Scholar and Scientist: Cosmos and Logos

What did the Anglo-Saxons and their neighbours know of their world? There was greater mobility than we might think and water was used as major highways, along with a reused network of prehistoric trackways and Roman roads. They inherited some knowledge of geography and natural history from ancient Rome through authors such as Pliny and Priscian and the cartographer Ptolemy. Bede's scholarship embraced the natural world as part of his quest to understand God's purpose. He wrote *On the Nature of Things*, building on the encyclopaedic approach to natural history of Pliny and Isidore of Seville, and the volumes *On Times* and *On the Reckoning of Time*. Bede knew from the ancients that the world was a globe in a cosmos of stars and planets, even if, in accordance with early Christian lore, he considered that stratified cosmos to revolve around the Earth. He also studied eclipses and the phases of the Moon, predicting tides using a nineteen-year lunar cycle and inspiring the compilation of tide tables.[1]

Numbers and calculation intrigued him, especially dating. One of the things that Bede is best remembered for is that he popularized a system of dating from the birth of Christ: AD ('Anno Domini', the year of the Lord), first introduced by Dionysius Exiguus (*c*. 470–544, a Scythian monk based in Rome), and undertook the complex calculations needed to reconcile the many different dating styles observed by his sources. Think of

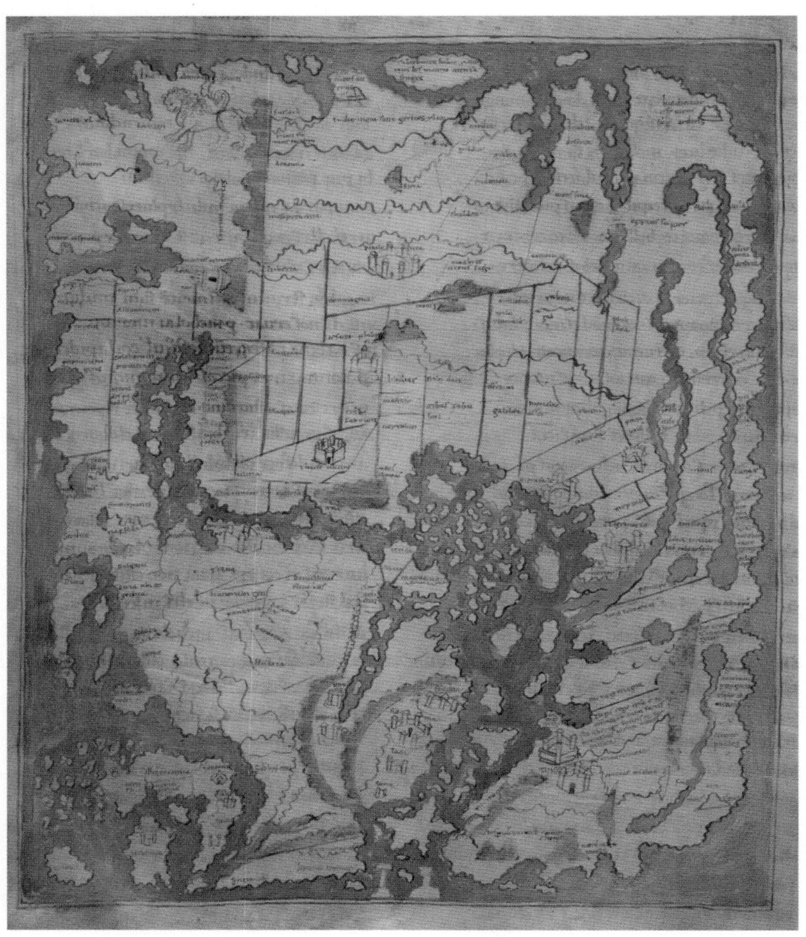

16 The Anglo-Saxon World Map (British Library, Cotton MS Tiberius B V/1, f. 56v), Canterbury, 1020s, conflating the received wisdom of the ancient cartographers and voyagers with the more recent experience of the Scandinavian trading empire of which England briefly formed a part.

doing such reckonings, long divisions and fractions, then imagine doing them using Roman numerals!

Bede's own biblical commentaries included studies of the Temple and Tabernacle in Jerusalem, of which he likely even produced a plan, probably inspired by or modified from that by the sixth-century monastic founder/publisher Cassiodorus, which features in the prefatory quire of the Codex Amiatinus (see illus. 11) and was later used as a frontispiece to his *On the Tabernacle* in at least one twelfth-century copy (BL, Add. MS 38817, ff. 1v–2r). From his cell, Bede sent forth his imagination to envision the wider world and the heavenly kingdom. The Frankish pilgrim-bishop Arculf is said to have been blown off course to Iona on his return by boat from the Holy Land. He drew ground plans of the holy places on wax tablets and dictated his pilgrim guide to Abbot Adomnàn of Iona in around 690.[2] Bede's *On Holy Places*, which reworks Adomnàn's account of *The Holy Places*, is one of the best early pilgrim guides, used by those who physically visited the Holy Land and those who, like Bede, journeyed spiritually in heart and mind.[3]

Insular missionaries helped to spread Christianity abroad. The foundations of the Irish saint Columbanus, who left Bangor in the North of Ireland on *peregrinatio* (voluntary exile for Christ) in 590, included Luxeuil in southern France, St Gall in Switzerland and Bobbio in Lombardic northern Italy. The trajectory of his mission was shaped by the vagaries of his relations with the rulers of Merovingian Gaul; he initially won the support of Childebert II but then fell foul of Theuderic and moved on to Lombardic territory, where he became increasingly embroiled in the Easter controversy and the tensions between Catholic orthodoxy and the Arian heresy. Columbanus's letter to Pope Gregory the Great pointing out errors in Roman observation may well have played a part in turning the focus of papal attention westwards to Britain and Ireland. In 690 the English saint Willibrord launched his work in Frisia, with the support of the Merovingian ruler Pippin II. There he founded Echternach (Luxembourg) and Utrecht as part of an Irish-led, part-Northumbrian mission instigated by an English bishop, Egbert, based in Ireland. During the first half of the eighth century Willibrord's work was consolidated by Boniface, 'Apostle to the Germans' (c. 675–754), from Devon. Prior to his martyrdom at pagan hands at Dokkum, he was assisted by a circle that included his kinswoman St Leoba (acclaimed as the greatest poetess of the age, none of her work is known to exist now).

Traditions from Britain and Ireland and the Christian East hint at visits in both directions, while Insular liturgy and litanies include numerous references to practices and figures from the Near East. There is a reference to the relief of famine in southwest Britain conducted on the back of tin-trading between Cornwall and Alexandria in the Life of St John the Almsgiver, Greek Patriarch of Alexandria (610–21). Certainly, pottery indicating continuing trade with the Mediterranean and North Africa during the post-Roman period has been found in sites along the Atlantic seaboard, such as Tintagel.

Benedict Biscop undertook six visits to Rome, gathering icons and books to stock one of the greatest western libraries at his twin foundations of Monkwearmouth and Jarrow. He was accompanied on various of these trips by Ceolfrith and Wilfrid, later Archbishop of York. It has been estimated that the Wearmouth-Jarrow library contained some three hundred volumes, two-thirds of which were consulted by Bede in his research.[4] But some areas, such as poetry, grammar and philosophy, were less populated by titles than the resources available to Aldhelm in southern England and there are gaps in Bede's knowledge, either because of lack of access or due to authorial agendas, for Bede's scholarship was, after all, monastic rather than scholastic.

The massive church that Wilfrid built at Hexham, in Roman masonry technique, contains a crypt modelled on the Holy Sepulchre, filled with relics collected during his travels. His other crypt at Ripon became the centre of Wilfrid's own cult from 709/710, the focal point of which was a purple codex he probably acquired abroad. Wilfrid's enduring monuments therefore assembled iconic references to *romanitas*, the Holy Places and imperial dignity, expressed through Byzantinizing visible consumption of costly materials in book form.

Wilfrid was but one of a number of Insular pilgrims to Rome. Pilgrimage to the Holy Land had escalated following St Helena's investigations of the biblical sites and discovery of the True Cross in the fourth century. That same century, the Spanish nun Etheria/Egeria recorded her journeys to the holy places, including Mount Sinai. In addition to Arculf's account, during the 780s the West Saxon St Willibald dictated to the nun Hugeburc/Hygeburg/Huneberc of Heidensheim an account of his visit to the Holy Land in the 720s–30s, including the monastery of Mar Saba, where St John Damascene was writing *The Fount of Knowledge*. This refutation of heresies included the first Christian discussion of Islam, presented as essentially a Christian heresy, like Arianism and Monothelitism. In the 730s St Boniface wrote from the Germanic mission-fields to the Archbishop of Canterbury asking him to stem the waves of unaccompanied Englishwomen travelling abroad, for many perished or wound up in the brothels of Lombardy and Gaul. In defence of the morals of said Englishwomen, Boniface was in part displaying erudition by quoting a passage from Eusebius (demonstrating that European women were already travelling widely in the fourth century). Women also risked life and limb in missionary endeavours, such as Leoba, Boniface's kinswoman, renowned for her learning and poetry. The Irish were also inveterate travellers, as missionaries, preachers and hermits, and in the ninth century were ridiculed in the Carolingian Empire as troublesome itinerants.

Travellers from the East might also take a westerly trajectory: an inscription on an ogham stone near St Olan's Well, Aghabullogue, Co. Cork, has been deciphered as 'Pray for Olan the Egyptian', although this may be a generic reference to local Egyptian-style hermits rather than an ethnic indicator. Likewise, at Templebrecan on Inishmore in the Irish Aran Isles, an early Christian stone marks the graves of the VII Romani (possibly seven anonymous Romans who may have studied there, or seven Irish clerics who followed the ways of Rome).

The Islamic conquest of the Near East, northern Africa and much of Iberia during the seventh century following the flight of the Prophet Muhammad and his followers to Medina (the Hijra, in 622) made such journeys harder, but the desire for trade and the toleration afforded to many existing communities meant that it still occurred. St Catherine's monastery in Sinai, for example, received permission (allegedly from Muhammad himself) to extend its safe conduct to anyone who visited en route.[5]

Post-prehistoric rural Ireland lacked towns prior to the Viking age, but trade flourished in northern European towns, including those familiar to the Germanic Anglo-Saxons such as Dorestad, Riga, Birka, London, Southampton and Ipswich. Monasteries and courts also served as distribution centres for imports and manufactured goods – some of them also made in situ. Exotic items from distant parts were greatly prized and brought some knowledge of other cultures. By around 800 in the kingdom of Mercia, the sculptures at the monastery of Breedon on the Hill in Leicestershire featured Syriac lion hunts, centaurs and a Byzantinizing icon of the Virgin in stone. Prayerbooks featured compilations of devotions composed by Celtic, Roman and Eastern authors (such as St Ephrem the Syrian).[6] Such Eastern influences built upon an exoticism and internationalism long apparent in Insular culture and further enhanced by King Offa (r. 757–96), who had embarked upon dynastic marriage alliances and trade wars with his 'cousin' Charlemagne and who, in 773/4, had minted a golden mancus modelled upon a dinar of the Abbasid Caliph al-Mansur minted in Baghdad that same year – such dinars circulated around the Mediterranean through trade

– featuring Ethiopic Axumite script and his own name alongside that of Allah. This is a supremely graphic and concise expression of the extent to which the Anglo-Saxons laid claim upon the world stage by the end of the eighth century.

The Insular experience of the world may have extended only as far as the Near East, but the Silk Road linked it, and Byzantium, to great Eastern centres such as XiangAn. The islands of Britain and Ireland were linked to those of Japan by an international trade network that converged upon Byzantium and the Near East, even if they did not know of each other's existence. Islamic areas provided a route for Eastern technology to reach the West. In the eighth century, paper-making was learned from Chinese captives, reaching Europe via Spain and Sicily in the twelfth century; the knowledge of porcelain manufacture travelled via a similar route. Aspects of Graeco-Roman learning and medicine were preserved by Islamic scholars and reintroduced to Europe during the late twelfth and thirteenth centuries following the Crusades and the establishment of universities in proliferating and expanding towns.

The classical and early Christian legacies continued to resonate in the farthest points of East and West but developed in different ways. It is important to compare like with like, as many of the scientific and artistic splendours of the East and Islam date from later periods than the eighth century. Others are much earlier. The Chinese had developed printing from woodblocks as early as the seventh century, while the West had to await the fifteenth century for moveable type printing. During the century of Bede's birth Buddhism was introduced to Japan from China (around 600), around the same time as Christianity was being reintroduced to southeast England from mainland Europe. The seventh century also witnessed the birth of Islam which, by 711, had swept into Iberia, a major part of the western Roman Empire and home to Bede's respected Isidore of Seville.

Other arts, such as poetry and music, flourished in both the far West and East. Celtic poets were the first in the West to celebrate nature, while the Anglo-Saxons brought the epic verse of the mead hall to bear upon both secular and religious themes, such as *Beowulf* (written down in its developed form around the year 1000) and *The Dream of the Rood*, the early core of which is inscribed on the Ruthwell Cross in Dumfriesshire, a Northumbrian-inspired monument on British soil (in the British kingdom of Rheged, southwest Scotland. Some of the finest Japanese poetry likewise survives from this period, notably that by Prince Shotoku, who introduced Buddhism, while the tenth-century Islamic physician-philosopher al-Razi (Rhazes, *c.* 854–935) introduced the concept of the ethical treatment of animals, a concern also reflected in some Celtic poetry and hagiography. Columbanus (*c.* 543–615) wrote that nature was a second Scripture in which we perceive God. An affinity with nature and the opportunities it afforded for solitary contemplation and communion with the divine are a distinctive feature of the 'Celtic' response to Christianity, stimulated by prehistoric tradition and the hagiographical visionary experiences of the desert fathers, who also sought spiritual encounter in wilderness. Such concerns also pervade the vitae of Insular saints such as Cuthbert, Fursey and Guthlac. Sts Paul and Anthony, their visionary models, are depicted on eremitic retreat on sculptures from Pictland and Ireland, along with paradisiacal landscapes featuring palm trees and ostriches, as on the ninth-century cross-slab at Fowlis Wester, Perthshire, on the eighth-century North Cross at Ahenny, Munster, and on the Ruthwell Cross.

Bede never travelled far, though he probably visited York, Hexham and Lindisfarne. Nonetheless, he dispatched research requests answered by Lastingham, East Anglia, Wessex, London, the Barking nuns and Canterbury. Nothhelm, a London priest and later Archbishop of Canterbury (735–9), even undertook research on Bede's behalf at Canterbury earlier in his career and later in Rome. Abbot Albinus of Canterbury particularly supported Bede in writing the *Ecclesiastical History of the English People* – Bede evidently attracted influential friends as well as jealous detractors.

The *Universal Ecclesiastical History* compiled by Eusebius during the fourth century may have been a source of inspiration for Bede's *Ecclesiastical History of the English People*. This is his most famous work and it is for this that he is principally remembered, for his pioneering methodology and because it remains the single most important source for the early Anglo-Saxon period. Through it, Bede sought to weave his people into the broader fabric of the Christian story, in sequel to Eusebius' *Ecclesiastical History* of the early Christian Church. Indeed, the very concept of Englishness stems from Bede's attempts to construct a collective identity for the mêlée of peoples inhabiting the former Roman province of Britannia, although in so doing he privileged his own people, the Angles.

To divine the will of the Divine, Bede also studied the workings of the natural world, of time and space. He wrote *On the Nature of Things* around 703, building on the encyclopaedic approach to natural history of Pliny and Isidore of Seville, and *On Times*, again in 703, and wove these two approaches to time and space together and extended his thinking on them in 725 in *On the Calculation/Reckoning of Time*. Such was the interconnectivity of his thought that Bede's *Reckoning of Time* also made reference to medical sources, such as the *Letter to Pentadius* by Vindicianus, a fourth-century North African physician, which discusses the relation of the four humours to the seasons, and the Letter to King Antiochus by pseudo-Hippocrates, which offers instructions on preserving health through changes in the seasons, making Bede the first writer to link computus and medical material. In the breadth of this approach, C. W. Jones has suggested

17 Christ adored by the Beasts, based on the Book of Habakkuk, from the Ruthwell Cross, an early 8th-century Northumbrian monument in the recently annexed British kingdom of Rheged (the region that is now southwest Scotland), inscribed in runes with part of the poem *The Dream of the Rood*.

that he was influenced by a genre of anthologies linking letters, didactic dialogues and tracts, from southern Ireland (notably Bodleian Library, Bodley 309, an eleventh-century copy), which linked historical, philological and computistical material.[7] By fusing the encyclopaedic reference approach of Pliny and Isidore with the didactic, questioning approach of the Irish masters, Bede effectively created a new tool for transmitting knowledge, teaching it and shaping the thought processes required to process it. No wonder Carolingian, Anglo-Saxon and Scholastic educators prized his works and that during the twelfth century they should have been supplemented with diagrams to compensate for the fact that Bede was no longer present *viva voce* to create his wonderful, memorable verbal images.

One of these diagrams illustrates Bede's prologue to *The Reckoning of Time*, helping to clarify calculations using finger reckoning. Intriguingly, it is supplemented in the twelfth-century copy by a parallel interpretation of the finger system as monastic sign language (illus. 18).

Another Irish source, *The Book of the Order of Creatures*, also joined Pliny and Isidore in influencing Bede's *On the Nature of Things* – for example, when examining the relationship between the Moon and tides in Chapter 39, which he expanded upon in *The Reckoning of Time*. His approach when addressing issues such as what causes the tides was generally that of the schoolroom

18 Diagram showing finger counting and monastic sign language, from a copy of Bede's *De temporum ratione*, included in a miscellany of compustical and astrological texts copied in northern France, late 11th–early 12th century (BL, Royal MS 13 A XI, f. 33v).

Q&A (although he talks of them in relation to what constitutes a port in very practical terms in Chapter 29, leading to the suggestion that he was involved in some sort of survey of coastal landing places). But when dealing with the nature of the Earth itself in chapters 46–7 he ventured further into proofs proposing, for example, that the world was demonstrably spherical because of variations in the length of shadows cast on sundials and the variation in the length of daylight according to latitude. The heavenly constellations were also perceived to vary according to location. Flat earthers beware!

In that same text, Chapter 21, in which he deals with the nature of the world according to the four elements, Bede went beyond other authors in providing a mathematical formula for finding the sign of the Moon in any age, and studied solar and lunar eclipses. Bede's eclipse records show that astronomical events could be used to explain unusual phenomena such as the postulated volcanic 'dust-veil' that enveloped Europe in 536, causing climate deterioration and one of its worst plague and famine periods before the fourteenth-century Black Death.[8] (It is now thought to have been caused by comet impact or volcanic eruption, and tallies with an acidity layer in the Greenland ice cores around this time.) Bede linked this to earlier references he found to two eclipses having occurred around this time. He would surely have made the link to the worsening conditions that led the Celtic missionaries he admired to set sail aboard 'the boat with no oars' to go where God sent them to minister to the bodies and souls of those suffering so sorely. The Anglo-Saxon Chronicle went on to record forty cosmic or meteorological events, which it viewed as portents, including Halley's Comet, which announced the Norman Conquest in 1066, as depicted in the Bayeux Tapestry.[9] In the complexity of his lunar and other computistical calculations, Bede was following an ancient tradition of astronomical observation and database compilation that extended back across time and space, from prehistoric stone circles and monuments such as Stonehenge, through ancient Mesopotamian and Babylonian star clocks and cuneiform tablet lists of eclipses, to Graeco-Roman astronomy; it would extend later, in an as yet unknown continent, to Mayan codices such as the eleventh- to twelfth-century Dresden Codex. His work forms a significant step along the road to modern space exploration and computing.

The Easter and Monothelete Controversies

Chronological miscalculations disrupted eternal harmony, especially when relating to Easter – the defining moment when God and humankind were reconciled. It was therefore crucial to Bede to correct any such inconsistencies. The biggest disruption was one that dragged on for many centuries, concerning the dating of the moveable feast of Easter – the defining moment of the Christian year – and the Church in Northumbria found itself at the heart of the debate during the seventh and eighth centuries. Feelings surrounding this ran high and many theologians and scholars had sought to address it. Bede succeeded.

In 325 the First Council of Nicaea first debated the Easter Controversy, which had arisen during the second century when Bishop Irenaeus of Lyon (from Smyrna in Anatolia) asserted the 'quartodeciman' Jewish/Johannine mode of calculation as part of his work in combating heresy and asserting orthodoxy in southern France. In Smyrna he had heard the preaching of St Polycarp, who was said to have heard St John, making him the last known living connection with the apostles. John had favoured the use of the Jewish lunar calendar. The Council of Nicaea, however, prescribed an Alexandrine single rule for Easter, computed independently of the Jewish calendar, but did not prescribe details of the computation, which took centuries to become standardized.[10]

A letter written by Irenaeus shows that the diversity of practice regarding Easter had existed at least from the time of Pope Sixtus I (*c.* 120). Irenaeus states that Polycarp observed the fourteenth day of the Moon, whatever day of the week that might be, following the tradition he claimed to have derived from St John (this may be why the Columban Book of Durrow adopts Irenaeus' ordering of the evangelist symbols, rather than what came to be the usual ordering of Matthew the man, Mark the lion, Luke the bull and John the eagle preferred by Augustine, Gregory the Great and Bede).

The monastic federation established by St Columba, with its caput of Iona, favoured the Johannine solution by virtue of its antiquity and the apostolic tradition, as did the British Church. Those churches within the orbit of the missions of Palladius to Ireland and Augustine to Anglo-Saxon England, both launched from Rome, and those of Frankish missionaries such as Felix, favoured the Nicene ruling, with calculations based upon the Roman solar calendar. Things came to a head in 664, when this and other conflicting practices (such as the method of tonsure) were debated at the Synod of Whitby. There the Alexandrine computus advocated at Nicaea was adopted by the English Church. Wilfrid argued successfully in its favour, asserting that 'it was the universal practice of the Church, even as far as Egypt.' Bishop Colman of Lindisfarne, having failed to assert the Columban Johannine tradition, returned with many followers to Ireland. The Columban and British Churches were thereby effectively deemed to be schismatic until they conformed, which in the case of the Columban paruchia took place in 715, when Iona was its last bastion to succumb. Some of the British churches of the north, of Wales and of the southwest held out longer – in Cornwall until the tenth century, for although St Athanasius specifically noted that the British Church assented to the decisions of the First

Council of Nicaea, they did not follow many subsequent developments.

The Easter Controversy was not the only matter of high-level international ecclesiastical importance in which the nascent Insular churches played a role. From 669 Archbishop Theodore of Tarsus and Abbot Hadrian set about reforming, organizing, regularizing, educating and growing the English Church. Cuthbert was persuaded to become Bishop of Lindisfarne in 685 and was given a leading role in the post-Whitby reconciliation process, while Eadberht and Adomnán led that of the Columban federation. Wearmouth-Jarrow became the principal northern exponent of their educational agenda.

In 679 Archbishop Theodore convened the Council of Hatfield (just north of London) as a pre-debate for the Sixth Ecumenical Council of 681, which met in Constantinople to resolve the monothelete controversy that revolved around the thorny issue of how Christ could be both human and divine. The Council declared that the divine and human nature of Christ were indivisible. I have suggested that the foundation of Jarrow very soon after, joining Monkwearmouth (founded 674) and forming the unusual phenomenon of a twin monastery, described by Bede as 'two places with but one will', was a symbolic statement of adherence to the Council and a commitment to international orthodoxy, as established by the Council of Chalcedon in 451. The traditional historical view of Wearmouth-Jarrow as a bastion of *romanitas*, in opposition to the 'Celtic' traditions of Lindisfarne and other ultimately Columban foundations, is evidently a distorting over-simplification (the 'Celtic Church' being a modern concept, not current at this time). They would have been united in the common purpose of reconciliation and eirenic collaboration, locally and throughout Christendom. This imperative can be detected throughout Bede's work and in his contributions towards framing the cult of St Cuthbert and espousing the cause of Lindisfarne in the face of opposition from Wilfrid and his supporters and successors.

In order to enable him to effectively contribute to the debate on calculating dates, Bede needed to draw upon previous learning in the fields of computus and astronomy and to grapple with the very nature of time. A major problem in so doing was the myriad of different methods of recording dating, from indictions (a fifteen-year cyclical taxation system first initiated by Julius Caesar in 48 BC) to eras of individual rulers' reigns or consulships, recorded on monuments, in letters and documents and in yearly records of events (annals, which originated as marginal annotation to Easter tables) and compilations thereof (chronicles). Bede's self-imposed task of writing a history of his people that transcended the genre of chronicles, with their bald statements of events, led him to process vast amounts of research materials, which needed to be synthesized and integrated into not just a continuous narrative, but a demonstration of cause and effect. The unified dating system that he chose to employ was that of dating from the Incarnation of Christ, in what was thought to be A(nno) D(omini) 1. This had been pioneered by the Scythian monk Dionysius Exiguus, the 'humble' or 'small' (*c.* 470–*c.* 544), who resided in Rome, was a friend to Cassiodorus and was also responsible for compiling the canons of the early Church synods and councils (including those from Nicaea to Chalcedon), composing and translating saints lives and writing a *Computus* – tables used to help calculate when Easter should fall.

The Council of Nicaea in 325 had decreed that both Eastern and Western churches should celebrate Easter simultaneously, but they calculated its date differently. Both agreed, however, that the Christian celebration should not be based upon the Jewish calendar and that it should fall on the Sunday after the first full moon that followed the vernal (spring) equinox (21 March) – a nasty bit of prejudice initiated in this case by Cyprian in his *On*

Computing the Paschal Feast in 243 – but this presented difficulties in reconciling the lunar and solar calendars. Dionysius decided to renumber the then current era, which began in the age of the martyrs, in order to displace the name of their persecutor, Emperor Diocletian. Thus 'Anno Diocletiani' was changed to 'Anno Domini nostri Jesu Christi', although some churches, including that of the Copts, retained the persecution by Diocletian as the marker of time. Dionysius then set dates for Easter in a 95-year cycle, using his own *computes*, spanning the years 532 to 627.

At the pope's behest, Dionysius accordingly sought to calculate when the birth of Christ had occurred and used that as the starting point for his system. This method had already been used by the Church of Alexandria (but not by the Church of Rome) from at least AD 311. What Dionysius did was convert its arguments from the Alexandrian calendar into the Julian calendar to give the Julian Easter, which is that still used by all Orthodox churches. The Gregorian Easter, which is that commonly used in the West today, arose from a reform of the calendar in 1582, undertaken under Pope Gregory XIII to address the problem of equinox drift and the resulting confusion over the date of Easter. When Julius Caesar established his calendar in 45 BC he set 25 March as the spring equinox, but since the Julian year (365.25 days) is slightly longer than the tropical year, the vernal equinox drift meant although it occurred around 21 March in AD 300, by 1500 it fell on 11 March. Thus by the sixteenth century, the Church's lunar calendar and the Julian calendar were off-kilter and Easter was being celebrated on the wrong day. To rectify this, the Gregorian calendar simply dropped ten days from the year 1582.[11]

And so, by building upon earlier work and paving the way for such future work, it had fallen to Bede to play a key role and to refine, systematically apply and establish the use of the Christian Era. In *The Reckoning of Time*, he ensured the popularization of his modified Dionysian system by firmly synthesizing computus, astronomy and cosmology with a theological significance.

On Times ends with a world chronicle, which may seem surprising until one realizes that this plays a key part, along with other aspects of his *computes* and his comment on the Apocalypse, in Bede's recalibration of the Christian Era to reinforce its rooting in the soil of Jewish prehistory and to establish that within the traditional six ages of the world (which correspond to the six days of Creation and are said to be each of 1,000 years' duration, based on Psalm 90:4 and 2 Peter 3:8 – 'with the Lord one day is as a thousand years'), Christ's incarnation fell within the fourth rather than the sixth age, as previously thought (calculating Christ's birth at 3952 in the age of the world, as opposed to the year 5199 given by Eusebius).[12] For Bede was no millennialist and refuted the idea that the end of the world was nigh; there was still a lot of work to do, not least on human nature and the trajectory of human history. He hoped that his own people would now play a positive role in this – though he displays misgivings about where things were currently heading in his own age, hence his reforming agenda.

Bede's pivotal emphasis upon the Synod of Whitby (*Ecclesiastical History*, III.25), and events leading up to and ensuing from it, is echoed in his placing of the Paschal cycle between the year and the ages of the world in his discussion of units of time in *On Times* (thereby integrating *computes* into a 'science of time').[13] It all becomes explicable in this wider context – for Whitby was not only a matter of local and immediate concern, but had a bearing on the international ecumen and on the correct time-setting of the cosmos.

It is not by chance that Bede structured the *Ecclesiastical History* to begin with a verbal word map – a description of Britain that consciously echoes material not only from Pliny, Solinus, Orosius and Gildas, but from the *Gallic Wars* by Julius Caesar, followed by an account of his expedition thence.

Chap. 1. Of the Situation of Britain and Ireland, and of their ancient inhabitants.

Britain, an island in the Atlantic, formerly called Albion, lies to the north-west, facing, though at a considerable distance, the coasts of Germany, France, and Spain, which form the greatest part of Europe. It extends 800 miles in length towards the north, and is 200 miles in breadth, except where several promontories extend further in breadth, by which its compass is made to be 4,875 miles. To the south lies Belgic Gaul. To its nearest shore there is an easy passage from the city of Rutubi Portus, by the English now corrupted into Reptacaestir [Richborough]. The distance from here across the sea to Gessoriacum [Boulogne], the nearest shore in the territory of the Morini, is fifty miles, or as some writers say, 450 furlongs. On the other side of the island, where it opens upon the boundless ocean, it has the islands called Orcades. Britain is rich in grain and trees and is well adapted for feeding cattle and beasts of burden. It also produces vines in some places, and has plenty of land and water fowl of divers sorts; it is remarkable also for rivers abounding in fish, and plentiful springs. It has the greatest plenty of salmon and eels; seals are also frequently taken, and dolphins, as also whales; besides many sorts of shell-fish, such as mussels, in which are often found excellent pearls of all colours, red, purple, violet and green, but chiefly white. There is also a great abundance of snails, of which the scarlet dye is made, a most beautiful red, which never fades with the heat of the sun or exposure to rain, but the older it is, the more beautiful it becomes. It has both salt and hot springs, and from them flow rivers which furnish hot baths, proper for all ages and both sexes, in separate places, according to their requirements. For water, as St. Basil says, receives the quality of heat, when it runs along certain metals, and becomes not only hot but scalding. Britain is rich also in veins of metals, as copper, iron, lead, and silver; it produces a great deal of excellent jet, which is black and sparkling, and burns when put to the fire, and when set on fire, drives away serpents; being warmed with rubbing, it attracts whatever is applied to it, like amber. The island was formerly distinguished by twenty-eight famous cities, besides innumerable forts, which were all strongly secured with walls, towers, gates, and bars. And, because it lies almost under the North Pole, the nights are light in summer, so that at midnight the beholders are often in doubt whether the evening twilight still continues, or that of the morning has come; since the sun at night returns to the east in the northern regions without passing far beneath the earth. For this reason the days are of a great length in summer, and on the other hand, the nights in winter are eighteen hours long, for the sun then withdraws into southern parts. In like manner the nights are very short in summer, and the days in winter, that is, only six equinoctial hours . . .

There are in the island at present, following the number of the books in which the Divine Law was written, five languages of different nations employed in the study and confession of the one self-same knowledge, which is of highest truth and true sublimity, to wit, English, British, Scottish, Pictish, and Latin, the last having become common to all by the study of the Scriptures. But at first this island had no other inhabitants but the Britons, from whom it derived its name, and who, coming over into Britain, as is reported, from Armorica [Brittany], possessed themselves of the southern parts thereof.

Starting from the south, they had occupied the greater part of the island, when it happened, that the nation of the Picts, putting to sea from Scythia, as is reported, in a few ships of war, and being driven by the winds beyond the bounds of Britain, came to Ireland and landed on its northern shores. There, finding the nation of the Scots, they begged to be allowed to settle among them, but could not succeed in obtaining their request. Ireland is the largest island next to Britain and lies to the west of it; but as it is shorter than Britain to the north, so, on the other hand, it runs out far beyond it to the south, over against the northern part of Spain, though a wide sea lies between them. The Picts then, as has been said, arriving in this island by sea, desired to have a place granted them in which they might settle. The Scots answered that the island could not contain them both; but 'We can give you good counsel,' said they, 'whereby you may know what to do; we know there is another island, not far from ours, to the eastward, which we often see at a distance, when the days are clear. If you will go thither, you can obtain settlements; or, if any should oppose you, we will help you.' The Picts, accordingly, sailing over into Britain, began to inhabit the northern parts thereof, for the Britons had possessed themselves of the southern. Now the Picts had no wives, and asked them of the Scots; who would not consent to grant them upon any other terms, than that when any question should arise, they should choose a king from the female royal race rather than from the male: which custom, as is well known, has been observed among the Picts to this day. In process of time, Britain, besides the Britons and the Picts, received a third nation, the Scots, who, migrating from Ireland under their leader, Reuda, either by fair means, or by force of arms, secured to themselves those settlements among the Picts which they still possess. From the name of their commander, they are to this day called Dalreudini; for, in their language, Dal signifies a part.

Ireland is broader than Britain and has a much healthier and milder climate; for the snow scarcely ever lies there above three days: no man makes hay in the summer for winter's provision or builds stables for his beasts of burden. No reptiles are found there, and no snake can live there; for, though snakes are often carried thither out of Britain, as soon as the ship comes near the shore, and the scent of the air reaches them, they die. On the contrary, almost all things in the island are efficacious against poison. In truth, we have known that when men have been bitten by serpents, the scrapings of leaves of books that were brought out of Ireland, being put into water, and given them to drink, have immediately absorbed the spreading poison, and assuaged the swelling . . .

Chap. 2. How Caius Julius Caesar was the first Roman that came into Britain.

Now Britain had never been visited by the Romans and was entirely unknown to them before the time of Caius Julius Caesar, who, in the year 693 after the foundation of Rome, but the sixtieth year before the Incarnation of our Lord, was consul with Lucius Bibulus. While he was making war upon the Germans and the Gauls, who were divided only by the river Rhine, he came into the province of the Morini, whence is the nearest and shortest passage into Britain. Here, having provided about eighty ships of burden and fast-sailing vessels, he sailed over into Britain; where, being first roughly handled in a battle, and then caught in a storm, he lost a considerable part

> of his fleet, no small number of foot-soldiers, and almost all his cavalry. Returning into Gaul, he put his legions into winter-quarters, and gave orders for building six hundred sail of both sorts. With these he again crossed over early in spring into Britain . . . In the second engagement, with great hazard to his men, he defeated the Britons and put them to flight. Thence he proceeded to the river Thames, where a great multitude of the enemy had posted themselves on the farther side of the river, under the command of Cassobellaunus, and fenced the bank of the river and almost all the ford under water with sharp stakes: the remains of these are to be seen to this day, apparently about the thickness of a man's thigh, cased with lead, and fixed immovably in the bottom of the river . . . Caesar at length, after severe fighting, took the town of Cassobellaunus, situated between two marshes, fortified by sheltering woods, and plentifully furnished with all necessaries. After this, Caesar returned from Britain into Gaul, but he had no sooner put his legions into winter quarters, than he was suddenly beset and distracted with wars and sudden risings on every side.

It was Caesar who had introduced the solar Julian calendar that led to the calendrical problems in the first place. The *Ecclesiastical History of the English People* might just as well have been entitled *The Faith Journey of the English People towards Orthodox Compliance* – but that would hardly have been as catchy.

Nor was it a coincidence that Bede's description of Britain in the *Ecclesiastical History*'s opening chapter (finished in 731) combines measurements and observations on natural history, the areas of study that Bede had explored in *On the Nature of Things* and *On Times*, or that his intellectual energies during his own last days should have been devoted to translating, and thereby rendering more accessible, Isidore of Seville's *The Nature of Things* (things needful to know about the material world, lest 'my children learn what is not true and waste their labour on this after I am gone') and the spiritual vision of St John's Gospel (things needful to know about the Divine).[14] For Bede had his own master plan, which he structured in accordance with his intellectual and spiritual perception of God's will, and he lived it to his earthly end. This is true vocation.

This thorny and extensive research had entailed deploying skills in the disciplines of mathematics, science, astronomy, theology and history. It demonstrated that scientific methods could be applied to problem solving – a lesson that has informed much modern research practice and which contributed to a trajectory of thought and theory testing that has led to quantum theories. It also showed that the control of time brought with it other forms of cultural, and political, ascendancy – though Bede would probably have been the first to affirm that this is essentially a human preoccupation born of mortality and that only God exerts any real measure of control over time, which is but one dimension to Creation. For time is not the only or best way of measuring things – especially eternity and infinity.

Science/*scientia* did not mean the same to Bede and this earlier age as it does to us. It meant 'knowledge' (rather in the way that the European Science Foundation uses the term, whereas for the ancients the humanities and sciences were grouped under the 'liberal arts') and literacy meant being well read in Scripture, the Patristics and other respected Latin texts. They were subordinate to *doctrina christiana*, the Christian learning needful to teach, preach and comment upon the Christian faith and worldview. 'Ratio' was the logical and mathematical reckoning of the natura/nature of things and mathematics performs the role of an allegorical means of explaining the natural world and of divining God's purpose within it.

Bede's computistical calculations, not surprisingly, led him perilously close to charges of heresy – for the early medieval mind sought to build upon the experience of the past rather than trusting innovative thought. In his *Letter to Plegwin*, Bede reveals his profound hurt and indignation at being accused by 'lewd rustics', at the table of Bishop Wilfrid, of introducing dubious ideas of his own in his *On Times* – overtones of the response and accusations that Galileo would later receive from his peers. Bede's rebuttal was cutting and drew upon theological, exegetical, philological and 'scientific' justification. The urgency and assertiveness of his reaction speaks not only of righteous indignation at this unsupported attack on his work's value, but of his deep concern over the need to heal the Easter controversy rift and to uphold the Alexandrine Paschal tradition. He was probably correct in suspecting that this was what had motivated the attack from Wilfrid's coterie in the first place and accusing a scholar dedicated to healing schismatic rift in Christendom of contributing to it was a low blow. But, as is the way of things if you remember that it is not what happens to you, but how you respond to it, the contretemps did help stimulate Bede to go on to produce his masterly *On the Reckoning of Time*, in which his arguments were consolidated and expanded onto a much wider canvas.

Bishop Acca of Hexham also had to encourage Bede to defend himself against similar criticism concerning his exegesis on the evangelists and their symbols.[15] As Bede was quick to point out, his critics' ignorance meant that they were less literate (which in Bede's terms meant less well read and latinate) and were unaware of his allusions to earlier authorities. In response, he effectively introduced footnotes, inserting s-shaped marginal marks beside biblical quotations (which interestingly find an early application in the Lindisfarne Gospels, in the planning of which I have suggested he may have been involved) and marginal alphabetic characters to denote the names of other authors cited (A for Augustine, and so on). He was also at pains to credit his sources, stating in his autobiographical note that the *Ecclesiastical History* was based on facts gleaned 'so far as I have been able to ascertain them from ancient writings, from the traditions of our forebears, and from my own personal knowledge', while his preface cites those who actually supplied data.

Bede relied wherever possible on the work of his early Christian forebears, be they the Church Fathers of East and West or scholars such as Isidore of Seville (the intellectual master of sixth-century Visigothic Iberia), Cassiodorus (who founded the monastic publishing house of the Vivarium in southern Italy during that same century) and the computistical masters Dionysius Exiguus and Cummian the Wise of Iona. But he also drew, where he could and where appropriate, on the works of the ancients. Aristotle's writings were lost to the West during the collapse of the western empire and the expansion of Islam around the eastern and southern shores of the Mediterranean during the seventh and eighth centuries, not to be reintroduced until the scholastic age, but the influence of Pliny, Virgil and perhaps a little Cicero and Dioscorides and others lingered on and was readily assessed, deployed and assimilated into the Christian mindset. For Christian scholars of Bede's calibre harboured no automatic antipathy towards pagan authors, with Bede praising 'that delightful book, the *Natural History*' of Pliny the Elder (whose authority he compares to observations based upon Genesis by Ambrose and Basil in the *Hexaemera*, in *The Reckoning of Time*, Chapter 31), but they did exercise caution in appraising and utilizing those of their works that came their way from the wreckage of the Roman Empire.

Bede's definitions of rhetorical figures (tropes – including allegory, metaphor, periphrasis, metonymy and synecdoche – alliterations, homonyms, rhymes, puns and the like) may be based on the Latin grammarians, but he also goes to great lengths to replace

Vergil as a prime poetic role model, substituting early Christian poets in his place. Vergil's texts had served as the schoolroom exercise examples during the Roman period and continued to do so. Bede would gradually replace them with worthy Christian successors, such as Prudentius, Sedulius and Paulinus. The Christian scholarship of Spain, with its perpetuation of classical Latin, perhaps more so than elsewhere, was an important influence upon Bede. Following Jerome, he even perceived an underlying poetic compositional structure in the Psalms (written in lyric metres) and much of the Book of Job (composed in hexameters), confirming him in his belief that an understanding of rhetoric was also essential to understanding Scripture.[16]

M.L.W. Laistner lists some 78 authors whose work Bede is likely to have known to varying extents.[17] Bede also named Solinus, a third-century Latin grammarian who wrote a work containing geographical and historical excerpts from earlier authors such as Pliny and referred to passages (unascribed) from Vegetius' *On the Art of War*. He was also familiar with the work of Irish cosmographers, such as Augustinus Hibernicus' *The Miracles of Holy Scripture* and pseudo-Isidore's *Book of the Order of Creatures*.[18] He would have been acquainted with classical exponents of the genre, for a magnificent anthology of the works of the cosmographers, obtained in Rome, was presented by Benedict Biscop to King Aldfrith of Northumbria in exchange for a valuable parcel of land.

Cosmography was the proto-science of mapping the general features of the cosmos, heaven and earth and is now applied to the ongoing effort to determine the large-scale features of the observable universe. It encompassed astronomy and the then related field of astrology. Aldfrith's book might conceivably have included the *Aratea*, Cicero's Latin translation of the Greek *Phaenomena* of Aratus (although this did not achieve renewed popularity until the Carolingian age), and Bede would doubtless have pored over it or a copy made in the Wearmouth-Jarrow scriptorium. His interest in the heavens was an essential component of his approach to time and computus – and the vexed questions of the dating of Easter and a unified chronology, in which the phases of the Sun and Moon were crucial. The early Christian concept of the universe was akin to that of Graeco-Roman antiquity: a spherical layering of celestial and terrestrial spheres, the former inhabited by stars and planets (imbued with mythological significance) and the latter by creatures, plants, minerals and oceans. But instead of a pantheon of deities, they believed in creation *ex nihilo* by the one God of the Hebrews, whom they equated with the eternal, cosmic Logos (the 'Word'), expressed in the opening words of St John's Gospel as: 'In the beginning was the Word and the Word was with God and the Word was God.'

In his exegetical and literary pursuits and in those relating to understanding the nature of the world, Bede was not content to tack Christian experience and scholarship onto that of the ancients, as Isidore had done to some extent. He sought to show that Christian culture and faith had a robust, joined-up approach to understanding the cosmos, the world, the humans and other creatures and things that inhabited it and their relationship with one another and their Creator: a theory of everything.

Coming from the ranks of the newly converted, the Anglo-Saxons were well aware that the validity of their pre-Christian culture was not negated by receiving the knowledge of God, but was reinterpreted through a Christian lens and integrated into a new reading of human history and divine purpose. Thus, the whalebone Franks Casket, made in Northumbria during Bede's lifetime, had scenes from world history and mythology integrated into its iconography: Achilles; Hengist and Horsa; the Temple in Jerusalem sacked by Emperor Titus; Weyland the Smith, about to rape the daughter of his enemy, Nithard, and to

19 The Franks Casket, Northumbria (British Museum), early 8th century, a whalebone casket based on late Roman/Byzantine models, perhaps made to contain a manuscript of a royal genealogy. The scenes on this panel depict Weyland the Smith, about to conceive a warrior with his enemy's daughter (left) and the Adoration of the Magi (right), inscribed in runes.

conceive a warrior hero before escaping on wings of bird feathers. The latter scene is adjacent to and juxtaposed with that of the Adoration of the Magi (preceded by a duck-like Holy Spirit, paralleling Weyland's birds) before a Byzantine-style depiction of the frontal Virgin and Child – the true saviour of the world, across all peoples and all ages. It may have contained a copy of the Northumbrian royal genealogy, in which its rulers were shown to be descended from historical and mythological Germanic forebears to the biblical Adam.[19]

Nature itself also offered valuable insight, as St Columbanus had stated. For those of an eremitic disposition, used to living, however frugally, off the land and sea, an experimental awareness of their properties would have been only natural, for these were the survivalists of their day. If Isidore mediated Pliny's work on natural history and the nature of things and introduced an encyclopaedic approach, then Bede went further to construct an authentically Christian approach to Creation in which everything is interconnected across time and space and governed by the mathematical principles of geometry and *computes*. Human history, which perpetually seeks to disrupt this divine harmony, is ultimately reconciled and harmonized by the sacrifice of the eternal Logos, through which God might know what it is to be human and might forgive and redeem.

Direct observation of the natural world and of human history had, however, to be reconciled with scriptural revelation and learning inherited, albeit piecemeal, from the ancients and patristics. For the principal route to fully comprehending divine reality lay, for Bede and his peers, in the study of Judaeo-Christian Scripture and its interpretation by the Church Fathers. He therefore devoted most of his research (some twenty works) to biblical exegesis, excavating the Old and New Testaments not only for literal meaning and archaeological detail but, in rabbinic fashion, to extract multiple layers of allegorical interpretation through which deeper meaning might be discerned.

Integrating the English into Eternity

The deepest meaning that ultimately most preoccupied Bede was the creation of a good relationship with God, on the part of the individual, society and the world. As a Christian, he equated this with the process of conversion and the longed-for completion of the apostolic mission to proclaim the message of the Gospel ('Good News') to the furthest ends of the Earth, for in Bede's day Britain and Ireland marked the westernmost parameters of the known world. Bede situated those islands and the Christian experience and witness of his own people, whom as a Northumbrian were Angles (from which stemmed the terms Anglo-Saxon and 'English') at the front line of the working out of redemption. Much of his scholarship was placed at the service of establishing their identity as a Christian people – the new children of

Israel, settled in the promised land after their wanderings in the displacement of the barbarian migrations – and in presenting a different way of recording events in their history so that the implications of cause and effect might be perceived and used to inform future developments. Cautionary tales relating to good and bad government, both secular and clerical, abound in the *Ecclesiastical History of the English People* and, along with his hagiographical role models and his expounding of the meaning of Scripture and of Bible history, they work towards constructing guidelines for the conduct of a unified state guided by Christian ethics and underpinned by prayer and social justice – an exhortation to work towards the construction of the heavenly kingdom, rather than the mirror of worldly excesses and ultimately doomed combat against the world serpent that is the pagan Germanic Valhalla.

In so doing, Bede seems to have drawn upon varying previous approaches: that of the Bible in respect of human history and the working out of God's plan, some of the histories of the ancients, such as Julius Caesar's *Gallic Wars*, and Eusebius of Caesarea's *Universal Ecclesiastical History* – an account of the international early Christian Church and the societies that hosted it, to which Bede's own *Ecclesiastical History* effectively serves as a codicil, situating the English and their neighbours within that world-view. He also drew upon more local sources such as the polemic of the Welsh monk Gildas, *The Ruin and Conquest of Britain* (the *De excidio*), and Germanic and Celtic annals (short yearly accounts of events which are thought to have begun as notes in the margins of tables used to calculate the date of Easter and liturgical calendars recording the feast-days of the Church year; annals might subsequently be compiled into continuous historical chronicles). Other sources he encountered in his sacred (*lectio divina*) and scholarly reading; correspondence and records unearthed in response to his research enquiries, addressed to repositories of knowledge such as the papal archives and the Barking nuns (who

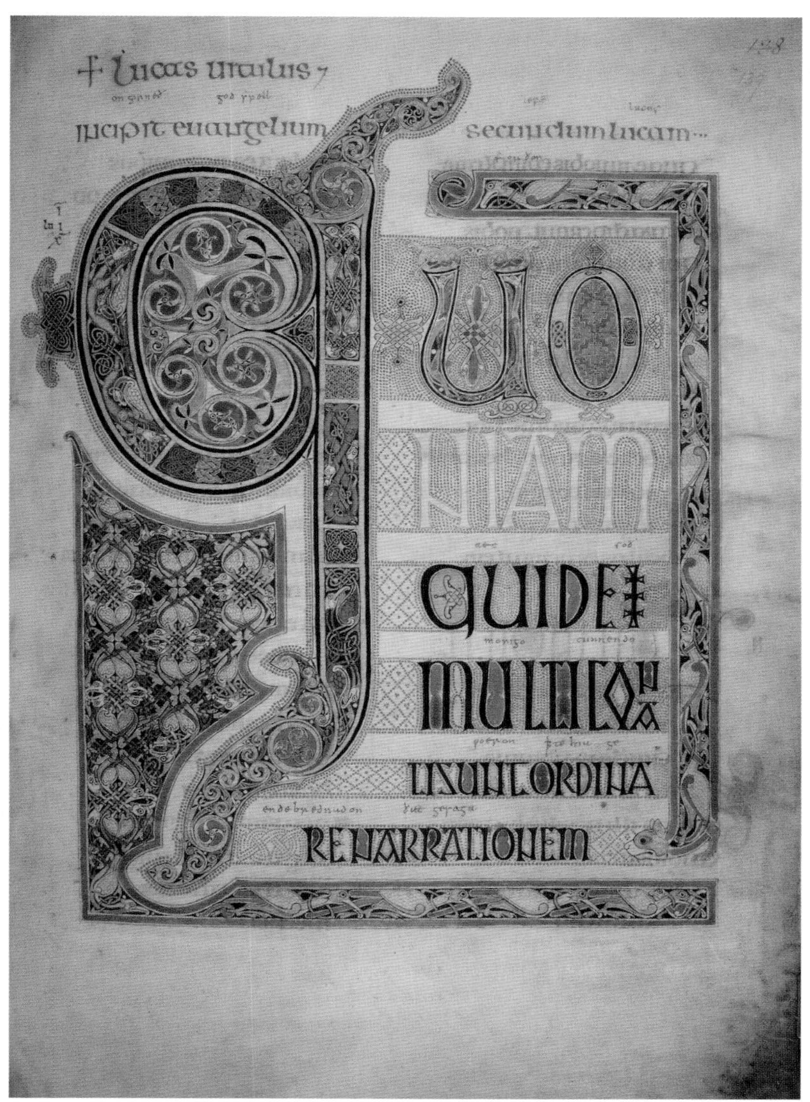

20, 21 Opening of St Luke's Gospel (cross-carpet page and incipit page), from the Lindisfarne Gospels, Lindisfarne, *c.* 715–22 (BL, Cotton MS Nero D IV, ff. 138v–139r).

responded with alacrity, increasing exponentially the amount known about early Essex in the *Ecclesiastical History*); and, as he says, the oral witness of those he interviewed or corresponded with and tales recounted across the generations around the fireside.

The academic and public approach to Bede's work is so often to raid and plunder it for details and to attempt to divide and pigeonhole it by subject classification. Historians will thus often cite the *Ecclesiastical History* without ever accessing his biblical or scientific scholarship, for example. But for Bede everything was interconnected, like the most complex yet mathematically structured designs of the decorated incipits and carpet pages of the great Insular Gospel books, such as the Book of Durrow, the Lindisfarne Gospels and the Book of Kells. Their geometric and numeric principles established a framework filled with Anglo-Saxon zoomorphic interlace inhabited by the creatures of the natural world, echoed in the abstraction of Celtic La Tène spiralwork with its shape-shifting ambiguity recollecting the flora and fauna and the movement of fire, wind and waves, and with human and identifiable animal forms conveying historical, mythological and/or moral meaning, unlocking references in the mind of the informed viewer to works such as the *Physiologus* or *Marvels of the East*, forerunner of the medieval bestiary, with its Christian moral interpretation of the symbolism of exotic peoples and creatures.

For Bede's mindset is characterized, it seems to me, by joined-up thinking and the long view, which extended across time and space and occasionally transcended it to glimpse the fourth dimension of eternity and the reconciliation and unification of all Creation, underpinned by Logos – the eternal, creative Word.

The key to reading much imagery, especially during the Insular period, lay in the principle of multivalence: why settle for only one, literal meaning when you can simultaneously explore other, deeper levels of allegorical meaning? The relentless rational pursuit of literal meaning espoused by the scholastics during the twelfth century was yet to come. John Cassian, a founding figure of Eastern and Western monasticism, advocated the deployment of three sorts of spiritual knowledge in order to understand Scripture: allegory, anagoge and tropology. History deals with real past events which have a literal meaning, whereas allegory relates to prefigured mysteries. Anagoge goes beyond such mysteries to penetrate the secrets of heaven, while tropology interprets all three for the moral edification and instruction of the present.

There may be a distant connection between the Jewish Kabbalistic tradition and the Christian interpretative tradition of the Scriptures. In the Kabbalistic concept of *Pardes* (orchard or paradise), 'P stands for *peshat* or the literal meaning, R for *remez* or the allegorical meaning, D for *derasha* or the Talmudic and Aggadic interpretation, and S for *sod* or the mystical meaning.'[20] It is, however, equally possible that this was derived by the Kabbalists from Christian hermeneutics – the 'fourfold allegorical scheme' or 'four senses of Scripture'.

This approach was favoured by Jerome and Gregory the Great and was adopted by Bede in his work on rhetoric, *On Tropes and Figures*. Such layered meaning might be difficult to 'read' to other than learned scholars – although the taste for riddles and conundrums probably inclined people towards it. Art rendered it more accessible.

To give an example, Bede wrote an allegory of the Temple in *On Tropes and Figures*, ch. 2.12:

> In the literal sense it is the house which Solomon built; allegorically, it is the Lord's body, of which Christ said: 'Destroy this temple and in three days I will raise it up', or his Church, to whom the apostle Paul said: 'For the

> Temple of the Lord is holy, which you are'; tropologically, it is each of the faithful, to whom the Apostle said: 'Know you not, that your bodies are the temple of the holy spirit, who is in you?'; anagogically, it is the joys of the heavenly mansion, for which the Psalmist sighed, when he said: 'Blessed are they that dwell in your house, O Lord; they shall praise you for ever and ever.'

It may be that the miniature of the Temptation of Christ in the Book of Kells, made probably on Iona circa 800 as a cult book of St Columba and continued at Kells, is a visualization of this teaching, with Christ appearing as the head of the body of the Temple building (depicted as an Irish portable house-shaped shrine, like the Tabernacle itself), with the faithful ranged around in a disposition that Carol Farr has related to the Communion of Saints, with the Church expectant at the foot, awaiting liberation, the Church militant on the left, doing the work in the world, and the Church triumphant giving eternal praise above.[21]

For if letters were the email and social media equivalents of their day, then the great illuminated manuscripts and carved monuments were the films. Then, as now, you did not need to be able to understand them completely, or penetrate all their nuances, in order to participate in the community of reading that they stimulated. For the visual literacy of the early Middle Ages is characterized by the interaction of words to be seen and images to be read.

The peoples of sixth- and seventh-century Britain and Ireland, who were brought up over centuries on a diet of rich storytelling, vibrant imagination and an art of personal adornment replete

22 The Temptation of Christ, which can also be interpreted as a sacred *figura* (diagram) of the Communion of Saints, with Christ as the head of the Church. From the *Book of Kells*, Iona (and continued at Kells), c. 800 (Trinity College Dublin, MS 58, f. 202v).

with encoded symbols and animal ornament, would have been a receptive audience for imagery associated with the spoken and written word. Exploitation of their visual memory would have assisted those introducing them to a new Christian cultural narrative – and a new way of thinking and living. Appreciation of the semiotic potential of motifs and symbols was inherent within pre-Christian Celtic and Germanic art and merged with Christian symbolism to great effect.[22]

Bede's thinking included one of the foremost examples of the application of the principle of multivalence. He wrote that there may be a literal meaning of a thing (a bare fact) but that, in order to understand it fully, you need to look beneath the surface and penetrate its deeper significance, meaning and context. This he did by applying the Jewish rabbinical concept of *Pardes* ('the Garden'), discussed above, in which the intellectual and literary tools of allegory, tropology (elaborations upon a theme) and typology (one thing foreshadowing another, for example, King David being the Old Testament 'type' or forerunner of Christ, or Moses setting up the brazen serpent in the wilderness being the 'type' of Christ raised up on the Cross – illustrations of which were among the continental images with which Biscop adorned the walls of his new basilicas at Wearmouth-Jarrow and through which Bede would have received instruction as a boy). A native familiarity with the kenning of Germanic riddles, which were adopted by Aldhelm and others as a means of schoolroom teaching, would also have taught Bede that you could not know what an onion was by simply looking at it. You need to peel off its skin, penetrate its layers and ultimately bite into it to really understand it, and then contextualize it by relating it to your knowledge of the natural world, be it in received or experimental wisdom. Thus you read Pliny and Isidore on natural history and an encyclopaedic approach to the world – and you also ate the onion! In conveying to others what the onion is and what it signifies, you might also then adopt the humorous approach of the riddler to fix it in the memory of your audience by creating a picture poem – a *figura* (or figurative image).

Hence the following risqué riddle, the answer to which is an onion, was inscribed in the Exeter Book (in Exeter Cathedral Library), an anthology of Old English poetry, composed around the year 1000, perhaps at Exeter, for teaching and entertainment in the schoolroom/monastic library or, as Patrick Conner has suggested, perhaps for recitation at a proto-guild feast.[23]

The Exeter Book, *Riddle 25*

I am a wondrous creature, a joy to women,
a help to neighbours; I harm none
of the city-dwellers, except for my killer.
My base is steep and high, I stand in a bed,
shaggy somewhere beneath. Sometimes ventures
the very beautiful daughter of a churl,
a maid proud in mind, so that she grabs hold of me,
rubs me to redness, ravages my head,
forces me into a fastness. Immediately she feels
my meeting, the one who confines me,
the curly-locked woman. Wet will be that eye.[24]

Even onions grow in the garden of paradise and the Anglo-Saxons were not squeamish in their humour – it is certainly a memorable picture poem.

The use of the *Pardes* principle is also deployed in the work of some patristics (such as Augustine and Gregory the Great) and was employed by Aquinas as one of his teaching, preaching and compositional methods in the world of the medieval universities and the mendicant friars. Aquinas also later taught that man became literate with the help of mental images (*phantasmata*) stored while reading and Pope Gregory the Great's approach to the didactic and mnemonic role of imagery presaged this thirteenth-century scholastic view. The Anglo-Saxons and Celts were no strangers to *phantasmata*, even if their images were traditionally received aurally – their literatures are replete with them.

Gregory the Great wrote (in his *Moralia in Iob*, 2 vols, CCSL 143, I.3.110–115 4):

> First we lay the foundation of history, then through typical signification we build the fabric of the mind into a stronghold of faith; last we clothe the edifice through the grace of morality, as if with overlaid colour. Clearly what else must the words of Truth be believed to be except food for rebuilding the mind?[25]

In terms of visual exegesis this meant that the representation of historical episodes in Scripture (*figurae*) should be interpreted and imbued with Christian moral meaning.

The application of these principles can be observed in the famous 'Ezra' miniature in the Codex Amiatinus, which should perhaps be read not only as an image of Cassiodorus adapted with reference to the great preserver of the Judaic Scriptures, Ezra the Scribe, but as a homage and exhortation to the ongoing process of rediscovery and emendation of sacred text inspired by the Spirit.[26]

The bookcase contains nine volumes, alluding to Cassiodorus' Novem Codices but labelled on their spines as the editions of others such as St Augustine, indicating a living tradition. Cassiodorus and those responsible for the Ceolfrith Bibles were not attempting 'authorized' editions, but authoritative ones, improving upon the best sources they could find to carry forward the process of revelation and understanding of the Word. It would have been anathema to them to view their work as the

CODICIBVS SACRIS HOSTILI CLADE PERVSTIS
ESDRA DÕ FERVENS HOC REPARAVIT OPVS

23 Ezra the Scribe, from the Codex Amiatinus (Biblioteca Medicea Laurenziana, Florence, MS Amiato 1, f. 5r), Wearmouth-Jarrow, early 8th century.

'last word', for the process of transmission and exploration was divinely inspired and perpetual.

The figure of the scribe is thus not only Ezra (who was thought to have memorized and 'reconstructed' the Judaic sacred books after their destruction by the Babylonians), but represents the Old and New Testament authors, Cassiodorus and other biblical editors and also Ceolfrith, Bede and other of their brethren, the prophetic priestly scribes. It also offers the viewer, across the ages, an open invitation to participate in the continuing transmission of Scripture. A seemingly narrative illustration can therefore encapsulate, at a deeper multivalent level of reading, the relationship of all things across time and space. Bede deployed mental images of a pictorial nature in his texts and was no doubt also instrumental in contributing to the formulation of the use of visual images at Wearmouth-Jarrow and beyond.

Hagiography and the Art of the Miraculous

As already stated, Bede also recounted and used the lives of saints as role models for society. He compiled a martyrology, improved the translation of the Greek Life of St Anastasius (a text probably introduced to England by Archbishop Theodore, whose Cilician monastery in Rome was dedicated to that saint), reworked Paulinus's metrical Life of St Felix in prose and composed verse and prose lives of a new English saint in the making, Cuthbert, Bishop of Lindisfarne (d. 687). When writing hagiography, it was unthinkable that miracles, the visible manifestation of sanctity, should be excluded, as audiences expected them from their superheroes; their omission would have been like Batman without the Batmobile or the X-Men without their superpowers. Yet when writing about his personal heroes, in the *History of the Abbots of Wearmouth-Jarrow*, Bede eschewed such hagiographical devices, for this was the history of saints in the making.

Modern audiences often marvel at the ability of the medievals – and especially scholars of the calibre of Bede – to believe in the power of saints and miracles, without pausing to question their own suspension of disbelief when interacting with the virtual entertainment environment, be it digital gaming or the media. The existence of a virtual reality is increasingly taken as read and sometimes the borders between this and physical reality become blurred. In an age when airborne disease was commonly thought to take the form of 'elf-shot', who are we to quibble at the belief in a supernatural dimension, without the benefit of the intervening 1,300 years of study and experiment? Elf-shot was airborne, behaved in strange ways and conveyed negative impact, as diseases such as coronaviruses continue to teach us. Without the benefit of virology, postulation of the agency of unseen malevolence is perhaps to be expected. Even Covid generates its conspiracy theories.

As quantum physics moves ever onward in exploring the existence of another dimension and of a spiritual component of being, we can perhaps be a little more forgiving of the attempts of other ages and cultures to construct their own contexts for the miraculous – that which apparently transcends the usual workings of the world and of physics. There are still signs, portents and wonders, if we but look for them, even if we do understand more of the mechanisms by which they have occurred. At the time of writing, two researchers, committed to helping to save the environment and culture of the Amazon, had been murdered by the forces of self-interest and greed, their bodies dumped in a hidden swamp. Such are our latter-day martyrs. The miracle is that more will arise to take their place.

For all his learning and his proto-science, Bede found the miraculous credible, because his God was miraculous and credible. That is not to say that he blindly attributed anything he did not understand to supernatural agency. He worked hard to verify and question. An example of his bottom line, however, is his proof that an eclipse could not have occurred at the time of the Crucifixion, when the sky turned black, the world trembled and the veil of the Holy of Holies, separating man and God, was torn asunder. Bede's own computistical and cosmological research had demonstrated that this could not be the case, for he had ascertained the working of the heavens that produced them and charted their occurrence and a solar eclipse could not have taken place during the Passover full moon (*The Reckoning of Time*, Chapter 27). But Scripture related that it did occur and that this was proof that the Almighty could transcend the very rules of materiality that He had set in motion – especially when accepting the human form in obedience to the divine will, even unto death on the Cross. What greater transgression could there be of the laws of nature?

FOUR

Bede, Poetry and the Origins of Written English

Bede and the English, like the Irish before them, had to learn Latin as a foreign language, as the lingua franca of the western Church and as a result of their conversion. Learning new languages entails studying different patterns of thought and speech, and those encountered in Scripture inspired Bede to compose a treatise *On Tropes and Figures*, which he appended to his book on *The Art of Poetry*. A *Book of Hymns* 'in various metres and rhythms', a *Book of Epigrams* 'in heroic or elegiac verse', a *Book of Orthography* 'arranged in alphabetical order' and a collection of letters complete Bede's oeuvre.

According to his disciple Cuthbert, in his letter to Cuthwin on Bede's death (the *Epistola Cuthberti de obitu Bedae*), Bede was 'doctus in nostris carminibus' (learned in our songs). Cuthbert records that Bede's last words were his *Death Song*. Bede loved to sing. He sang the offices eight times every day and night and his last recorded words – fittingly enough, on Ascension Day on 26 May – are his death song (which occurs in some 45 manuscripts, but only some of the later ones ascribe the words to Bede) and the response 'Glory be to the Father and to the Son and to the Holy Spirit', which he sang to greet death, sitting on the chill floor of his cell.

His love of song and poetry had landed him in trouble on at least one occasion when Bishop Wilfrid's coterie accused him of practices bordering upon the heretical – including his love of verse sung in his own language, Old English. The Wearmouth-Jarrow refectories likely rang to the sound of him joining the singing round the table, including heroic poetry in English. The earliest recorded example of this occurs in the pages of the *Ecclesiastical History of the English People*, where he gives us Caedmon's hymn, the first poem in English, which is sung when the Lord opens the mouth of the herdsman who was too shy to take his turn at singing in a similar context in the mead-hall and who then joined Whitby Abbey.

There would have been so much more poetry and song circulating, in such a richly oral society, but it is typical of Bede that it should be he who has preserved for us a shining example, which may even be a literary device of his own composition rather than a 'true' account, in writing, and it is significant that this example of literary creativity should have been as part of a work designed to establish the identity of the English on the international Christian stage.

Bede also composed verse in Latin and wrote instruction manuals on its composition for his, and others', students. One such was *The Art of Poetry*, which taught composition of Latin verse, drawing upon the work of earlier Roman grammarians. It drew upon Donatus' *De pedibus* and Servius' *De finalibus* and gave models taken from Vergil – one of the main Roman schoolroom sources for such texts – and primarily from Christian poets. Bede's work likewise became a standard text for the teaching of Latin verse over following centuries. It is dedicated to one of Bede's own students, Cuthbert, his 'beloved son', to whom Bede said, 'I have laboured to educate you in divine letters and ecclesiastical statutes.'

The *Book of Orthography* is Bede's aid to contemporary readers who were unfamiliar with the vocabulary, spelling and abbreviations used in classical Latin and biblical works and could serve both as a teaching manual and as a reference work. Both these works are undated. Another of Bede's didactic works, *On Tropes and Figures*, discuss the Bible's use of rhetoric, for, as C. B. Kendall has said, familiarity with 'the "schemes" and "tropes" of rhetoric was equally essential in order not to be misled about the literal and figurative meanings of the Bible' – it is a pity that this is not often the case today.[1] As in his *The Art of Poetry*, he emphasized the primacy of Christian models in comprehending and emulating Christian Scripture and literature.

Bede can be seen applying his own teaching in the body of Latin poetry that has been credibly ascribed to him and edited by Michael Lapidge: *Versus de die iudicii* (Verses on the Day of Judgement), which is found complete in 33 manuscripts and in fragmentary form in ten; the metrical *Vita Sancti Cudbercti* (Life of St Cuthbert); and two collections of verse mentioned in the *Ecclesiastical History* Book v.24.2. Bede names the first of these collections as 'librum epigrammatum heroico metro siue elegiaco' (a book of epigrams in the heroic or elegiac metre). The second is named as 'liber hymnorum diuerso metro siue rythmo' (a book of hymns, diverse in metre or rhythm); Lapidge's reconstruction of the latter contains ten liturgical hymns and four compositions that resemble hymns in structure. Bede has also left us a hymn for the Feast of St Æthelthryth, embedded in his account of this saintly queen of Northumbria and foundress of Ely in the *Ecclesiastical History*.

Book 4, Chap. 19. How Queen Ethelthryth always preserved her virginity, and her body suffered no corruption in the grave. [AD 660–696]

King Egfrid took to wife Ethelthryth, the daughter of Anna, king of the East Angles, of whom mention has been often made; a man of true religion, and altogether noble in mind and deed. She had before been given in marriage to another, to wit, Tondbert, ealdorman of the Southern

Gyrwas; but he died soon after he had married her, and she was given to the aforesaid king. Though she lived with him twelve years, yet she preserved the glory of perfect virginity, as I was informed by Bishop Wilfrid, of blessed memory, of whom I inquired, because some questioned the truth thereof; and he told me that he was an undoubted witness to her virginity, forasmuch as Egfrid promised to give him many lands and much money if he could persuade the queen to consent to fulfil her marriage duty, for he knew the queen loved no man more than himself. And it is not to be doubted that this might take place in our age, which true histories tell us happened sometimes in former ages, by the help of the same Lord who promises to abide with us always, even unto the end of the world. For the divine miracle whereby her flesh, being buried, could not suffer corruption, is a token that she had not been defiled by man . . .

Book 4, Chap. 20. A Hymn concerning her.

It seems fitting to insert in this history a hymn concerning virginity, which we composed in elegiac verse many years ago, in praise and honour of the same queen and bride of Christ, and therefore truly a queen, because the bride of Christ; and to imitate the method of Holy Scripture, wherein many songs are inserted in the history, and these, as is well known, are composed in metre and verse.

'Trinity, Gracious, Divine, Who rulest all the ages; favour my task, Trinity, Gracious, Divine.

'Let Maro sound the trumpet of war, let us sing the gifts of peace; the gifts of Christ we sing, let Maro sound the trumpet of war.

'Chaste is my song, no rape of guilty Helen; light tales shall be told by the wanton, chaste is my song.

'I will tell of gifts from Heaven, not wars of hapless Troy; I will tell of gifts from Heaven, wherein the earth is glad.

'Lo! the high God comes to the womb of a holy virgin, to be the Saviour of men, lo! the high God comes.

'A hallowed maid gives birth to Him Who gave the world its being; Mary, the gate of God, a maiden gives Him birth.

'The company of her fellows rejoices over the Virgin Mother of Him Who wields the thunder; a shining virgin band, the company of her fellows rejoices.

'Her honour has made many a blossom to spring from that pure shoot, virgin blossoms her honour has made to spring.

'Scorched by the fierce flames, the maiden Agatha yielded not; in like manner Eulalia endures, scorched by the fierce flames.

'The lofty soul of chaste Tecla overcomes the wild beasts; chaste Euphemia overcomes the accursed wild beasts.

'Agnes joyously laughs at the sword, herself stronger than steel, Cecilia joyously laughs at the foemen's sword.

'Many a triumph is mighty throughout the world in temperate hearts; throughout the world love of the temperate life is mighty.

'Yea, and our day likewise a peerless maiden has blessed; peerless our Ethelthryth shines.

'Child of a noble sire, and glorious by royal birth, more noble in her Lord's sight, the child of a noble sire.

'Thence she receives queenly honour and a sceptre in this world; thence she receives honour, awaiting higher honour above.

'What need, gracious lady, to seek an earthly lord, even now given to the Heavenly Bridegroom?

'Christ is at hand, the Bridegroom (why seek an earthly lord?) that thou mayst follow even now, methinks, in the steps of the Mother of Heaven's King, that thou too mayst be a mother in God.

'Twelve years she had reigned, a bride dedicated to God, then in the cloister dwelt, a bride dedicated to God.

'To Heaven all consecrated she lived, abounding in lofty deeds, then to Heaven all consecrated she gave up her soul.

'Twice eight Novembers the maid's fair flesh lay in the tomb, nor did the maid's fair flesh see corruption in the tomb.

'This was Thy work, O Christ, that her very garments were bright and undefiled even in the grave; O Christ, this was Thy work.

'The dark serpent flies before the honour due to the holy raiment; disease is driven away, and the dark serpent flies.

'Rage fills the foe who of old conquered Eve; exultant the maiden triumphs and rage fills the foe.

'Behold, O bride of God, thy glory upon earth; the glory that awaits thee in the Heavens behold, O bride of God.

'In gladness thou receivest gifts, bright amidst the festal torches; behold! the Bridegroom comes, in gladness thou receivest gifts.

'And a new song thou singest to the tuneful harp; a new-made bride, thou exultest in the tuneful hymn.

'None can part her from them which follow the Lamb enthroned on high, whom none had severed from the Love enthroned on high.'

Bede's greatest work of Latin poetry, as far as we know, was his metrical Life of St Cuthbert. This was based upon the anonymous Life of Cuthbert, written between 698 and 705, within two decades of Cuthbert's death in 687. Bede's metrical Life is undated but is thought to date from sometime between 705 and 716. It was prefaced by a letter to a deacon, John, who is about to depart on pilgrimage to Rome. In his preface to his subsequent prose Life of Cuthbert, completed around 721 and dedicated to Bishop Eadfrith and the brethren of Lindisfarne, Bede's tone implies that there may have been some suggestion of impropriety in his writing about their saint unsolicited. Bede is at pains to note that the heroic verse Life was written for his own community, Wearmouth-Jarrow, and that it was based upon his own research, without the involvement of the Lindisfarne community, which he had to consult at length to obtain its permission to publish his prose Life. Only in the prologue to the *Ecclesiastical History* does he mention his use of the anonymous Life, not in either of his own versions. There may be a sense of scholarly pride and competition between communities here, along with a possessiveness surrounding 'ownership' of a developing saint's cult. Bede is usually scrupulous and transparent about referencing his sources, but evidently not in this instance, which suggests that some circumspection was deemed prudent. It has been suggested that Herefrith, who was abbot of Lindisfarne at Cuthbert's death, may have authored the Anonymous Life. Bede certainly names him, and only him, as a reviewer of Bede's Life of Cuthbert and that they came together to work on it. We lose sight of Herefrith as abbot after Cuthbert's death in 687 and it may be that he fell foul of Wilfrid, who succeeded Cuthbert as bishop for one turbulent year, during which some members of the community left. A Herefrith appears as an anchorite in the Durham *Liber vitae*, the book of remembrance of the Lindisfarne community which was copied in the ninth century (in which Bede's name was inscribed, in fulfilment of his plea), and perhaps this was he. Might Bede's purpose in citing Herefrith have been, in part, to assure the Lindisfarne community and his wider audience that his first version of the Life, in verse, was fully informed by an eyewitness report (the anonymous Life, supplemented by Bede's *viva voce* exchanges with its author) originating from Lindisfarne itself? Bede eloquently expressed his own close relationship with the island monastery:

Prose Life of St Cuthbert, Preface [c. 721]

To the holy and most blessed Father Bishop Eadfrid, and to all the Congregation of Brothers also, who serve Christ in the Island of Lindisfarne, Bede, your faithful fellow-servant, sends greeting.

Inasmuch as you bade me, my beloved, prefix to the book, which I have written at your request about the life of our father Cuthbert, of blessed memory, some preface, as I usually do, by which its readers might become acquainted with your desire and my readiness to gratify it, it has seemed good to me, by way of preface, to recall to the minds of those among you who know, and to make known to those readers who were before ignorant thereof, how that I have not presumed without minute investigation to write any of the deeds of so great a man, nor without the most accurate examination of credible witnesses to hand over what I had written to be transcribed. Moreover, when I learnt from those who knew the beginning, the middle, and the end of his glorious life and conversation, I sometimes inserted the names of these my authors, to establish the truth of my narrative, and thus ventured to put my pen to paper and to write. But when my work was arranged, but still kept back from publication, I frequently submitted it for perusal and for correction to our reverend brother Herefrid the priest, and others, who for a long time had well known the life and conversation of that man of God. Some faults were, at their suggestion, carefully amended, and thus every scruple being utterly removed, I have taken care to commit to writing what I clearly ascertained to be the truth, and to bring it into your presence also, my brethren, in order that by the judgment of your authority, what I have written might be either corrected, if false, or certified to be true. While, with God's assistance, I was so engaged, and my book was read during two days by the elders and teachers of your congregation, and was accurately weighed and examined in all its parts, there was nothing at all found which required to be altered, but everything which I had written was by common consent pronounced worthy to be read without any hesitation, and to be handed over to be copied by such as by zeal for religion should be disposed to do so. But you also, in my presence, added many other facts of no less importance than what I had written, concerning the life and virtues of that blessed man, and which well deserved to be mentioned, if I had not thought it unmeet to insert new matter into a work, which, after due deliberation, I considered to be perfect.

Furthermore, I have thought right to admonish your gracious company, that, as I have not delayed to render prompt obedience to your commands, so you also may not be slow to confer on me the reward of your intercession; but when you read this book, and in pious recollection of that holy father lift up your souls with ardour in aspiration for the heavenly kingdom, do not forget to entreat the Divine clemency in favour of my littleness, in as far as I may deserve both at present with singleness of mind to long for and hereafter in perfect happiness to behold the goodness of our Lord in the land of the living. But also, when I am defunct, pray ye for the redemption of my soul, for I was your friend and faithful servant; offer up masses for me, and enrol my name among your own. For you, also, most holy prelate, remember to have promised this to me, and in testimony of such future enrolment you gave orders to your pious brother Guthfrid, that he should even now enrol my name in the white book of your holy congregation And may your holiness know that I already have written in heroic verse, as well as in this prose work, which I offer to you, the life of this same our father beloved by God, somewhat more briefly indeed, but nevertheless in the same order, because some of our brethren entreated the same of me: and if you wish to have those verses, you can obtain from me a copy of them. In the preface of that work I promised that I would write more fully at another time of his life and miracles; which promise, in my present work, I have, as far as God has allowed me, done my best to perform.

Wherefore it is my prayer for you, that Almighty God may deign to guard your holinesses in peace and safety, dearest brethren and masters of mine. Amen.[2]

Clare Stancliffe has proposed another compelling scenario, however.[3] She suggests that the Life of St Wilfrid by Stephen of Ripon (previously known as Eddius Stephanus), written shortly after Wilfrid's death in circa 709, was intended not only to rival the nascent cult of St Cuthbert at Lindisfarne, but to pick up and amplify passages in the anonymous Life that demonstrated the unorthodoxy of Cuthbert and his episcopate and of the Lindisfarne community and its remaining Columban traditions. Bede's prose Life of St Cuthbert was commissioned by Bishop Eadfrith of Lindisfarne and sought in turn to rebuff these criticisms. In the process, the anonymous Life, and Herefrith's likely authorship, were played down, as, to some extent, was Bede's own verse Life, which was heavily indebted to it. In defending

Cuthbert, Lindisfarne and the contribution of the Columban missionaries to this new version of Cuthbertine hagiography, Bede had to be circumspect, for it would seem that Wilfrid's successor, Bishop Acca of Hexham, whom Bede seems to have admired and with whom he was in dialogue, was intent upon regularizing the Northumbrian episcopacy, eliminating the phenomenon of the bishop-monk – which Cuthbert embodied so well – and asserting the primacy of the bishopric of Hexham within the kingdom.

As a priest, Bede felt the bonds of obedience to his bishop keenly, but as a monk he was fully aware of the synergy between the contemplative life and active work in the world. As a Northumbrian he harboured a deep respect for the role of Sts Aidan, Cuthbert, Hild and their followers in converting his people to the faith, in caring for and nurturing their bodies and souls and in helping to forge a healthy Christian state. He would not join in denigrating or forgetting them and did what he was most skilled at – praying on it, covering them with the shield of faith and defending them with his sharp pen. In so doing, Bede recreated Cuthbert as an indigenous hero for the Christian age – a hero worthy, like Beowulf and Cú Chulainn, of the halls of kings, capable of passive heroism, physical and spiritual endurance and benign diplomacy; a home-grown father of the Church, combining the traditions of the desert fathers, their Celtic counterparts and the intrepid missionary bishops of Pope Gregory; and a domestic soul-friend of the hearthside – the St Cuddy who is still spoken of affectionately as a family member in so many Northumbrian households today.

As already noted, Bede also had an interest in poetry and song in his own language, Old English. According to his pupil and assistant, Cuthbert, Bede was *doctus in nostris carminibus* (learned in our songs). In his letter on Bede's death, the *Epistola Cuthberti de obitu Bedae*, Cuthbert also implies (although he does not state it definitively, and Bede's authorship, rather than his quotation of another author, is debated by some scholars) that Bede composed a five-line vernacular poem known to modern scholars as *Bede's Death Song:*

> And he used to repeat that sentence from St. Paul, 'It is a fearful thing to fall into the hands of the living God,' and many other verses of Scripture, urging us thereby to awake from the slumber of the soul by thinking in good time of our last hour. And in our own language – for he was familiar with English poetry – speaking of the soul's dread departure from the body:
>
> Fore ðæm nedfere nænig wiorðe
> ðonc snottora ðon him ðearf siæ
> to ymbhycgenne ær his hinionge
> *hwæt his gastæ godes oððe yfles*
> *æfter deað dæge doemed wiorðe.*
>
> Facing that enforced journey, no man can be
> More prudent than he has good call to be,
> If he consider, before his going hence,
> What for his spirit of good hap or of evil
> After his day of death shall be determined.

Another of Bede's labours in those final weeks of illness, with mortality lurking in the shadows of his cell, was to translate John's Gospel – which he described as 'the little Gospel which treats of the things that work of love' (that is, by God's love) – into Old English to instruct and evangelize his people in their own tongue, adding that people learn better that way. This was a characteristically pragmatic and sympathetic approach. In addition to his pastoral concern for his people's spirit, he was also concerned for its mind and gave himself the task of translating tricky excerpts from Isidore of Seville's encyclopaedic work into English. Bede certainly died in the scholarly saddle.

In his discussion of Bede and education, Calvin B. Kendall writes of the end of Bede's life:

> The fact that Bede does not gesture in the direction of the life of the hermit demonstrates a paradigm shift, a complete reorientation of his mental map of the uses and purposes of life on earth. From this final perspective, Bede's importance as an educator is that he embodied an alternative model of Christian monasticism – the ideal of the educated, as opposed to the ascetic, Christian monk . . . It is hardly an exaggeration to claim that, in validating the life of the mind and the importance of education, his model helped redirect the course of Western civilization.[4]

While the final statement here may be valid, the former assumption may be a projection of the modern mindset. For Bede was fully aware and respectful of the place of hermits and anchorites as one of the very highest echelons of spiritual maturity and of the religious life. His treatment of St Cuthbert's ministry, and his prayerful and politically effective passive resistance to the ills of secular government from his hermitage on Inner Farne, attests to that. Bede, with his avowed monastic humility, would not have aspired to such heights but he certainly asserted the bedrock of scholarship in discerning the how and the why of God's purpose and what made Creation tick. He preferred to dwell amid his beloved books and in the choir, rather than in the wild as a frontline spiritual survivalist.

Bede, the First Translator of Part of the Bible into English

The Insular approach to the role of language in relation to unity and diversity has more in common with the polyglot traditions of the Middle East than with that of Latinate Europe. Social and ecclesiastical attitudes in early medieval Britain were very different from those that prevailed later, when Wycliffe and Tyndale were condemned for publishing Scripture in English, for Latin had emerged as the principal scriptural language of the medieval West; it was the adopted vernacular of a diverse empire encompassing Rome, the Carolingians and their successors.

Throughout the medieval world a plethora of collections of canonically sanctioned biblical books circulated in many different languages. This made for a 'Babel of bibles', much as exists today. The early Western biblical scholars and scribes who most faithfully preserved the Latin Vulgate, the result of their dedicated reconstruction of Jerome's painstaking research in the Holy Land during the late fourth century, were those of northern England, as is witnessed by the Codex Amiatinus and the Lindisfarne Gospels, both of which were produced in early eighth-century Northumbria. The former was one of three pandects made for Abbot Ceolfrith at Wearmouth-Jarrow, and the latter was made at Lindisfarne, probably by Bishop Eadfrith. These books drew upon a Gospel book from Naples and other exemplars, including editions by Cassiodorus, which were edited at Wearmouth-Jarrow to produce the 'Italo-Northumbrian' family of texts.

One of the foremost advocates of the use of vernacular languages in the service of the apostolic mission, Bede was particularly interested in the Pentecost episode in which the apostles spoke in different tongues. In his Commentary on Acts (Acts 2:6) he said that this passage could be read as meaning either that the apostles went to many different peoples and preached in their various tongues, or that they spoke only once and the Holy Spirit simultaneously translated their words. He was criticized for this opinion by peers less well read than he, and was accused of innovating rather than building upon earlier patristic thought. Bede subsequently justified himself (in his *Retractatio*/Retraction) by emphasizing that he was quoting from an authoritative source, namely the Eastern Church Father Gregory of Nazianzus. Bede was not alone in his perception of the value of sharing Scripture in the vernacular, in both oral and written forms. Indeed, some of the earliest examples of written vernaculars come from precisely this evangelizing context: witness Ulfilas and his use of Gothic, Mesrop and his use of Armenian, Cyril and Methodius and their use of Cyrillic, and Augustine and his receptivity to Old English.

Bede's interest in the vernacular relates to his recognition of the generosity of the Jews in sharing the Word with gentiles through the Greek Septuagint, an impulse shared by the gentile races of Britain and Ireland, who sought to share their faith with others (*Commentary on Tobias*, 12 and 2:6). On his deathbed, in 735, Bede was still sharing the Word by translating the Gospel of St John into English. This original work has not survived but, as we shall see, it may be recollected in parts of the gloss that Aldred added to the Lindisfarne Gospels circa 950–60 – the oldest surviving translation of the Gospels into English. Another gloss was added to the Macregol Gospels, a work written and illuminated in Ireland by MacRegol, Abbot of Birr, during the early ninth century and thereafter glossed in English by the priests Owun and Farmon in mid-tenth-century England. By adding their names in colophons – a practice of Eastern derivation – Aldred, Owun and Farmon situated themselves, and the English language, in direct line of transmission from the divine to humankind. Colophons are comparatively rare in the West, but they occur with some frequency in Insular manuscripts (especially

24 St Cuthbert's or Cuddy's Isle (Hobthrush), a place of retreat where it is probable that the Lindisfarne Gospels were made, just offshore of the Holy Island of Lindisfarne. The remains of a small medieval chapel are marked with a cross.

those of Irish background). In Armenian books, however, they are common and detailed, rendering the book an intercessory vehicle for scribe and patron. Redeeming such intercessors from captivity by non-Christians and restoring them to the Church was a pious act also recorded within Armenian manuscripts, as well as in two Insular Gospel books retrieved from Vikings during the ninth century: the Lichfield Gospels and the Stockholm Codex Aureus.

A son of the Germanic and Celtic North, Bede's imagination was also nurtured by oral tradition, vernacular poetry and song. In a letter recounting Bede's death – a genre that promoted his posthumous saintly status – one of his pupils, Cuthbert, describes his last days, spent in study, prayer, chanting psalms, antiphons and Old English verse, for he 'knew our poems well'. This included Bede's *Death Song*, the earliest recorded example of Old English poetry, along with a verse ascribed by Bede to Caedmon, who became a monk at Abbess Hild's Whitby, who was so embarrassed at the prospect of taking his turn at singing at feasts that he hid with the beasts in the byre until God inspired him to sing:

Book 4, Chap. 24. That there was in her monastery a brother, on whom the gift of song was bestowed by Heaven. [680]

There was in the monastery of this abbess a certain brother, marked in a special manner by the grace of God, for he was wont to make songs of piety and religion, so that whatever was expounded to him out of Scripture, he turned ere long into verse expressive of much sweetness and penitence, in English, which was his native language. By his songs the minds of many were often fired with contempt of the world, and desire of the heavenly life. Others of the English nation after him attempted to compose religious poems, but none could equal him, for he did not learn the art of poetry from men, neither was he taught by man, but by God's grace he received the free gift of song, for which reason he never could compose any trivial or vain poem, but only those which concern religion it behoved his religious tongue to utter. For having lived in the secular habit till he was well advanced in years, he had never learned anything of versifying; and for this reason sometimes at a banquet, when it was agreed to make merry by singing in turn, if he saw the harp come towards him, he would rise up from table and go out and return home.

Once having done so and gone out of the house where the banquet was, to the stable, where he had to take care of the cattle that night, he there composed himself to rest at the proper time. Thereupon one stood by him in his sleep, and saluting him, and calling him by his name, said, 'Cædmon, sing me something.' But he answered, 'I cannot sing, and for this cause I left the banquet and retired hither, because I could not sing.' Then he who talked to him replied, 'Nevertheless thou must needs sing to me.' 'What must I sing?' he asked. 'Sing the beginning of creation,' said the other. Having received this answer he straightway began to sing verses to the praise of God the Creator, which he had never heard, the purport whereof was after this manner: 'Now must we praise the Maker of the heavenly kingdom, the power of the Creator and His counsel, the deeds of the Father of glory. How He, being the eternal God, became the Author of all wondrous works, Who being the Almighty Guardian of the human race, first created heaven for the sons of men to be the covering of their dwelling place, and next the earth.' This is the sense but not the order of the words as he sang them in his sleep; for verses, though never so well composed, cannot be literally translated out of one language into another without loss of their beauty and loftiness. Awaking from his sleep, he remembered all that he had sung in his dream, and soon added more after the same manner, in words which worthily expressed the praise of God.

In the morning he came to the reeve who was over him and having told him of the gift he had received, was conducted to the abbess, and bidden, in the presence of many learned men, to tell his dream, and repeat the verses, that they might all examine and give their judgement upon the nature and origin of the gift whereof he spoke. And they all judged that heavenly grace had been granted to him by the Lord. They expounded to him a passage of sacred history or doctrine, enjoining upon him, if he could, to put it into verse. Having undertaken this task, he went away, and returning the next morning, gave them the passage he had been bidden to translate, rendered in most excellent verse. Whereupon the abbess, joyfully recognizing the grace of God in the man, instructed him to quit the secular habit, and take upon him monastic vows; and having received him into the monastery, she and all her people admitted him to the company of the brethren, and ordered that he should be taught the whole course of sacred history. So he, giving ear to all that he could learn, and bearing it in mind, and as it were ruminating, like a clean animal, turned it into most harmonious verse; and sweetly singing it, made his masters in their turn his hearers. He sang the creation of the world, the origin of man, and all the history of Genesis, the departure of the children of Israel out of Egypt, their entrance into the promised land, and many other histories from Holy Scripture; the Incarnation, Passion, Resurrection of our Lord, and His Ascension into heaven; the coming of the Holy Ghost, and the teaching of the Apostles; likewise he made many songs concerning the terror of future judgement, the horror of the pains of hell, and the joys of heaven; besides many more about the blessings and the judgements of God, by all of which he endeavoured to draw men away from the love of sin, and to excite in them devotion to well-doing and perseverance therein. For he was a very religious man, humbly submissive to the discipline of monastic rule, but inflamed with fervent zeal against those who chose to do otherwise; for which reason he made a fair ending of his life.

For when the hour of his departure drew near, it was preceded by a bodily infirmity under which he laboured for the space of fourteen days, yet it was of so mild a nature that he could talk and go about the whole time. In his neighbourhood was the house to which those that were sick, and like to die, were wont to be carried. He desired the person that ministered to him, as the evening came on of the night in which he was to depart this life, to make ready a place there for him to take his rest. The man, wondering why he should desire it, because there was as yet no sign of his approaching death, nevertheless did his bidding. When they had lain down there, and had been conversing happily and pleasantly for some time with those that were in the house before, and it was now past midnight, he asked them, whether they had the Eucharist within? They answered, 'What need of the Eucharist? for you are not yet appointed to die, since you talk so merrily with us, as if you were in good health.' 'Nevertheless,' said he, 'bring me the Eucharist.' Having received It into his hand, he asked, whether they were all in charity with him, and had no complaint against him, nor any quarrel or grudge. They answered that they were all in perfect charity with him, and free from all anger; and in their turn they asked him to be of the same mind towards them. He answered at once, 'I am in charity, my children, with all the servants of God.' Then strengthening himself with the heavenly Viaticum, he prepared for the entrance into another life, and asked how near the time was when the brothers should be awakened to sing the nightly praises of the Lord? They answered, 'It is not far off.' Then he said, 'It is well, let us await that hour;' and signing himself with the sign of the Holy Cross, he laid his head on the pillow, and falling into a slumber for a little while, so ended his life in silence.

Thus it came to pass, that as he had served the Lord with a simple and pure mind, and quiet devotion, so he now departed to behold His Presence, leaving the world by a quiet death; and that tongue, which had uttered so many wholesome words in praise of the Creator, spake its last words also in His praise, while he signed himself with the Cross, and commended his spirit into His hands; and by what has been here said, he seems to have had foreknowledge of his death.

Here is Caedmon's Hymn in Old English, based on that in the earliest extant manuscript version, the Moore Bede, deemed by Malcolm Parkes to have been copied at Wearmouth-Jarrow within a decade of Bede's death:

Nū scylun hergan hefaenrīcaes Uard,
metudæs maecti end his mōdgidanc,
uerc Uuldurfadur, suē hē uundra gihwaes,
ēci dryctin ōr āstelidæ
hē ǣrist scōp aelda barnum
heben til hrōfe, hāleg scepen.
Thā middungeard moncynnæs Uard,
eci Dryctin, æfter tīadæ
firum foldu, Frēa allmectig.

Now we must honour the guardian of heaven,
the might of the architect, and his purpose,
the work of the father of glory
as he, the eternal lord, established the beginning of wonders;
he first created for the children of men
heaven as a roof, the holy creator,
Then the guardian of mankind,
the eternal lord, afterwards appointed the middle earth,
the lands for men, the Lord almighty.[5]

Another English verse of this era is carved in Roman capitals and Germanic runes on the Ruthwell Cross in the ancient British kingdom of Rheged in southwest Scotland. This monument, a visual meditation in stone on the Passion of Christ and the religious life, reflects Northumbrian influence in a recently annexed region. In the late tenth century this verse was expanded to form *The Dream of the Rood*, in which the cross laments its role in the crucifixion of the young warrior, Christ. Bede's aspirations for reframing heroic northern culture in Christian guise were being fulfilled. The words uttered by the Rood itself are eloquent and moving, relating how it is felled by enemies, forced to become an instrument of torture and then buried ignominiously, like Christ himself, until, like him, it arises when Empress Helena excavates it during the fourth century and it is transformed into the Crux Gemmata, the golden and gem-adorned symbol of salvation and eternal life.

The visual imagination, the poetic eloquence and the knowledge of Scripture and early Christian history displayed in this proto-poem, carved into the otherwise mute stone of the Ruthwell Cross, is of such a calibre that I cannot help wondering if it was composed by Bede himself (or was based on something composed earlier by Caedmon).[6] The sculpture is usually dated to the first half of the eighth century and is likely contemporaneous with Bede. It has been contextualized by some scholars as a meditation upon the contemplative and active Christian life and on salvation, perhaps standing within a monastic enclave. It may be that the Roman capitals and runes carved upon it were intended to signal the imposition of Northumbrian authority, both religious and secular, upon the recently annexed British kingdom of Rheged. The Romanizing figure-style of the carving, indebted to ancient Roman and early Christian sculpture and portable antiquities such as ivories, has led to speculation that Wearmouth-Jarrow's influence was at work here. It cannot be proven that those houses, or Bede, had a direct involvement in planning this complex monument, but neither can it be precluded.

Here is a translated extract from the fully developed poem, of around 1000, preserved in the Vercelli Codex, an anthology of English verse:

> I trembled as the warrior embraced me.
> But still I dared not bend down to the earth,
> fall to the ground. Upright I had to stand.
> A rood I was raised up; and I held high
> the noble King, the Lord of heaven above.
> I dared not stoop. They pierced me with dark nails;
> the scars can still be clearly seen on me,
> the open wounds of malice.[7]

The advantages of communicating orally in the vernacular, as well as being literate (that is, latinate) in the Mediterranean fashion, were fully appreciated by Bede. His letter to Bishop Ecgbert evinces deep concern that most of the thinly spread priesthood could not read Latin, leading him to translate the *Pater Noster* and Creed into Old English to help such 'illiterate' priests to conduct services and to teach their flocks.

Even during his final illness Bede was translating into English things needful to know, to stock the shelves of the believer's inner library or ark: dictating extracts from Isidore's *On the Nature of Things*, and John's Gospel, that the Good News (OE *Godspell*) might better be shared with all, free from elitism. For Bede, like fellow missionaries with the pen, such as Ulfilas, Cyril and Methodius, recognized the necessity for vernacular translation.

In 2003 I suggested that Aldred's gloss added to the Lindisfarne Gospels in circa 950 utilized two different inks – one black, the other red – to differentiate two sources. The use of crimson ink might be taken to accord one of the series of glosses a higher

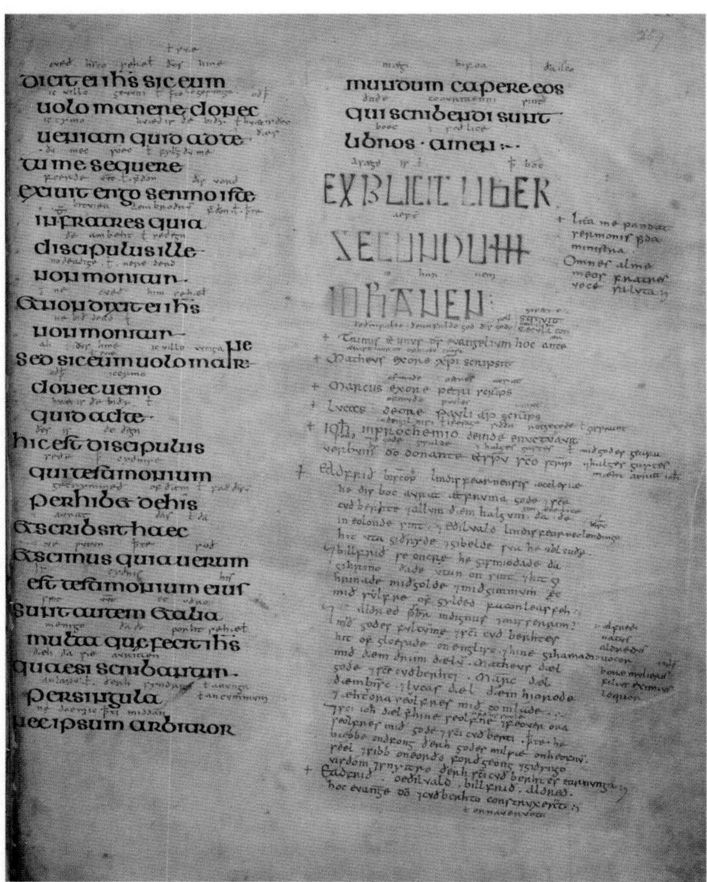

25 Aldred's colophon and the end of his gloss to St John's Gospel in the Lindisfarne Gospels, preserving, in part, Bede's otherwise lost deathbed translation of St John (BL, Cotton MS Nero D IV, f. 259r).

status and I speculated that this might be because it was a fossilized recollection of Bede's deathbed work in translating John into English.[8]

There are several signs supportive of this theory: f. 241r has the characteristic Bedan marginal quotation marks adjacent to the Isaiah passage that is quoted in the text. In addition, on ff. 257r–v the gloss often omits the names of the disciples, such as Thomas, that are given in the Latin text and refers to them simply as thegns, while on f. 257v it adds the names of the sons of Zebedee, though they are not given in the text. This is not consistent with Aldred's word-by-word or phrase-by-phrase schoolroom-based approach to translating the Latin text into Old English gloss, by which he would surely have adhered closer to what he saw before him. It seems more consistent with Bede's rapid translation work, introducing some short cuts due to pressure of time, with death approaching fast, and interpolating some details from memory.

Recent research by Julia Fernández-Cuesta and Nieves Rodríguez-Ledesma on the linguistics of these glosses have picked up on and substantiated my proposal, for they find that the red glosses in John align with Bedan style and linguistic usage:

> Perhaps the most salient finding of this study is that the degree of syncretism is not even throughout the Lindisfarne gloss, with John showing the lowest degree of syncretism in a statistically significant way. This is particularly interesting because John has also been shown to be different from the rest of the gloss both linguistically and palaeographically. Linguistically, it presents a higher percentage of contracted negative forms and of self-forms, third person singular possessive sin (besides his) is occasionally used, and prefixal gi- is more frequent than ge-. At the lexical level, this section is also different in that it appears to be more concerned with legal terminology. From a palaeographical point of view, John also stands apart from the rest of the gloss by the use of red ink and of pointed <v> instead of <u>. In addition, Aldred himself draws a distinction between John and the other gospels, stating in the colophon that he glossed this section for the salvation of his soul. Some of these features, such as the

> low degree of syncretism, seem to be more 'conservative', i.e. closer to the standard West-Saxon, whereas others, such as the use of self, appear to be more 'progressive', i.e. in the direction of Middle English.
>
> The linguistic differences between John and the other sections strongly suggest that in the composition of the gloss Aldred relied on already existing translations of the gospels that were available to him. As mentioned previously, there seems to be some evidence that the section corresponding to John might have been based on a previous translation made by Bede.[9]

I am excited by this confirmation of my theory (which Elliot and Ross had started to explore), for it is tantalizing, and fitting, to think that Bede's work in helping to establish the written Old English vernacular should be preserved, if only in part, in the oldest extant translation of the entire Gospels into English – in the Lindisfarne Gospels, which he seems to have played a role in helping to shape. This makes Bede the first translator of any of the books of the Bible into the English language. A major piece of work needed now is for someone to compile an edition of the Old English glosses in red that occur in St John's Gospel in the Lindisfarne Gospels, to reconstruct Bede's translation.

Aldred's continuous interlinear gloss in Old English between the lines of the original Latin Vulgate text of the Lindisfarne Gospels is written in the Northumbrian dialect. A further Anglo-Saxon translation is preserved in the form of later (twelfth-century) manuscript copies and is known as the West Saxon or Wessex Gospels, being written in the West Saxon dialect. Another gloss, added during the tenth century to an early ninth-century Irish Latin Gospel book, the Macregol Gospels, by Farmon, a priest from Harewood (West Yorkshire or near Ross-on-Wye or Lichfield), relies upon Aldred's gloss, or a source, and is in the Mercian dialect. The Lindisfarne Gospels may contain the earliest extant translation, but we know that work on disseminating the biblical texts in the English vernacular had commenced earlier. Apart from Bede's own work translating St John's Gospel on his deathbed, the Vespasian Psalter (BL, Cotton MS Vespasian A I), a Kentish work made in Bede's time around 730, was also given an interlinear Old English gloss during the second quarter of the ninth century (probably at Canterbury by one of the scribes who also worked on the Royal Bible, BL, MS Royal I E VI, sometime between 820 and 840). The spirit of evangelization that engendered such an openness to spreading the Word by any means was very different to the official intolerance encountered by Wycliffe and Tyndale in the less-tolerant late Middle Ages/early modern period.

This work may have been Aldred's way of establishing his credentials and of making a contribution to the community which he seems only recently to have joined. He glossed Matthew, Mark, Luke and the beginning of John in a neat, tiny, pointed cursive hand using black ink. From 5:10, and mid-verse (from 'tibi tollere', f. 220v, line 2), John's Gospel is glossed in the same hand, but using red ink. The Prefaces are also in red, up to the beginning of the 'Plures fuisse', as are some further glosses added to Matthew. There are also a few additional glosses in red on f. 140v (Luke 1). The change in ink may simply have resulted from some unpredictable change in Aldred's circumstances, or it may be that he

overleaf: 26 The Vespasian Psalter (BL, Cotton MS Vespasian A I, ff. 30v–31r) depicting King David composing the Psalms and with his secretaries taking notes on a scroll and wax tablets and his musicians playing and dancing. The text, in uncials, opens with one of the earliest historiated (storytelling) initials, showing David and Jonathan concluding peace. It was made in Kent in the 720s, perhaps by the nuns of Minster-in-Thanet, who around this time were supplying opulent manuscripts bearing gold for the mission of St Boniface to Germany. In the mid-9th century the volume received an interlinear gloss, translating the Psalms into Old English.

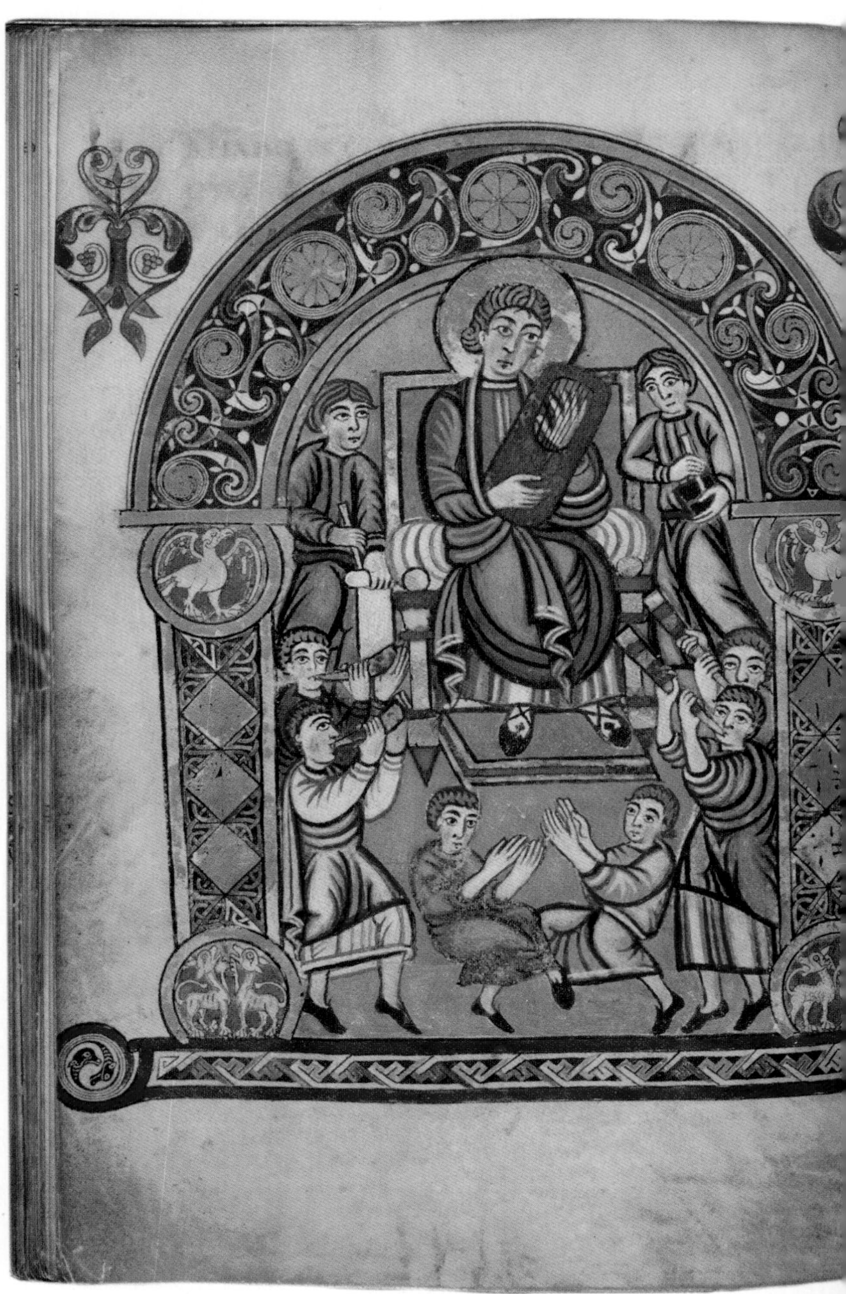

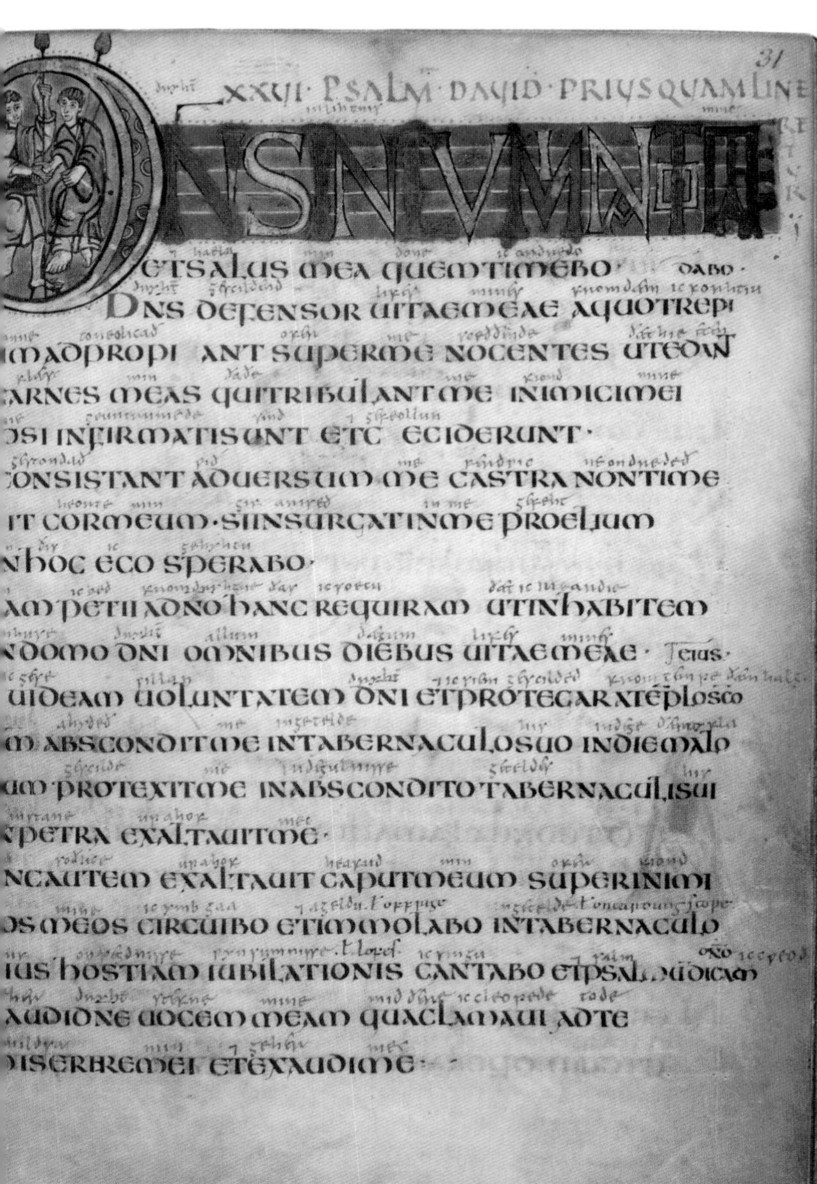

31

XXVI· PSALM̄ DAVID· PRIUSQUAM LINE

DNS INLUMINATIO

ETSALUS MEA QUEMTIMEBO· DABO·
DNS DEFENSOR UITAEMEAE AQUOTREPI
IMADPROPI ANT SUPERME NOCENTES UTEDANT
ARNES MEAS QUITRIBULANT ME INIMICIMEI
OSI INFIRMATISUNT ETC ECIDERUNT·
ONSISTANT ADUERSUM ME CASTRA NONTIME
IT CORMEUM· SIINSURGATINME PROELIUM
NHOC EGO SPERABO·
AM PETII ADNO HANC REQUIRAM UTINHABITEM
NDOMO DNI OMNIBUS DIEBUS UITAEMEAE· Tetus·
UIDEAM UOLUNTATEM DNI ETPROTEGAR ATEPLOSCO
M ABSCONDITME INTABERNACULOSUO INDIEMALO
UM PROTEXITME INABSCONDITO TABERNACULISUI
PETRA EXALTAUITME·
NCAUTEM EXALTAUIT CAPUTMEUM SUPERINIMI
OS MEOS CIRCUIBO ETIMMOLABO INTABERNACULO
IUS HOSTIAM IUBILATIONIS CANTABO ETPSAL DICAM
XAUDIDNE UOCEM MEAM QUACLAMAUI ADTE
ISERERE MEI ETEXAUDIME·

decided to accord John's Gospel the particular distinction that it often seems to have attracted, especially in the context of the cult of St Cuthbert (who studied it with his master, Boisil, and who was interred with a copy of it), by glossing it in a higher grade of ink.

I do wonder though whether Aldred's model for the gloss on John might even have been indebted, if only in part, to the translation to which Bede devoted his last days on Earth and that the red ink might honour such a source. William Boyd outlined the sources to which Aldred may have had access, including Bede's Old and New Testament commentaries and his homilies upon the Gospels.[10] However, in his 'gloss 62' (John 19:38) Boyd notes that Aldred glossed the passage 'post / .i. est in die examinis iudicii. Districti iudicis. đus beda đe bróema bóecere cućđ' (thus said Bede, the famous scribe), and states that 'It has proved impossible to pin down the precise reference in Bede. Aldred may have derived his explanation from Bede's *Explanatio Apocalypsis*,' his commentary on the Book of Revelation, composed around 703. The great value of this marginal explanation is that Aldred confirms Bede as one of the sources of his scholarship.[11] He signalled his use, and preservation, of Bede's otherwise lost translation of John's Gospel by the use of red ink when incorporating it into his glossing of John's Gospel in the Lindisfarne Gospels. Later in the Middle Ages deluxe volumes would often be ruled in red or purple ink as a sign of status, and the popular expression 'red-letter day' derives from the practice of grading liturgical feast days by the use of different coloured inks in calendars. Aldred might then have gone on to gloss the ancillary, prefatory texts and have decided to make a few additions to Matthew and Luke, correcting/supplementing his initial gloss and still using his red ink.

Aldred seems to have been building a reputation as a glossator/translator and his hand can also be observed in the Durham

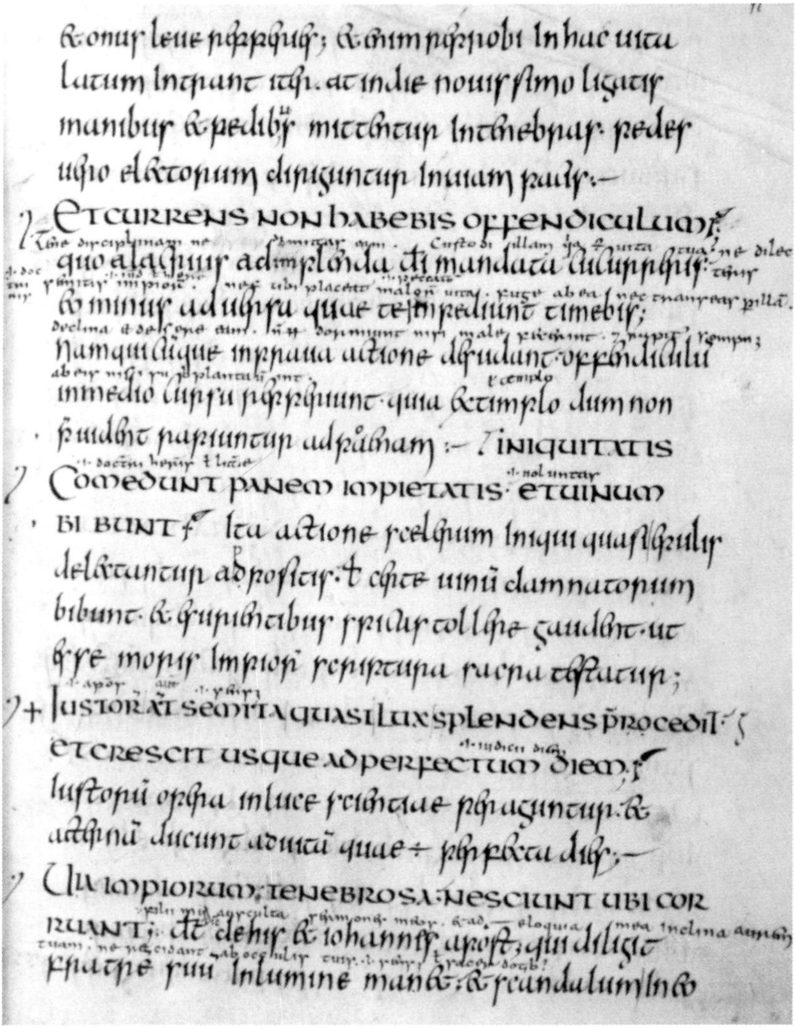

27 A late 8th-century copy of Bede's *Commentary on the Proverbs* (Bodleian Library, Oxford, MS Bodl. 819, f. 11r), written at Wearmouth-Jarrow in Insular minuscule script, used for the commentary, and uncial for the psalm texts with ivy-leaf (hedera) punctuation marks in classical fashion. It was glossed between the lines in the mid-10th century by Aldred, as were the Lindisfarne Gospels, and probably passed to the community of St Cuthbert as part of its absorption of Wearmouth-Jarrow's properties in the late 9th century.

Ritual (Durham, MS A.IV.19), where he glossed some of the collects between the text lines and added red initials to the text, and in Latin glosses to Bodleian Library, Oxford, MS Bodl. 819, a late eighth-century copy of Bede's *Commentary on the Proverbs* written at Wearmouth-Jarrow (which probably passed to the community of St Cuthbert as part of its absorption of Wearmouth-Jarrow's properties in the late ninth century).

Following in Bede's footsteps, Aldred emerges as something of a champion of the written English vernacular in northern England at a time when it was being reintegrated into the new, unified England. This process had been initiated by Alfred and was considerably advanced by his successors, Athelstan effectively reclaiming the North. It was not, however, an inevitable one and encountered much opposition. At around the time that Aldred was glossing the Lindisfarne Gospels, Eric Bloodaxe (died 954), ruler of Viking York, was advancing his 'kingdom' in Northumbria. Alba (Scotland) and Strathclyde also posed a threat to English control of the North. The community of St Cuthbert seems to have been doing its bit to keep the region 'English' and the promotion of Old English may have been part of this. The use of the vernacular would also, of course, have served to further enhance the popularity and accessibility of the cult of St Cuthbert and to have strengthened Christianity in the region. The visits of kings Athelstan and Edmund to the shrine of St Cuthbert over the preceding decades can also be viewed in the light of fostering the process of reintegration and may have helped to stimulate Aldred to perpetuate King Alfred's agenda of translation as an essential adjunct to unification, national spiritual well-being and an earlier Insular tradition of glossing texts. This may subsequently have been reinforced by Aldred's own visit to southern England as a scribal notary in the train of his bishop in 970, during which time they may have obtained the Durham Ritual, made in southern England earlier in the century, for the community. The visit may have been partly motivated by diplomacy to ensure the stability of the North, Bishop Aelfsige and Aldred accompanying Kenneth, King of Alba, to Wessex, perhaps as diplomatic mediators and presumably with the intention of safeguarding the community of St Cuthbert's interests in negotiations concerning the English–Scottish frontier zone and in perpetuating the Christian identity of the North, despite the Northmen.

FIVE

Bede the English Patristic

Bede wrote in his autobiographical note at the end of the *Ecclesiastical History of the English People*, v.24:

> Spending all the remaining time of my life a dweller in that monastery, I wholly applied myself to the study of Scripture; and amidst the observance of monastic rule, and the daily charge of singing in the church, I always took delight in learning, or teaching, or writing. In the nineteenth year of my age, I received deacon's orders; in the thirtieth, those of the priesthood, both of them by the ministry of the most reverend Bishop John, and at the bidding of the Abbot Ceolfrid. From the time when I received priest's orders, till the fifty-ninth year of my age, I have made it my business, for my own needs and those of my brethren, to compile out of the works of the venerable Fathers, the following brief notes on the Holy Scriptures, and also to make some additions after the manner of the meaning and interpretation given by them.

His tremendous respect for and indebtedness to the Church Fathers – the patristic authorities – was rewarded by him being the first English person effectively to be counted in their ranks.

Although they are sadly probably the least read of his works today, his commentaries on Scripture, along with his hagiography, are among his major contributions to the development of Western thought and formed the backbone of his other work. It is this, not the *Ecclesiastical History*, and his work on computus and teaching manuals that won him continued transmission in Christian scholarship and the title of Doctor of the Church.

Biblical exegesis is not preferred reading for everyone, but rest assured that Bede was a master of it. His finely attuned and nuanced mind skipped nimbly in the flower meadow of Scripture, made heady by its scent and not afraid of grasping its thorns and nettles. Following the injunctions of Cassiodorus, Bede devoted the might of his intellect to owning and honing the tools necessary for the effective study and transmission of the Bible.

His work on schemes and tropes was undertaken primarily to help distinguish the literal and figurative meanings of Scriptural passages, so essential to avoid the pitfalls of misapplication, literalism and hardlining that are so often made.[1] His work on orthography served to ensure accuracy in copying and commenting. In his *The Art of Poetry*, he stressed the primacy of Christian models in comprehending and emulating Christian Scripture and the literature that it generated, while his hagiographical output placed the moral exemplars of lives well lived before his readers, that they too might live better (plus, as we shall see in the case of St Cuthbert, addressing the contemporary relevance and ongoing significance of their work).

So, the choice of biblical books to which Bede chose to devote his time is of considerable significance. Some are verse-by-verse examinations of whole books, others of select passages, and often with more than one interpretation given, using the *per cola et commata* system (in which line length was used to help convey sense and sententia, in the absence of systematic punctuation) of Jerome's Vulgate to define sections. He worked on both Old and New Testaments, which he characterizes as the Law and the Gospel, and had a penchant for the Apocrypha. Several of his works had no precedent and were exegetical unbroken ground in which Bede was a pioneer: *On Ezra and Nehemiah*, *On the Temple*, *On the Tabernacle*, *On the Proverbs of Solomon* and *On Tobias*. Some took several years to complete, others were quicker, and he often seems to have worked on more than one project simultaneously.

He plucked all the flowers from the rabbinical garden of *Pardes* to help him to read and interpret intelligently and sensitively – the literal meaning, the allegorical, the typological, the tropological and the anagogical, of which the allegorical most often prevails. He had fully imbibed Gregory the Great's injunction that internalization of exterior details can bring the reader towards a transformation of earthly behaviour and thought into an anticipation of their heavenly counterparts. Numerology and verbal iconographies are also frequently used to this end. In his Commentary on Acts, he writes of 20:8, where Paul is teaching in a lamplit upper room: 'We can speak allegorically here, for the upper room is the loftiness of spiritual gifts; night is the obscurity of the scriptures; the abundance of lamps is the explanation of the more enigmatic sayings.'

It is appropriate that he should have linked his own modus operandi to that of the great exegetical apostle Paul. He always carried on learning and was not afraid to revise his own work, returning between 725 and 731 to his *Commentary on the Acts of the Apostles* of circa 709 to write a second *Retractation on the Acts of the Apostles* (as had Augustine) to deploy his improved knowledge of Greek and to correct his earlier errors or linguistic infelicities. Bede was working to transmit, interpret (in ways that both inexperienced readers and scholars might find accessible, and excerpting and summarizing lengthy works for those unable to digest them whole), critically revise, compile, interrogate and supplement the work of the patristics, of whom his sources ranged across figures such as Jerome, Basil, Ambrose, Augustine, Gregory the Great, Origen, Eusebius, Isidore, Eugippius, Victorinus, Pachomius and Tychonius, supplementing them where appropriate with non-Christian sources such as the Jewish historian Josephus and Pliny. In so doing, he effectively became one of them.[2]

Etymology was another of Bede's great interests, as may be expected, and his pursuit of it in his exegesis evinces a growing ability in Greek through his career and some Hebrew, especially for names and terms. He was, of course, supremely latinate and evidently also concerned with placing the English vernacular in this line of sacred languages used for transmitting Scripture – the *lingua sacra* – with his final bold step of translating St John into English, six and a half centuries before Wycliffe. No wonder it was a deathbed act of audacity and, yes, innovation (but in the tradition of the churches of the East), for it would surely have called down further censure upon him, even if this more tolerant age did not subject him to the constraints and persecutions faced by Wycliffe and Tyndale in the more restrictive late medieval and early modern ages. But, like Alfred a century and a half later, he was also concerned practically with meeting the needs of those 'illiterate' rural priests about whom he had lamented, in his Letter to Ecgbert, that he had found it necessary to translate the *Pater Noster* and the Creed into their native Old English. As it was in the early stages of Anglo-Saxon England, so it would be again at the birth of its new age.

Bede wrote commentaries on the Gospels of Sts Luke and Mark, the former composed between 709 and 716 with the latter following after 716. They are prefaced by letters showing that they were undertaken at the request of Bishop Acca of Hexham and it is here, in the letter accompanying Luke, that Bede outlined his system of marginal annotation of sources and enjoined others to retain and use them when quoting – a truly scholarly perspective. Here we also find him refuting accusations of dangerous innovation in an earlier work, the *Commentary on the Apocalypse*, namely what was to become the usual medieval interpretation of the ordering of the evangelist symbols, which he points out was based upon Augustine's work *On the Consensus of the Evangelists*.

In the Prologue to *The Commentary on Luke* Bede thus outlines the system that he devised for indicating his primary sources (the patristic authors) by writing their initial in the margin next to the thoughts he ascribes to them. In so doing, Bede effectively invented footnotes:

> Having gathered together the work of the Fathers, as if they were the most eminent and most worthy craftsmen of such a great gift, diligently undertook to examine what blessed Ambrose, what Augustine, and then what Gregory, the apostle of our nation who was 'most watchful' in accordance with his [Greek] name, what Jerome the interpreter of sacred history, [and] what the rest of the Fathers thought and said about the words of blessed Luke . . . Because it was laborious to insert their names every time and to indicate by name what had been said by which author, I found it convenient to note the first letters of their names in the margin and in this way to show where the discourse I have transcribed from each of the Fathers individually begins and where it ends. [This I have done] carefully throughout, lest it be said that I was stealing the words of my predecessors and putting them forth as my own. I very much pray and beseech my readers through the Lord that if anyone should perhaps judge these works of ours to be in any way worthy of transcription, they might remember also to add the

aforementioned signs of the names as they find them in our exemplar.

He also introduced the practice of putting a series of symbols like lightning flashes in the margins next to passages where he is quoting other authors, rather like the modern practice of highlighting. This was his answer to those who had previously accused him of the heresy of innovation, making sure to emphasize that he had done so 'carefully'. Interestingly, Bede also states that Luke, 'this most holy Nazarene from the mother's womb . . . performed the office of historian'.

Surely, had time permitted, a commentary upon Matthew might have followed – or would it? For perhaps he felt that Origen, Jerome, Augustine and Gregory had already trodden well the ground of what was long considered the first Gospel to have been written. But 716 saw the departure for Rome of Bede's beloved lifelong mentor, Abbot Ceolfrith, an event that caused him great personal distress and to which he seems to have paid tribute by throwing himself, after a pause, back into his other work. Underway at that time was the *Commentary on Samuel*, the first three books of which were completed by June 716, when Abbot Ceolfrith departed for Rome, and the fourth book of which was begun after Ceolfrith's successor, Hwaetberht, had been appointed. Samuel, of course, enjoyed the biblical role of serving as mentor to King David.

As previously stated, on his deathbed in 735, Bede returned to the task, this time not commenting on St John, but taking the bold step of translating it into his native Old English, that it might be more readily accessible to his people; a last offering from the teacher, preacher and priest. Today, the rising provision of translations of Bede's works, some of them also available online, is perpetuating Bede's agenda of using the vernacular and publishing to spread the Word, and his wisdom, more effectively.

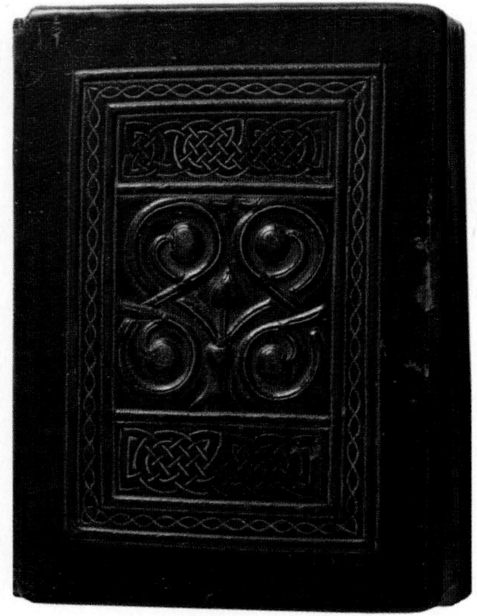

et non uenit ad lucem
ut non arguantur opera eius
Qui autem facit ueritatem
uenit ad lucem ut manifes
tentur eius opera
quia in deo sunt facta
Post haec uenit ihs et discipuli
eius in iudaeam terram
et illic morabatur cum eis
et baptizabat
Erat autem et iohannes
baptizans in aenon
iuxta salim
quia aquae multae erant illic
et adueniebant et baptizabantur
Non dum enim missus fuerat
in carcerem iohannes
Facta est ergo questio ex disci
pulis iohannis cum iudaeis

28, 29 The St Cuthbert Gospel (BL, Add. MS 89000; formerly known as the Stonyhurst Gospel of St John), written in uncial script at Wearmouth-Jarrow, bound in Coptic fashion and perhaps placed in St Cuthbert's coffin when his relics were translated in 698.

John's gospel, of course, was that used in ministering to the sick and the dying, a pastoral and spiritually visionary non-synoptic deep masterpiece that St Cuthbert had spent formative time studying with his master, Boisil, at Melrose. The significance of 'the little Gospel that speaks of the things that work of love' is attested to by the probable placing of a tiny copy of that Gospel (the St Cuthbert Gospel, BL, Add. MS 89000, formerly known as the Stonyhurst Gospel),[3] copied at Wearmouth-Jarrow, in the coffin of St Cuthbert, perhaps in 698 at the translation of his relics, wherein it was discovered in 1104. This was made in the codicological format of the small Irish pocket Gospel books, used in travelling ministry and for personal study, but it was bound in the Coptic fashion of the desert fathers as a pan-global statement of the collaboration of churches.

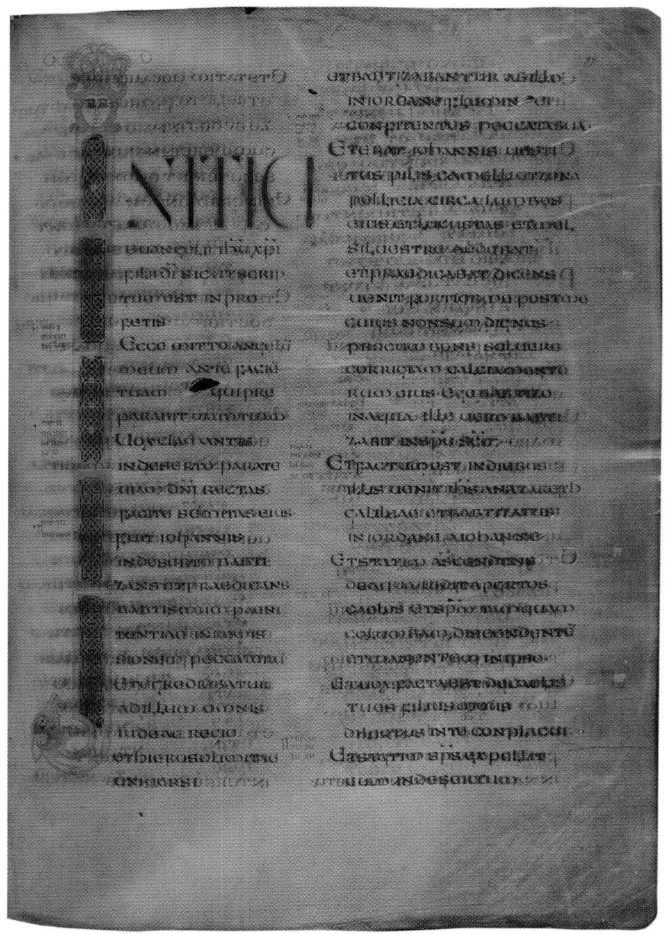

30 An early 8th-century Northumbrian Gospel book (Durham Cathedral Library, MS A.II.16, f. 37r), which is thought to have been written at Wearmouth-Jarrow and which employs both the uncial script seen here at the opening of St Mark's Gospel (with its classicizing antique mask at the head of the initial 'I') and a hybrid half-uncial/set minuscule script for its Gospel of St John. It may be the Gospel book referred to in Durham Cathedral's 1392 Spendement inventory as 'de manu Bede' ('in the hand of Bede'), which Alan Piper suggested may have been removed from the shrine after Bede's relics were translated from there to the Galilee Chapel in 1370. It dates to Bede's lifetime and, like the Ceolfrith Bibles, may contain his own hand writing a different grade of script.

Another fragmentary Gospel of John, thought to have been copied at Wearmouth-Jarrow, is appended to Durham Cathedral Library MS A.II.16, an early eighth-century Northumbrian Gospel book also from their scriptorium. This may indicate that Wearmouth-Jarrow was publishing and distributing copies of this fine Vulgate edition of John's text.[4] Bede himself is known to have distributed copies of at least some of his work and the publishing programme adopted at the twin monasteries, not least in distributing Bede's own work, undoubtedly played a key role in shaping Alcuin's publication of his edition of the Bible at his abbey of Tours. This was modelled on Wearmouth-Jarrow's campaign of producing massive single-volume Vulgate Bibles, which was ultimately indebted to the publication programmes of Jerome and Cassiodorus. We owe a considerable amount to them for ensuring the transmission of a reliable Latin version of the Bible.

The *Commentary on Revelation* (*In Apocalypsis*), devoted to John's other major work, was Bede's first venture into biblical exegesis. Written around 703, in an atmosphere of heightened speculation and anxiety about the imminent end of the world at the end of what was believed to be its sixth millennium, it was an ambitious choice. Bede placed the climax of Creation, human history, salvation and time at the beginning of his work. Resisting the temptation to calculate the time of the end, for we are enjoined in Scripture not to look for it, as it is too horrific to wish upon our generation, the Commentary argues that Revelation symbolizes the perennial struggle of the Church in this world, rather than literally predicting the end. In this, Bede's work is complemented by his counter-millennialist stance in *On Times*.

Also written around 702–3 was Bede's tract *On the Holy Places* (*De locis sanctis*), intended to better familiarize his audience with the backdrop for events and their symbolic significance. He did not include it in his list of his own works though, perhaps in honour of Abbot Adomnán of Iona, on whose own work it drew.

Bede's other New Testament works, *The Commentary on the Act of the Apostles*, completed shortly after 709 and dedicated to his fellow monk Hwaetberht, whom Bede calls 'Eusebius' and who succeeded Ceolfrith as abbot in 716, is one of the two books referred to in his list of own works as *In actus apostolorum libros II*. The other was *The Retractation (or Retractatio)*, probably composed between 725 and 731, in which he revised his earlier work. His *Commentary on the Catholic Epistles* (*In epistolas VII catholicas libros singulos*) comprises seven commentaries, one of which (on 1 John) was written at the same time as *The Commentary on Acts*, completed shortly after 709. It is possible that the commentaries were not all completed at the same time. The epistles in question are those by James, Peter, John and Jude, called 'catholic' or 'universal' as they are not addressed to particular churches – which may have commended them to Bede as appropriate for his own gentile race. It was ambitious for this stage in his writing career, for the only previous work in this area was Augustine on 1 John.

Bede's own intellectual and spiritual curiosity and his desire to open up such instruction to nascent early Christian churches and to his own people, especially on the avoidance of heresy and schism, probably had more to do with this choice than scholarly ambition. Interestingly, he did not feel the need to comment fully on the Pauline Epistles, despite the dedication of Jarrow to the saint, perhaps feeling that Augustine, with some additional matter from Eugippius, sufficed; he therefore contented himself with compiling *Excerpts*. Described in Bede's list as *In apostolum quaecumque in opusculis sancti Augustini exposita inveni, cuncta per ordinem transscribere curavi*, this is his *Collectaneum on the Pauline Epistles*.

But to return to the beginning and Bede's Old Testament work, his *Commentary on Genesis* expounds the first twenty chapters of Genesis and the first ten verses of the 21st chapter. It exists in two forms: an early version in two books, and a later, revised version in four books that benefited from Bede's deeper thinking on Creation in light of his intervening work on matter and time.

On the Tabernacle sees Bede commenting on the tabernacle of Moses, which he interpreted as a symbolic figure of the Christian Church. Written in the early 720s, it was the first Christian work devoted entirely to this topic and the first verse-by-verse commentary on the relevant portions of the Book of Exodus. It was one of Bede's most popular works, copied throughout the Middle Ages. Bede followed it with his commentary *On the Temple*, which treats of the passage in 1 Kings 3:1 to 7:51 in which Solomon builds the Temple with the help of gentile workers. This was probably composed shortly before 731, the same year as the *Ecclesiastical History*, and its allegorical significance for Bede's account of the building of the English Church is palpable.

Laistner suggests that the *Commentary on Tobias* was composed around the same time as *On the Temple*, as Bede stresses allegorical interpretation in both. As with the commentary on *The Prayer/Canticle of Habakkuk*, he draws on the work of Jerome and on Augustine's *City of God*. It is not known when Bede composed it, but he dedicated the work to 'his dearly beloved sister and virgin of Christ', a nun and perhaps abbess who remains unidentified. Perhaps she was Abbess/St Ælflæd of Whitby (654–714), daughter of King Oswy of Northumbria, to whom Bede refers in Chapter 24 of his prose Life of St Cuthbert as 'a most holy virgin, and mother of the virgins of Christ'.[5]

The biblical Book of Habakkuk was popular in early Anglo-Saxon England. One passage that particularly appealed, and which occurs in the Septuagint version of Habakkuk 3.2,[6] 'in the midst of two lives/ living things thou shalt be known', which can be interpreted as a prophesy of Christ crucified between the two thieves. This interpretation has also been applied to the iconography of Christ adored by two beasts, seen for example on the early eighth-century Ruthwell Cross (illus. 17), and is thought also to account for the presence of the ox and ass in Nativity scenes. I suspect that Bede may have drawn upon it himself in the prose Life of St Cuthbert, in the much-loved passage in Chapter 10 relating two sea otters drying the saint's feet after his nocturnal sea penance, thereby acknowledging his status as chosen by God:

> How Cuthbert passed the night in the sea, praying; and when he was come out, two animals of the sea did him reverence; and how the brother, who saw those things, being in fear, was encouraged by Cuthbert.
>
> When this holy man was thus acquiring renown by his virtues and miracles, Ebbe, a pious woman and handmaid of Christ, was the head of a monastery at a place called the city of Coludi, remarkable both for piety and noble birth, for she was half-sister of King Oswy. She sent messengers to the man of God, entreating him to come and visit her monastery. This loving message from the handmaid of his Lord he could not treat with neglect, but, coming to the place and stopping several days there, he confirmed, by his life and conversation, the way of truth which he taught.
>
> Here also, as elsewhere, he would go forth, when others were asleep, and having spent the night in watchfulness return home at the hour of morning-prayer. Now one night, a brother of the monastery, seeing him go out alone followed him privately to see what he should do. But he when he left the monastery, went down to the sea, which flows beneath, and going into it, until the water reached his neck and arms, spent the night in praising God. When

31 St Cuthbert's feet being dried by otters (the two living creatures who in Habakkuk identify the Lord's anointed one) after he had spent the night in prayer in the sea at Coldingham, from a late 12th-century Durham copy of Bede's *Prose Life of St Cuthbert* (BL, Yates Thompson MS 26, f. 24r).

> the dawn of day approached, he came out of the water, and, falling on his knees, began to pray again. While he was doing this, two quadrupeds, called otters, came up from the sea, and, lying down before him on the sand, breathed upon his feet, and wiped them with their hair after which, having received his blessing, they returned to their native element. Cuthbert himself returned home in time to join in the accustomed hymns with the other brethren. The brother, who waited for him on the heights, was so terrified that he could hardly reach home; and early in the morning he came and fell at his feet, asking his pardon, for he did not doubt that Cuthbert was fully acquainted with all that had taken place. To whom Cuthbert replied, 'What is the matter, my brother? What have you done? Did you follow me to see what I was about to do? I forgive you for it on one condition – that you tell it to nobody before my death.' In this he followed the example of our Lord, who, when He showed his glory to his disciples on the mountain, said, 'See that you tell no man, until the Son of man be risen from the dead.' When the brother had assented to this condition, he give him his blessing, and released him from all his trouble. The man concealed this miracle during St. Cuthbert's life; but, after his death, took care to tell it to as many persons as he was able.[7]

Bede was a priest, with pastoral and preaching roles, and his *Homilies*, sermons arranged by order of the Church's liturgical feasts, give us a valuable insight into his approach, which was to compile extracts from the Church Fathers on the Gospels and to add his own comments and interpretations – new treasure discovered from old – so that they might be of use to others, including the famous later Anglo-Saxon homilist Aelfric. The universal, non-location-specific nature of most of the homilies may indicate that he intended them to serve as an aid for other preachers and perhaps also for private devotional reading (*lectio divina*) and use in the refectory and the night office (as outlined in Benedict Biscop's version of the Benedictine Rule observed at Wearmouth-Jarrow). Use of Bede's work as a mainstay of the Carolingian homiliary by Paul the Deacon ensured that his words would be read during the monastic night office for many centuries to come.[8] Needless to say, he focuses upon the most liturgically significant seasons of Advent–Christmas and Lent–Easter–Pentecost. It has been noted that there is very little overlap between Bede's fifty homilies and Gregory the Great's *Forty Gospel Homilies* and that perhaps Bede intended his series to serve as a supplement to that of Pope Gregory, one of his great heroes.[9]

His homilies are intended to be read, but that does not preclude them having an earlier existence in Bede's own oral delivery. We do not have any references to him actually preaching, but as a priest it is likely that he would have, especially when the abbot (who did the bulk of the in-house preaching) was absent from Wearmouth-Jarrow. It is pleasing to think of him guest-preaching on Holy Island during his visit to the monastery of Lindisfarne.

However, we are given an insight into Bede's approach to those imbued with teaching, pastoral and preaching gifts, be they religious or lay, as part of his discussion of imagery concerning the human body, to which he relates them allegorically in his *Commentary on the Song of Songs*:

> They can rightly be called eyes, since they perceive the secrets of mysteries; rightly are they called teeth, since in reproving the ungodly it is as though they are chewing them and, once softened and humbled, transforming them

> into the body of the Church; rightly are they called a neck, since in preaching eternal joys it is as though they provide the whole body of the Church with the breath of life and prepare the doctrinal food with which she is nourished unto salvation; and they are also quite aptly referred to as breasts, since they supply the milk of the saving word to those who are still infants in Christ.[10]

Bede was very aware of the pressing needs of society for physical and spiritual care and of the impact of good or bad government and leadership, be it by state or Church. His tribute to the saints, many of whom had themselves performed such roles and whose feast days formed anchors in the ebb and flow of the year, included a lost Life of St Anastasius, of which a manuscript survived as late as the fifteenth century,[11] a Life of St Felix, which was essentially a prose reworking of four poems on St Felix by Paulinus of Nola, and the verse and prose Lives of St Cuthbert (the verse Life composed between 705 and 716 and the prose Life around 721). He also compiled a Martyrology, probably written between 725 and 731, which he says included his research into when each of the saints therein were actually martyred, linking the historical with the miraculous. It was arranged in calendrical order and proved very influential in the genre.

Bede's allegorical *Commentary on the Song of Songs* is his love song to the Church he served, the Bride of Christ. This was in the tradition of the spiritual, typological and anagogical interpretation adopted earlier by Origen and Gregory the Great, when interpreting this text, but only Bede's version is complete. It is his longest commentary and consists of an introduction on Divine Grace, five books of *Commentary on the Song of Songs* and a final section of extracts from the works of Gregory the Great. It seems to have been followed soon after by his *Commentary on the Parables of*

Solomon (*Commentary on Proverbs*, *In proverbia salomonis libros III* or *In parabolas Salomonis*, or *Super parabolas Salomonis*), but it is not known exactly when they were composed.

A related work was the *Thirty Questions* (*Regum librum XXX quaestionum*), described in Bede's list as *In regum librum quaestiones XXX* but which also appears in some manuscripts as *In parabolas Salomonis*, or *Super parabolas Salomonis* (On the Parables of Solomon). Its date of composition is uncertain, but Laistner suggested that its style resembles that of Bede's later biblical commentaries and that it may have been composed around 725.[12] It consists of answers to thirty questions posed to Bede by Nothhelm (who assisted Bede by undertaking research for him in Canterbury and who subsequently became Archbishop of Canterbury from 735 to 739) on passages from I and II Samuel and I and II Kings. Another of Bede's works, *On Eight Questions* (*De octo Quaestionibus*), may have been written for Nothhelm and treats both Old and New Testament subjects.

Further examples of writings expressly made to answer pleas from others for clarification and insight are Bede's *Resting Places of the Children of Israel* (*De mansionibus filiorum Israel*) and *On the Words of Isaiah* (*De eo quod ait Isaias*), both of which were addressed to his sometime supporter Bishop Acca of Hexham, who shared his exegetical interests. It would be wonderful to have more of Bede's thoughts on Isaiah and also on the Psalms, but he did leave us an *Abbreviated Psalter* in which he selects verses from each Psalm as vehicles for meditation and prayer. Priests at this time were required to be *psalteratus* – to have memorized the Psalms by heart – and they formed both a mainstay of the divine office and the mass and were the bedrock of personal prayer. Bede's approach is echoed – or perhaps followed – at Lindisfarne, where Bishop Æthilwald, who succeeded Bede's friend Eadfrith in 722–40, made his own abbreviated version, which is preserved for us in the early ninth-century Mercian Book of Cerne

(Cambridge University Library, MS LL.I.10). This was made for his namesake, Bishop Æthelwald of Lichfield (d. 830), as part of an important new genre of thematic prayerbooks that appears to have originated in Anglo-Saxon Mercia.[13]

Bede has left us his own little creed, I feel, when he speaks of what the cowherd Caedmon sang of when the Lord opened his lips – tellingly, at Whitby, where unity was proclaimed:

> He sang about the Creation of the world, the origin of the human race, and the whole history of Genesis, of the departure of Israel from Egypt and the entry into the promised land and of many other of the stories taken from the sacred Scriptures: of the incarnation, passion, and resurrection of the Lord, of His ascension into heaven, of the coming of the Holy Spirit and the teaching of the Apostles. He also made songs about the terrors of future judgement, the horrors and the pains of hell, and the joys of the heavenly kingdom. (*Ecclesiastical History*, IV.24)

This is pretty much what Bede did and what guided his exegetical agenda.

Bede's biblical scholarship exerted a profound influence upon his approach to contemporary society and was employed in directing it in accordance with the will of God. His choice of Ezra and Nehemiah as a vehicle for this is particularly telling. Composed between 725 and 731 (while he was working on the *Ecclesiastical History*), his is the first commentary devoted to this text and its focus is the restoration and reform of the Jewish people as they return from their exile in Babylon to rebuild the Temple and reconstruct Scripture. For Bede, the English are the new children of Israel and, like Ezra the supreme priestly 'doctor' (leader), Bede takes on the role of healing what ails his people spiritually, morally and, by extension, politically. Ezra's role was to restore, preserve and transmit the Word and to interpret it through study, teaching and preaching to bring his people together as a community before God. Bede calls him pontifex ('high priest'), a forerunner or type of Christ, the 'great high priest'. Bede presents St Cuthbert in such a light and humbly sought to assume a similar role himself in respect of his teaching of the English and his calls for reform of their pastoral leaders, the bishops.

Nehemiah, who was appointed governor of Judea by King Artaxerxes I of Persia in 468 BC, rebuilt Jerusalem's walls and regulated the life of its people. He was, likewise, a symbol of Bede's recognition of and longing for good government. In his commentary Bede writes:

> And it should be carefully noted and used as an example of good works that while some leaders sinned and caused the common people who were entrusted to them to sin, other leaders who were men of more wholesome view for their part did their best to correct those sins; but because they cannot do this themselves they refer the matter to their pontifex (i.e. their archbishop) through whose authority so grave, so manifold, and so long-lasting a sin can be expiated.[14]

The role of the Church in serving as the conscience and corrective of the state is clearly stated. Thus, just as Bede's commentaries on the Temple and the Tabernacle present a symbolic reading of their construction and adornment as forerunners of the heavenly Jerusalem, and serve as an injunction to the English to work for the coming of the eternal Kingdom of God, so his interpretation of Ezra and Nehemiah emphasizes the role of secular rulers and their high priests – archbishops and bishops such as Egbert of York, to whom Bede addressed his letter calling for reform of abuses in eighth-century Northumbria. It will not have escaped notice that, in reminding both kings and senior churchmen of their duties in this respect, it is Bede who is cast in the role of the prophetic scholar-priest and doctor Ezra.

As Scott DeGregorio has pointed out, Bede was likely working on *Ezra and Nehemiah*, *On the Temple* and *On the Tabernacle* and the *Ecclesiastical History* in tandem, as part of a joined-up programme.[15] In his choice of these biblical vehicles for study and explication, Bede was instructing and exhorting the English in the establishment of an earthly kingdom and people with their own story and identity, one which should work for the coming of God's kingdom in which peace, justice and unity would prevail.

SIX

Bede the Historian and Reformer

Bede writes, in the preface to the *Ecclesiastical History of the English People*:

> Should history tell of good men and their good estate, the thoughtful reader is spurred on to imitate the good; should it record the evil ends of wicked men, no less effectively the devout and earnest listener or reader is kindled to eschew what is harmful and perverse, and himself with greater care pursue those things which he has learned to be good and pleasing in the sight of God.

The role of history, like hagiography, was for him in significant part the placing of worthy moral exemplars and cautionary tales before his audience, for their betterment and that of society. As Alfred and his scholars would later seek to stiffen the moral purpose and backbone of the English, in the face of renewed pagan onslaught by the Vikings, so Bede sought to help lead his own people into a place of spiritual robustness and safety.

We have come a long way in our reading of Bede and his purposes since the eminent historian J. H. Wallace-Hadrill wrote of him as one of the first of a species of medieval local historian – alongside figures such as Jordanes, Cassiodorus, Isidore, Fredegar, Paul the Deacon and Gregory of Tours – who recorded events in one of several post-Roman successor states in accordance with their own agendas. He saw them in contrast to the pagan, classical historians, such as Ammianus Marcellinus, and the first great ecclesiastical historian, Eusebius, and his immediate followers, saying, 'We cannot call them ancient historians, and only in a qualified sense are they ecclesiastical historians.'[1] We can now excavate something of Bede's wider vision of time and space, in which he sought to locate his people and their history.

The Aftermath of Empire: The Early Anglo-Saxons and Their Conversion

By the beginning of the fifth century the empire's borders were beginning to collapse under pressure from raiders and migrants seeking to move into it to participate in its economy. In 410 Emperor Honorius issued a rescript withdrawing Roman military, administrative and economic support from the provinces of Britannia, which was left to look to its own defences. Subsequent appeals for assistance to Consul Aetius met with little response, although Bishop Germanus of Auxerre did visit to help combat Pelagianism. Patterns of reversion to Celtic tribalism and of attempts to preserve the Romano-British status quo can be detected from the writings of British writers, notably the sixth-century monk Gildas, author of *The Ruin and Conquest of Britain* (*De excidio et conquestu Britanniae*), and the ninth-century Welsh cleric Nennius, who composed *The History of the British* (*Historia Brittonum*), which has become synonymous with the 'Age of King Arthur', a figure who has become more a heroic ideal than a historical reality and who came to embody British hopes of resurgence. An equally shadowy figure is King Vortigern, the British warlord who is said to have employed German mercenaries to uphold his rule – a practice that perpetuated the Roman use of federal auxiliaries. These are said by Gildas to have bitten the hand that fed them, seizing territory on their own behalf and encouraging widespread Germanic immigration and settlement, which in turn led to British migration westwards and abroad to Brittany. Determined British resistance, culminating in their victory at the Battle of Mount Badon (attributed to Arthur's leadership) around 500, stemmed the tide for a generation or two, but by the end of the sixth century a series of pagan Germanic kingdoms had been carved out around the eastern seaboard: Wessex, Sussex, Kent, Essex, East Anglia and Northumbria (composed of two parts, the more northerly Bernicia and the southerly Deira). Many smaller kingdoms – both Germanic and British – were gradually swallowed up by bigger fish, with the kingdom of Mercia consuming ever more of central England and pushing its way westwards into British territory, while Northumbria likewise annexed more and more territory from neighbouring British kingdoms such as Catterick, Elmet, Rheged (southwest Scotland and Cumbria), Strathclyde (around Glasgow) and the Gododdin (around Edinburgh). These peoples from Germany, Frisia and southern Scandinavia were later characterized by Bede as Angles, Saxons and Jutes – although many groups were probably of mixed origin and assumed any collective identity from their leader(s) – and imbued with a collective identity named for his own Anglian roots: the English (*Angli*).

Not surprisingly, therefore, Bede has often been accorded the title 'the father of English History'. He sought to imbue the aspirational ideological concept he had created with historical context and certainly imbued it with a sense of prophetic mission when he recounted the alleged origins of the name, ascribing to Pope Gregory the Great the words, upon seeing angelic blonde Anglo-Saxon children (from Deira, the southern part of Northumbria) in a slave market in Rome, 'Non Angli sed Angeli', not Angles but angels.

Ecclesiastical History, Book II, Chap. 1.
Of the death of the blessed Pope Gregory. [AD 604]

Nor must we pass by in silence the story of the blessed Gregory, handed down to us by the tradition of our ancestors, which explains his earnest care for the salvation of our nation. It is said that one day, when some merchants had lately arrived at Rome, many things were exposed for sale in the market place, and much people resorted thither to buy: Gregory himself went with the rest, and saw among other wares some boys put up for sale, of fair complexion, with pleasing countenances, and very beautiful hair. When he beheld them, he asked, it is said, from what region or country they were brought? and was told, from the island of Britain, and that the inhabitants were like that in appearance. He again inquired whether those islanders were Christians, or still involved in the errors of paganism, and was informed that they were pagans. Then fetching a deep sigh from the bottom of his heart, 'Alas! what pity,' said he, 'that the author of darkness should own men of such fair countenances; and that with such grace of outward form, their minds should be void of inward grace.' He therefore again asked, what was the name of that nation? and was answered, that they were called Angles. 'Right,' said he, 'for they have an angelic face, and it is meet that such should be co-heirs with the Angels in heaven. What is the name of the province from which they are brought?' It was replied, that the natives of that province were called Deiri. 'Truly are they De ira,' said he, 'saved from wrath, and called to the mercy of Christ. How is the king of that province called?' They told him his name was Aelli; and he, playing upon the name, said, 'Allelujah, the praise of God the Creator must be sung in those parts.'

This is presented as the trigger for the despatch of Augustine and his mission to Kent. It is a clever, memorable, punning piece of prose and also powerful propaganda, imbuing Bede's vision of a united race and kingdom (not to be achieved politically until the tenth century, after the spur of Viking invasion and settlement) with a prophetic sense of divine purpose.

More convincing, and moving, is Bede's poignant quotation (at the end of the passage below) of something that really sounds like Gregory's voice, to judge from his correspondence and complaints to the Eastern emperor and patriarchs at his fate in being left at the helm of the leaky ship of the West:

Chap. I. Of the death of the blessed Pope Gregory. [AD 604]

He was by nation a Roman, son of Gordianus, tracing his descent from ancestors that were not only noble, but religious. Moreover Felix, once bishop of the same Apostolic see, a man of great honour in Christ and in the Church, was his forefather. Nor did he show his nobility in religion by less strength of devotion than his parents and kindred. But that nobility of this world which was seen in him, by the help of the Divine Grace, he used only to gain the glory of eternal dignity; for soon quitting his secular habit, he entered a monastery, wherein he began to live with so much grace of perfection that (as he was wont afterwards with tears to testify) his mind was above all transitory things; that he rose superior to all that is subject to change; that he used to think of nothing but what was heavenly; that, while detained by the body, he broke through the bonds of the flesh by contemplation; and that he even loved death, which is a penalty to almost all men, as the entrance into life, and the reward of his labours. This he used to say of himself, not to boast of his progress

> in virtue, but rather to bewail the falling off which he imagined he had sustained through his pastoral charge. Indeed, once in a private conversation with his deacon, Peter, after having enumerated the former virtues of his soul, he added sorrowfully, 'But now, on account of the pastoral charge, it is entangled with the affairs of laymen, and, after so fair an appearance of inward peace, is defiled with the dust of earthly action. And having wasted itself on outward things, by turning aside to the affairs of many men, even when it desires the inward things, it returns to them undoubtedly impaired. I therefore consider what I endure, I consider what I have lost, and when I behold what I have thrown away, that which I bear appears the more grievous.'

Bede, from the comparative safety of his monastic cloister, sought to recount and try to make sense of the ways of men – and women – without becoming mired in their affairs, although his appreciation of the symbiotic relationship of past, present and future and his supreme belief in God's will and justice would lead him to challenge them for the greater good. Bede may sometimes appear to the modern mind to resemble certain old-school Oxbridge dons, buffered from the storms of the world by a privileged, serviced academic environment, with guaranteed bed and board, a superb library and the funded time to pursue their research and teaching interests. Maybe, but this is to overlook Bede's monastic pledges of obedience, prayer and *opus Dei*, not to mention celibacy and humility, with its injunction to undertake hard manual labour. If Bede were such a figure, he was not an ivory tower academic, but an activist whose research was focused upon changing the world for the better and who had the courage to challenge it when he saw it going awry – as his letter to Bishop Ecgbert pushing for Church reforms shows. In it Bede urged

Ecgbert to study Gregory the Great's *Pastoral Care*, and held up Aidan and Cuthbert as examples of model bishops in the face of attempts by the successors of Wilfrid of York (notably Bede's own friend-cum-patron, Bishop Acca of Hexham) to write the contribution of Lindisfarne and the Columban monastic federation out of the equation, a trend that Bede had sought to oppose in his hagiographies of St Cuthbert and by emphasizing their vital contribution and positive role-modelling in the *Ecclesiastical History*.[2]

Bede has attracted increasing criticism for racism in creating an English ethnic identity. He was not alone in this and it should be remembered that his was another age and that it would be revisionist to try to write such aspects out of the discussion. The Britons or Welsh, so named from the Old English term *Wealas* (stranger), were equally keen to distinguish themselves from the Germanic invaders and in Ireland there were contemporary references to monastic centres with a high density of Anglo-Saxons, such as 'Mayo of the English'. Bede's perspective is that of a committed member of the Church, of Germanic stock, wedded to the consolidation of English rule and its Christian establishment, convinced of the primacy of the papacy in Rome and afraid of the divisive propensities of religious schism – all too apparent within the successor to the Eastern Roman Empire, Byzantium, and its territories.

His view of the British Church was certainly a negative one. It, like parts of the Irish Church which it had helped to found, favoured certain observances, notably the calculation of the celebration of the moveable feast of Easter, which had become out of step with those of Rome. This, coupled with ongoing British armed resistance to his own people, predisposed Bede against it. He therefore downplayed what historians and archaeologists are increasingly coming to view as a significant level of post-Roman British continuity. Wine and olive oil from the Mediterranean continued to flow throughout the fifth and sixth centuries in high-status halls around the coast of western Britain, and at feasts or wakes for the dead in places such as Tintagel churchyard in Cornwall, and the sherds of the amphorae and promotional tableware with which they were marketed and transported are still being excavated on sites such as Tintagel Island and Glastonbury. The law codes of the Anglo-Saxon kingdoms of Kent and Wessex preserve indications of surviving British populations, of diminished legal status in comparison to their Germanic neighbours, which, along with evidence such as place names, support a picture of at least partial ethnic integration or co-existence as a corrective to Gildas's suggestion of British mass emigration to Brittany and to Bede's image of total segregation, with the British shirking their responsibility to try and convert the Germanic incomers.

Bede's conversion narrative is presented, rather, as a pincer movement conducted by two major protagonists: the missions launched by Pope Gregory the Great, whose emissary, St Augustine, reached Canterbury in 597, and that of the Irish prince-turned-monk St Columba. Augustine's entrée to Kent was facilitated by the marriage of its king, Ethelbert, to a Christian princess from Merovingian Gaul, Bertha, who was guaranteed the right to worship. The remains of the Roman mortuary chapel outside the walls of the Roman city of Canterbury used by Bertha and her confessor, Liudhard, can still be seen in the chancel of the church that Augustine and his followers built around it. Its dedication to St Martin of Tours reflects the importance of the links to the early church in Gaul.

Female influence through diplomatic marriage continued to play a part in the success of the Roman mission. The union of Kentish princess Ethelburga to King Edwin of Northumbria assured the welcome extended to missionary Paulinus, enabling his subsequent evangelization in centres such as York (Deira) and the hilltop royal hall and ampitheatre at Yeavering (Bernicia), following Edwin's eventual conversion in 627/8. Conversion as a manifestation of overlordship also played its part. As top dog, or 'bretwalda', as Bede termed the most powerful Anglo-Saxon ruler at any time, King Ethelbert of Kent compelled King Redwald of East Anglia to accept baptism, himself standing as his godfather. Redwald took his christening gifts and set them up in his temple alongside his ancestral Germanic deities. The silver spoons used at his baptism may be those preserved in the famous Sutton Hoo ship burial that dominates the cemetery close to the royal palace of Rendlesham, near Woodbridge on the banks of the River Deben in Suffolk. They were part of an extensive collection of grave goods deposited in the mighty ship: 37 Merovingian coins (tremissis) found in an elaborate purse form a snapshot of Frankish mints in the 620s, providing the earliest possible date for burial and bearing witness to trade links across the Channel, while the iconic helmet was a family heirloom from Scandinavia, the whetstone sceptre and hanging bowl were of Celtic craftsmanship and the gold and garnet fittings of the sword were English work, as were the ornate shoulder-clasps with their interlaced Germanic animal art (known as Salin's Style II, with amorphous beasts that resemble the offspring of an elephant and a vacuum cleaner). These clasps, like the royal standard and helmet, ape Roman parade armour, reflecting their owner's wish to appear as an heir of Rome – a Caesar.[3] The bronze bowl from Coptic Egypt and the Byzantine silver bowls inscribed with crosses, like the Byzantine spoons with their Saulos and Paulos inscriptions (perhaps signifying conversion), attest not only to the geographic extent of this ruler's economic relations, but to his reception of Christian goods and, to some extent, ideas.

Another high-status burial chamber, recently excavated at Prittlewell, near Southend in Essex, has yielded a similarly impressive array of exotic and local goods, including a Coptic bowl, a Byzantine bronze flagon adorned with a depiction of a military

32 St Cuthbert's pectoral cross (Durham Cathedral), Northumbria, late 7th century, which had suffered damage and repair before being placed in the saint's coffin.

saint, glowing blue glassware from Kent, Germanic weaponry, a hollow golden belt buckle which, like that from Sutton Hoo, may have contained a relic in Gaulish fashion, and two tiny gold crosses of a sort placed upon the eyelids of the Christian dead in Lombardic Italy. It has usually been considered that burials with grave goods are pagan, although such artefacts introduce an element of ambiguity and saints such as St Cuthbert certainly continued to be buried with an impressive assembly of artefacts elevated by their status as relics, such as his pectoral cross, which had suffered damage and repair before it was interred with him.

When one of the Roman missionaries, Mellitus, re-established the diocese of London on the site of St Paul's Cathedral in 604, he wrote to Pope Gregory seeking guidance, for the Essex folk had religion already. The essence of Gregory's reply was: if there's a party going on, join in; if there is a site hallowed by centuries of prayer, adopt it as your own in the name of Christ. The scene was set for the subtle rescoping of English society. One of

Augustine's earliest tasks, alongside the baptism of members of the Kentish court, was to commit the law code of its kings to the safe-keeping of writing, transliterating Old English into Latin script, one of a number of examples of the use of indigenous languages as an aid to evangelization of a sort also employed by Ulfilas, Apostle to the Goths, Mesrop, Apostle to Armenia and Cyril and Methodius in their conversion of the Slavs.[4] This use of the vernacular to spread the 'Godspell' (Old English 'Good News') was a far cry from the charges of heresy levelled against Wycliffe and Tyndale when they tried to do likewise at the end of the Middle Ages, in the face of control by a powerful centralized Church hierarchy.

The status of women in Anglo-Saxon law, which was the highest and most egalitarian afforded to any women by law, worldwide, until the 1930s – with that of their Irish counterparts not far behind – probably contributed greatly to the role that they too played in the conversion process, at home and abroad. Nuns served as 'evangelists with the pen', like their monkish scribal counterparts, Abbess Eadburh of Minster-in-Thanet supplying St Bonifaces's requests for books to serve in the German mission fields from the scriptorium of her double monastery of nuns and monks – an English, Irish and northern Frankish phenomenon, always governed by an abbess rather than an abbot. St Brigid's sixth-century foundation at Kildare featured male and female prayer halls in the manner of the Christian Orient, and she is even said by one near-contemporary hagiographer to have been accorded the status of bishop.

The process of conversion was a long and painful one, however, with some areas, notably Essex and East Anglia, reverting to traditional pagan ways whenever the vagaries of dynastic politics meant that those currently in power rejected Christianity. This was the case when Mellitus was ejected from London in 616 by the sons of the late King Saebert, who objected that he would not give them the 'white bread' he had shared with their father – evidently missing the point of the Eucharist and seeing it simply as a sign of endorsement or talismanic protection. The ambiguity surrounding the Christian status of some high-status burials, such as Sutton Hoo and Prittlewell, might be accounted for by the funerary arrangements of Christian rulers being undertaken by pagan relatives, or vice versa. There was also staunch pagan resistance to Christianity on occasion, especially the military campaigns led by King Penda of Mercia, which caused the defeat and death in battle of two of Northumbria's kings: Edwin at Hatfield in 632 (the year of the Prophet Muhammad's death) and Oswald at Maserfelth (Oswestry, perhaps) in 641. Penda finally met his own end combatting King Oswy of Northumbria at Winwaed (possibly near Leeds) in 655. That the expansionism of other, Christian kingdoms – notably Northumbria – was a major factor in such aggression is apparent from the pagan Penda's alliance with the Christian king Cadwallon of Gwynedd in Wales. Evidently mutual self-interest and a common enemy transcended Christian solidarity for this British ruler when faced with an expansive, aggressive Christian power of a different ethnicity and churchmanship.

The remarkable cache of over 3,000 items of high-quality metalwork – most of it of gold and garnetwork – known as the Staffordshire Hoard, which was discovered in 2009 by a metal detector at Ugley Hay (Hammerwich) in a field beside Roman Watling Street some 9 miles from Lichfield, speaks eloquently of troubled times. It may represent war booty or tribute payment (*heriot*) exacted by or from Mercia during the turbulent seventh and early eighth centuries, although it is also possible that it was a war cenotaph, a ritual votive burial of weaponry akin to those encountered in Scandinavia, or (perhaps most likely) the cache of a high-status metalworker. The hoard consists mainly of disassembled weaponry – sword and dagger (scramasax) hilts – and

33 The Staffordshire Hoard, a range of pieces from a saddlebag containing some 3,000 pieces of broken metalwork, mostly of gold and garnetwork (including a crumpled processional cross, a gold strip inscribed with a psalm extract and sword and helmet fittings) dating from throughout the 7th century, with pieces made in different Anglo-Saxon kingdoms. It was concealed to the side of a Roman road near Lichfield. The style of art and lettering are paralleled in contemporary manuscripts, notably the Book of Durrow.

an intriguing group of overtly Christian artefacts: a processional cross, perhaps four other crosses, one evidently a bishop's pectoral cross resembling that found in St Cuthbert's tomb, panels from what may be a book shrine or reliquary, and a gold strip from a shrine, cross or weapon inscribed with a quote from Psalm 68:1 (also found in Numbers 10:35): 'Rise up, O Lord, and may thy enemies be dispersed and those who hate thee be driven from thy face' – the same invocation of the Psalm that St Guthlac used as a spiritual defence against the demons who beset him. A similarly protective invocation is to be found on the eighth-century Coppergate helmet from York.

There was often a clerical presence on the battlefield and relics were carried into combat to ensure victory. The Cathach or Battler of Columcille was certainly used in this way later in the Middle Ages, while the early Armenian Church had adopted such practices and the Byzantines bore an icon known as the palladium before their troops. The inscription is inlaid with silver niello, with a variant version of its text written more cursively and lighter on the back (as a trial for layout or as an invocation that faced both ways, protecting the bearers and fending off enemies), and is in an early form of half-uncial script akin to that found in manuscripts thought to date to the second half of the seventh century, such as the Book of Durrow, which also provides a close parallel to some of the hoard's zoomorphic interlace.[5] The hoard as a whole represents the war gear of several generations, extending from perhaps the late sixth to early eighth centuries, and contains items probably made in Kent, East Anglia, Mercia, Northumbria and on the Continent. Weapons and reliquaries were often cherished and bequeathed by one generation to the next, swords often bearing names, like the famed sword Excalibur. However, gold was in limited supply and was frequently melted down for reuse, and another possibility is that the hoard represents the stash of a high-status metalworker, surely in royal service (perhaps his king, or 'gold-giver' wished to equip his comitatus with more fashionable modern war-gear), who was in the process of recycling the materials but needed to conceal them in a hurry by burying them in a field and who was then prevented from retrieving them. Whatever the circumstances, this highly significant hoard – a king's ransom – speaks of troubled, warlike times, which marched in tandem with the conversion process.

It was not lost upon Bede that the year of Augustine's arrival in Kent – 597 – also witnessed the death of another key figure in the conversion process: St Columba, or Columcille (the 'dove of the Church'), the princely scion of one of the great Irish tribes, the Uì Neill (O'Neills). Much of Bede's narration of subsequent events is concerned with the legacy of the Columban and other Irish missions and their integration into the multi-stranded process of converting the Germanic settlers, thereby transforming them into legitimatized heirs of Rome whose landscape of Christian successor states offered the promise of a cohesive entity – Anglo-Saxon England. It may have taken until the tenth century and the stimulus of the Viking raids and partition of England into the Danelaw to eventually achieve this, but in his presentation of the emerging imperium or quasi high-kingship of what he termed the 'bretwalda' (or overlord) Bede envisages and urges this process. Respecting the Irish contribution to the process of Christianization in Ireland and mainland Britain and its offshore islands, in the way that Bede does, carried the double benefit (from the Anglo-Saxon perspective) of easing good internecine relationships and collaboration with Ireland, Pictland and Dalriada and also of downplaying the seminal contribution of the British Church in southern Scotland, northwest England, Wales and the southwest, since Bede and his peers viewed it as schismatic and antipathetic.

In circa 560 Columba occasioned the great battle of Cúl Dreimne when he was accused of claiming a copy of the Psalter in Latin owned by his mentor, St Finian of Moville, as his own work. The Irish jurists ruled, 'to every cow its calf, to every book its copy,' thereby upholding the first case of copyright law, but the two tribes went to war – for such literary concerns were probably a symptom of bigger territorial rivalries. In repentance Columba left Ireland on *peregrinatio* (voluntary exile for Christ), a self-imposed punishment that equated to one of the harshest legal penalties, placing the punished outside of the social structure, the protection of law and the succour of kith and kin, effectively as an outlaw. He went just far enough so that he could no longer gaze upon his homeland and founded the monastery of Iona on a little cockle-shell-beached islet off the Hebridean island of Mull. This became the mother house of a monastic federation that would extend throughout the Irish expat kingdom of Dalriada into Pictland (which had already been exposed to Christian teaching by the early fifth-century Briton St Ninian of Whithorn in southwest Scotland) and on into Anglo-Saxon England. Columba's family of monasteries eventually came to include Derry, Durrow and Kells in Ireland, Iona, Lindisfarne, Melrose, Jedburgh, Whitby and Hartlepool, and was carried further southwards to Lastingham, Lichfield, Bradwell-on-Sea and Tilbury in Essex by a team of missionary siblings from Lindisfarne – Sts Cedd, Chad, Cealin and Cynibil.

Augustine's mission had targeted political court conversions, its missionaries entering via mixed-faith households. King Ethelbert of Kent and King Edwin of Northumbria had both married Christian wives and Augustine's follower Paulinus was sent to Edwin's court. As a model Christian king, Edwin became famed for good government and the stability of his rule. Bede says that a woman with a babe in arms could travel unmolested from one side of his kingdom to the other and that drinking fountains were set up along highways. Edwin fell in battle around 632 and Paulinus's mission cannot have penetrated society deeply, for he and the royal family then fled to Kent and it was left to Edwin's successor, Oswald, a member of a rival dynasty who had been in exile among the Irish of Dalriada, to invite monks from Iona to establish the monastery of Lindisfarne in 635 and to convert Northumbria's people, not just its royal household and court.

Meanwhile, British bishops continued to care for their native flocks, but often avoided contact with their pagan Germanic neighbours. Frankish bishops from Gaul also participated, such as the Burgundian bishop Felix (died 648), who founded his see at Dunwich on the Suffolk coast, and the Frankish bishop Agilbert, who was eventually expelled from Wessex by its ruler for his failure to learn the local language. Nor were Columban monks the only Irish presence. Around 633, an abbot from the West coast of Ireland, St Fursey, along with followers including his brothers, Sts Foillan and Ultan, arrived in East Anglia and were welcomed by King Sigebert and given a site called 'Cnobheresburg', thought to be the Roman 'Saxon shore' fort of Burgh Castle near Yarmouth, in which to establish religious communities. Thus Fursey became the earliest recorded Irish monastic leader to work in England. Other Irish participants included Dicuil, who evangelized in Sussex, and Diuma, who is said to have been active at Lichfield prior to St Chad. Meanwhile, Wales, Cornwall and Brittany had experienced Irish missionary activity from the fifth century onwards.

Bede recounts an escalating conflict between the 'Roman' and 'Celtic' churches. 'Celtic' in this context refers more specifically to centres founded by St Columba and his followers, for many other churches in Ireland already followed Roman practice. The respective adherents of both parties observed different traditions, including physical appearances, with Roman clerics having a circular tonsure, or shaved patch, on the top of their heads and Celts favouring a more flamboyant shaved tonsure running across the head from ear to ear with a mane of hair behind. They also had alternative methods of calculating the date of Easter. In 664 a synod was held to resolve the matter, held at St Hild's monastery of Whitby. The Columban cause was argued by Bishop Colman of Lindisfarne and the Roman by the promising young priest Wilfrid. King Oswy of Northumbria (who had succeeded his brother, Oswald) decided in favour of Rome – with Bede having him say that this was because St Peter held the keys to heaven. Much was at stake, for uniformity of purpose and practice was important for a young Church and schism was to be avoided at all costs if England and its rulers were not to be marginalized from the European and Near Eastern mainstream.

Disgruntled clergy – some led by Bishop Colman of Lindisfarne but also others, many of them English – left for Ireland, where monasteries such as Mayo of the English, Tullylease, Rath Melsigi and Armagh were noted for their presence. But within a generation the rest of the Irish Church, including Columban centres, had conformed – Iona being the last to comply, in 715. In Northumbria the great rallying point for reconciliation became a charismatic figure bridging both traditions – St Cuthbert.

Rebuilding Rome – and Jerusalem – in Britain

In 668 a new archbishop of Canterbury was appointed: Theodore of Tarsus (in Asia Minor). He and Hadrian, Abbot of St Augustine's Canterbury (who came from northern Africa, latterly via Naples), established a school of learning that was the envy of Europe, producing scholars such as Aldhelm, Abbot of Malmesbury and Bishop of Sherborne (d. 709), and (at a distance) Bede. Theodore and Hadrian taught Latin and Greek and perhaps some Hebrew, theology and biblical exegesis, computistics (especially calendrical calculations, so crucial to the Paschal controversy), poetry, astronomy, medicine and Gregorian chant. That Bede could have mastered his classical Latin and the rules of metrical composition and pronunciation speaks of great powers of analysis and intuition, especially without the benefit of first-hand linguistic exposure to native speakers (whose own Latin would by now have become localized, if not vulgarized) other than occasional visitors, notably John the Archcantor, who came to the monasteries for a year or so to teach chant.

Theodore's protégés, Benedict Biscop, Ceolfrith and Wilfrid, were filled with an ardour for Rome, adorning their churches with relics, artworks and books acquired on their journeys there.

Their imposing dressed stone masonry and their fittings proclaimed its influence, with Wilfrid's Hexham achieving renown as the largest church north of the Alps. Such structures and their deeply carved, naturalistic sculptures and paintings had not seen their like on British soil since the Roman Empire's withdrawal nearly three hundred years earlier.

Theodore had taken in hand the ecclesiastical and educational development of the early English Church – a truly cosmopolitan melting-pot of people and influences. The arrival of these international players in England came on the heels of the Synod of Whitby of 664, with its debate of the calculation of the dating of Easter. As discussed previously, such matters were of vital import to the early Christian Church in East and West. The First Paschal Controversy had been one of the key issues addressed at the First Ecumenical Council of Nicaea in 325, as it raised the threat of schism, the great spectre at the Eucharistic feast of the early Church. Establishing a common observance for the dating of Easter carried many implications. The avoidance of schism was a particularly vibrant concern, and one of the factors that coloured English relations with Rome during the period in question was the Monothelete controversy which had caused schisms to open among the Eastern churches. In 679 Archbishop Theodore convened the Council of Hatfield, which affirmed the faith of the English Church: that Christ had a fully human will, accompanied by human courage, thereby rejecting the Monothelete heresy, which denied him any such will, as this would have brought him into conflict with the perfect divine will of which he partook. Pope Agatho accordingly sent a senior member of his household, John the Archcantor, to represent him at this council and he accompanied Benedict Biscop and Ceolfrith on the return journey from Rome to Northumbria – not only to sing, evidently, but to help ensure the Catholic orthodoxy of the English. England was evidently considered an international player worthy of holding important pre-meetings, for Hatfield was one of a number of European councils that prepared the way for the Sixth Ecumenical Council held in Constantinople in 681, which was convened to resolve this crisis that had divided the Church in East and West and had even led to the martyrdom of a pope – Martin I (649–55). The Council proclaimed that in Christ the divine and human wills were coherently united and that as Christ was incorrupt he never conflicted with the divine will. It was stressed that this incorruptibility lay in his conception, without corruption, from the Virgin Mary by the Holy Spirit. The Church politics of the East therefore reverberated in the wild West, and it is from the 650s onwards that we find the cult of the Virgin and the veneration of the Cross developing in Rome (from earlier Eastern roots) and influencing its liturgy and art. These also rapidly become major themes in Insular culture, whether introduced via Rome or directly from the East.

Wilfrid's eloquent pro-Roman stance may have won the day at Whitby, but his autocratic manner and wealthy churches provoked discord, causing his deposition. His travels to Rome to seek papal intervention led to his temporary reinstallation, but dispute continued. England needed some powerful PR if the progress of the previous hundred years was not to be damaged.

SEVEN

Bede the 'Scribe of Scripture' and the Making of the Ceolfrith Bibles

In 715 the final bastion of Columban tradition, Iona, conformed to orthodox practices and, tellingly, within the year the elderly Abbot Ceolfrith left Jarrow for Rome, ostensibly to retire. He took with him one of three massive complete Bibles that he had commissioned from the Wearmouth-Jarrow scriptorium – leaving the others as reference works, one for each community – to present to his friend, the newly appointed librarian-pope Gregory II, who had facilitated Bede's own research requests. Bede wrote, in the *History of the Abbots*, ch.15:

> Ceolfrith was a man of acute mind, conscientious in everything he did . . . He doubled the number of books in the libraries of both monasteries . . . He added three copies of the new translation of the Bible . . . One of these he took with him as a gift when he went back to Rome in his old age, and the other two he bequeathed to his monasteries [Monkwearmouth and Jarrow, for reference and copying].

He was surely acutely aware of the mission he was undertaking, with the Bible as the eloquent and monumental ambassador, to the Pope and before God, of the English nation and of the orthodoxy of observance throughout these islands. Ceolfrith died en route in Langres in Burgundy and the book disappeared. In 1782 it was rediscovered in an Italian monastery – Monte Amiata, on one of the major pilgrimage routes that crossed the Alps and headed on through Italy to Rome.

That Bible still survives as the Codex Amiatinus (Florence, Biblioteca Medicea-Laurenziana, MS Amiatino 1). Christopher de Hamel, in *Meetings with Remarkable Manuscripts*, argues that the Codex Amiatinus never reached Rome but was left at Monte Amiata by Ceolfrith's companions after he had died on the way.[1] This is unlikely as Monte Amiata monastery was not founded until 743; perhaps the volume was a later papal dedication gift to that new foundation and Ceolfrith's dedication inscription was tampered with there, his name being erased and replaced with that of a local saint. The Codex Amiatinus certainly seems to have reached papal hands, for Pope Gregory II (715–31) – Ceolfrith's old friend and the former papal librarian – wrote an effusive letter of thanks to Ceolfrith's successor, Abbot Hwaetberht, thanking him and the community for a most acceptable gift of the codex, from which it was apparent that they were true 'Romans'. The book had served its role as an ambassador for the English well.[2] Nonetheless, this remarkable tome was not recognized as English work until the late nineteenth century, so convincing is its Italo-Byzantine stylistic cloaking mechanism, with its Gregorian-style Roman uncial script and its classicizing painterly style (redolent of the Syriac frescoes found in parts of Sta Maria Antiqua in the forum, painted at the beginning of the eighth century). Its text, incorporating that of the gospels as also preserved in the Lindisfarne Gospels, is considered the best extant witness to St Jerome's editorial work on the Latin Vulgate, undertaken in the Holy Land during the fourth century, and represents a masterly work of scholarly reconstruction and editorship on the part of the Wearmouth-Jarrow school and scriptorium, of which Bede undoubtedly formed a part. It was not until 1888 that the scholar G. B. de Rossi began to question

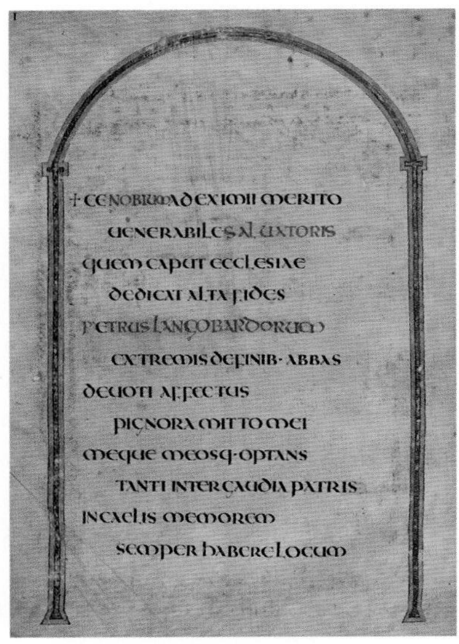

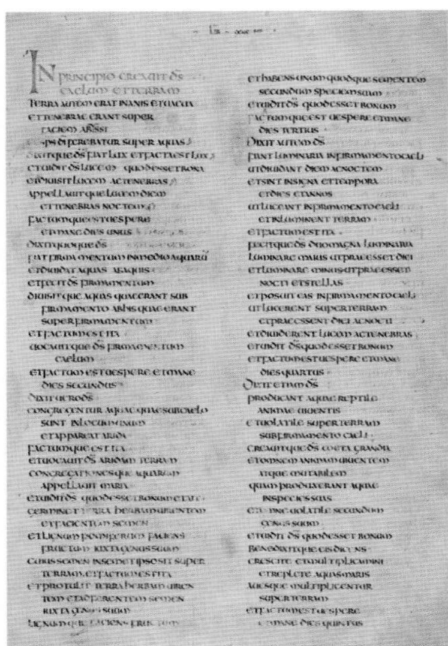

Left: 34 Ceolfrith's dedication inscription, with his name erased and replaced by that of a local Lombardic saint, from the Codex Amiatinus (f. 1v).

Right: 35 Uncial script in the Codex Amiatinus (f. 11r) of the sort that Bede would have used when writing Scripture – it could even be his hand as he would surely have participated in writing parts of the Ceolfrith Bibles.

the assumption that it was the work of Italo-Byzantine scholars, scribes and artists, leading eventually to the recognition that this triumph of *romanitas* was in fact of English workmanship. When, following the Council of Trent (1546), a scholarly equipe painstakingly sifted through the corpus of surviving late antique, medieval and Renaissance manuscripts to ascertain which best reflected St Jerome's original Latin Vulgate edition, that it might be authoritatively committed to print, they finally alighted upon two books as their purest exemplars: the Codex Amiatinus and the Lindisfarne Gospels, both from early eighth-century Northumbria.[3] Britain was no provincial outpost, but the only place capable of producing a remarkable monument of biblical scholarship and book production. The apostolic mission had made it to the furthest corners of the known world and was reflected back to its Mediterranean centre.

Amiatinus proclaims the fulfilment of the Apostolic mission: the Word had been preached to the farthest ends of the Earth, as it was then known, and the precondition for the Second Coming was fulfilled. Only in these far-flung islands on the edge of the world could such a feat of biblical transmission and scholarship have occurred in the post-Roman age, building upon the vestiges of Cassiodorus' library and his vision for biblical scholarship and publication.

To see the Codex Amiatinus is an unforgettable experience. It has a presence, a gravitas; its very size and seriousness compels you to bend the knee, if not physically then emotionally. For this massive single-volume Bible – known as a pandect – has an imposing and dignified presence worthy of the most venerable prelate or distinguished political leader. Early eighth-century Rome had not seen its like. Each of the three Bibles would have measured 515 mm × 340 mm × 230 mm and weighed 35–40 kg, and the skins of 515 calves would have been needed to produce the vellum for the Amiatinus's 2,060 pages. The heavy wagon that bore it would have trundled along the Appian Way and two or more reverent bearers would have strained under its weight as they unloaded it and carried it into the papal residence of the Lateran.

Fragments of the others have resurfaced, some discovered by Canon Greenwell as binding fragments in a Newcastle antique shop (now BL, Add. MS 37777 – the Greenwell leaves). These formed part of one of the volumes retained by the communities, while other pieces (BL, Add. MS 45025 and Loan MS 81 – the Middleton leaves and Bankes leaf) may be from the other, donated by King Offa later in the century to Worcester, where it was already thought to have been made in Rome, so 'romanizing' were the Ceolfrith Bibles in style.[4]

In response to a letter from Bishop Acca of Hexham, Bede writes, concerning his commentary on Luke, 'I have subjected myself to that burden of work in which, as in innumerable bonds of monastic servitude [or humility] which I shall pass over, I was myself at once dictator, notary, and scribe.' This reveals that he regarded such work as *opus Dei* (work for God) and differentiated between the functions of author (who usually dictated rather than write themselves), secretary/copyist and scribal evangelist. The sixth-century monastic founder/publisher Cassiodorus wrote that in those who translate, expand or humbly copy Scripture the Spirit continues to work, as in the biblical authors. Bede elaborates this theme in relation to Ezra the Scribe, who fulfilled the Law by rewriting its destroyed books, thereby opening his mouth to interpret Scripture and teach others. The act of writing is therefore presented as an essential, personal act for the scribe/preacher/teacher – Bede.

It is quite remarkable that he should have achieved his intellectual stature, given that his people, from the pagan Germanic North, were such relatively recent arrivals on the scene of the post-Roman Empire in the West (however long their forebears had engaged in contact with Rome as federal auxiliaries, trading partners and opponents). The infrastructure of Roman Britain had largely collapsed, save for the perpetuation of Christianity and literacy within the orbit of the British and Irish churches, although Bede does point to some intriguing attempts to perpetuate some of its elements, such as his reference, in the prose Life, to Cuthbert being given a civic tour of Carlisle, which included the still-functioning Roman fountains and water supply, when the news of King Ecgfrith's death in battle against the Picts was received.

One thing that had not survived, in Britain or Gaul, was much of the liberal arts education system and schoolrooms of the Roman age. Vestiges of them lingered on in parts of Italy and Spain – and in the East, of course – and to some extent in British and Irish monastic teaching centres such as St Illtud's Llantwit Major, Llanbadarn and Llandaff (Cardiff).[5] St Patrick, coming probably from a background in the British Church of northeast Britain and writing in the second half of the fifth century in his *Confession*, laments his lack of education, much of it received once he had escaped from Ireland to Gaul and the Eastern-influenced island monastery of Lérins. Ireland still possessed trading links with the Mediterranean and as early as 431 (as recorded in the Chronicle of Prosper) Pope Celestine sent Palladius as bishop from Rome to those in the southern littoral who already believed. It soon caught up, with its impressive tradition of ancient oral education, and during the sixth and seventh centuries cultivated a learned Christian tradition of scholarship of its own, which included consulting the works of some of the late antique Grammarians' works. This was shared and enhanced through its missions to Britain and the Continent. Columban foundations such as Lindisfarne provided a conduit for this into Anglo-Saxon England, especially Northumbria.

Bede benefited from this, but even bigger factors in preparing the soil for his mental and spiritual growth were the arrival in Britain of Theodore of Tarsus and Abbot Hadrian, shortly before his birth, the energy and education with which they imbued the nascent English church and the impetus this gave to Biscop's twin foundation of Wearmouth-Jarrow and the generous provision that he and Abbot Ceolfrith made for its library provision, constructed over the course of six visits to Rome. There and perhaps in other centres in northern Italy and Gaul, they and Wilfrid hungrily purchased or were given the precious relics in book form of the late antique and early Christian world. They were, in a sense, the forerunners of the English aristocrats of the eighteenth-century Grand Tour, intent upon reconstructing that world in their northern climes. But theirs was not only a cultural or even a political or ideological mission – it was focused upon the spiritual health of their people and the role that they might play in being part of a flourishing body of a unified international Church, fit to be the Bride of Christ. Given his opportunity, from the time he entered this remarkable new foundation as a boy, Bede worked with all his intellectual and spiritual might to be a blessing to this union.

Pope Agapetus I and Cassiodorus had planned to form a new library in Rome in the aftermath of its ravages by incoming barbarian rulers. They had even got as far as planning the decor of the entrance hall, which was to be adorned with mosaics depicting fictive books representing fictive authors, who were to be dispatched as long-distance teachers to the ends of the Earth. That never came to pass, but some of the wreckage of earlier learning washed up upon the shores of islands at the farthest limits of the known world and fulfilled their mission in a new library – that of Wearmouth-Jarrow – where they found a particularly avid and receptive reader: Bede.

It is likely that the Wearmouth-Jarrow library included some actual remnants of the library established by an earlier influential monastic founder, Flavius Magnus Aurelius Cassiodorus Senator (*c*. 485–*c*. 585), whose influence pervades the former's works and ethos of study, writing and publication of works devoted to biblical studies. Cassiodorus had abandoned his role in public life as praetorian prefect for Italy in the face of Ostrogothic Arian heretical obduracy (and having witnessed the fate of the philosopher Boethius at their hands) and headed far south to Squillace in Calabria, his country estate. There he founded the monastery of the Vivarium – the place of the living things (named for the fishponds which were a feature of its civilized lifestyle and for its role in feeding the life of faith) – and constructed a remarkable programme of religious life with a particular mission of studying, editing, accurately copying and disseminating Scripture. This was the first publishing drive of the post-Roman age – an impetus that began with Emperor Constantine's request to Eusebius of Caesarea in 326–7 to produce fifty copies of the Bible for the imposing churches he was constructing. Ceolfrith took up this mantle when he devoted the human and bibliographical resources of Wearmouth-Jarrow to perpetuating this initiative in the production of the Ceolfrith Bibles, which reconstructed and perpetuated the transmission of the Vulgate.

We do not know for sure whether Wearmouth-Jarrow possessed a copy of Cassidorus' *Institutiones*. In this work he outlined his publishing programme and the rule of life governing his community and in which he praised the scholarship of Dionysius Exiguus, whose computistical work so influenced Bede, and wrote eloquently of the sacred role of the scribe of Scripture. Bede and his brethren certainly seem to have drunk deeply from its knowledge and approach and the Wearmouth-Jarrow library is known to have possessed several of his works, perhaps from the Vivarium itself. It may also have copied some of his works, such as his *Commentary on the Psalms*, which still survives at Durham Cathedral Library, MS B.II.30 (see illus. 14).

Jennifer O'Reilly draws attention to the patristic concept of the 'inner library' and the necessity for each believer to make him or herself an ark or library of the Word, which Cummian the Wise of Iona referred to as 'entering the Sanctuary of God' through studying and transmitting Scripture.[6] Books are the vessels that fill the believer's inner library and are, as I have said, 'enablers of direct, contemporary Christian action, channels of the Spirit, and gateways to revelation'.[7]

O'Reilly also suggested that Wearmouth-Jarrow was adapting material drawn from sixth-century exemplars from the Vivarium to produce an illustrated prefatory quire for its single-volume Bibles and that this represented a process of informed choice and conscious adaptation. Bede probably played a leading role in this programme, and, as O'Reilly, Carol Farr and others have demonstrated, the concerns manifest in editing and in 'illustration' by means of complex *figurae* (sacred images that embody theological concepts) tie in with the preoccupations that Bede exhibits in his commentaries, written around this time. I have suggested that this programme was drawn upon and strategically adapted further in the Lindisfarne Gospels, around 715–22. It is highly likely, in my opinion, that Bede had a hand in this too, in collaboration with the book's maker, Bishop Eadfrith of Lindisfarne.[8]

The act of copying and transmitting the Gospels was to glimpse the divine and to place oneself in its apostolic service. This may have been seen as a solitary undertaking on behalf of the community, rather than a communal collaboration, in Eastern fashion, as with other aspects of Celtic eremitic monasticism. As such these books are portals of prayer, during the acts both of making and studying. Like the hermit or anchorite, the scribe preached with the pen in the 'desert' of the book. As St Cuthbert struggled with his demons on Inner Farne on behalf of all, so the monk who produced the Gospel book for his cult undertook a feat of spiritual and physical endurance as part of the apostolic mission of bringing the Word of God to the farthest outposts of the known world, enshrining it there within the new Temple of the Word and embodiment of Christ – the Book.

As I have written elsewhere:

> What might it actually have meant to those who dedicated their lives to God's service to be entrusted with the transmission of his Word, as preachers and as scribes? I would propose the extension of the metaphor of the scholar-priest to that of the scribe-priest. In a letter to Bishop Acca of Hexham concerning his commentary on Luke, Bede says that 'I have subjected myself to that

> burden of work in which, as in innumerable bonds of monastic servitude which I shall pass over, I was myself at once dictator, notary, and scribe.' This revealing passage shows that he regarded such work as an expression of monastic humility, an act of *opus Dei*, and that he differentiated between the functions of author, note-taker and formal scribal transmitter. Cassiodorus, again in the *Institutiones*, said that each word written by the monastic scribe was 'a wound on Satan's body', thereby ascribing to the scribe the role of *miles Christi*, or soldier of Christ. In the same work he says that in those who translate, expand or humbly copy Scripture the Spirit continues to work, as in the biblical authors who were first inspired to write them. Indeed, as Jennifer O'Reilly has pointed out, Scripture lends the scribal analogy to the Lord himself (see Jeremiah 31:33; Hebrews 10:16; Ps. 44/45:1–2). Cassiodorus says (in his Commentary on Psalm 44/45:1–2 and in the *Institutiones*) that the scribe could preach with the hand alone and 'unleash tongues with the fingers', imitating the action of the Lord who wrote the Law with his all-powerful finger (bringing to mind the pointing hand of God which features in later Anglo-Saxon evangelist miniatures). Bede pursues this theme in relation to Ezra the Scribe, who fulfilled the Law by restoring/writing its destroyed books, thereby opening his mouth to interpret Scripture and teach others. The act of writing is therefore presented as an essential, personal act for the scribe/preacher/teacher.[9]

There is an analogy here with the Jewish *sofer* – the priestly scribe of Scripture – and this may be what Bede meant when he separated the term 'scribe' from 'author' or 'copyist' and claimed that honour and duty for himself.

et libauit ea dño

Lxxx uiiii Ab asai frater ioab qui leuauit manum
contra trecentos uiros inter
fecit eos et ceteris fortes uiri
in quibus unus leones absque ferro
occidit et aegyptium fortem
hasta sua eum puniit

xc Indignatur ds contra israhel
iussit dinumerari et post dinume
rationem iubet eum per dilationē
electione plagarum trium
e quibus una euenit in populo
tribus diebus . et iubetur angelo
a dño quiescere et ut non sit
offerendum holocausta
nisi de proprio
la
bo
re

EXPLICIT BREUIS .

INCIPIT REGUM

LIBER PRIMUS

QUI HEBRAICE APPEL

LATUR SAMUHEL

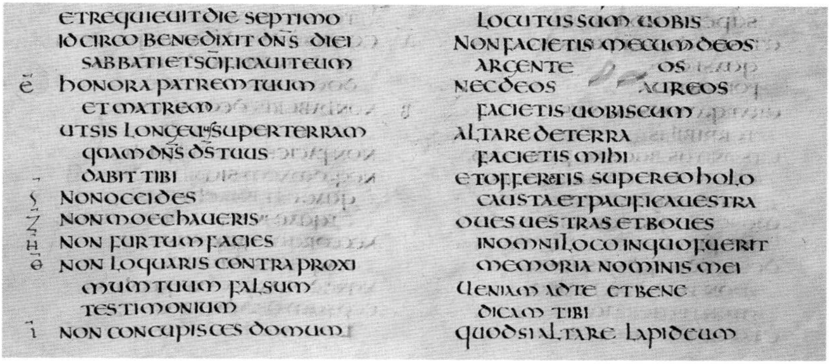

37 Detail of the uncial script of the Codex Amiatinus (f. 67v). The Greek letters in red in the margin might indicate that this is Bede's hand, as he knew Greek and was experimenting with his own systems of marginal annotation for referencing and highlighting quotes.

Bede, the scribe, would surely have taken his turn at the scriptorium desks in physically penning the Ceolfrith Bibles. We cannot firmly identify his hand, but it is probably one of the seven that wrote Amiatinus in a stately, romanizing uncial script modelled upon that of Gregory the Great's Rome, with Roman rustic capitals being employed for rubrics and titles.[10] I do wonder whether the Greek letters (alpha, beta, gamma, delta, epsilon, zeta, eta, theta and iota) in red in the margins of ff. 67r and v, marking Exodus 20:2–8 in Amiatinus, might indicate the presence of Bede's hand, as he knew Greek and was also experimenting with his own systems of marginal annotation for referencing and highlighting quotes, which occurs here at the beginning of

Opposite: 36 Bede's handwriting? The preface to the Book of Kings in the Codex Amiatinus (f. 221r, column 1) is written by a hand that often introduces Greek letter-forms and shows an interest in Greek and Hebrew terms. It uses graphic marks to highlight them, in a manner known to have been pioneered by Bede for marking quotations; his distinctive lightning flash marks used for this occur here, drawing attention to the word labore ('work'), which he has divided into syllables in the manner of the schoolteachers of late antiquity. This would be particularly apt for Bede, the inveterate teacher and hard worker, forming a colophon for his own work on this great endeavour.

38, 39 The same hand (Bede's) was responsible for writing the text on ff. 218r and 219r. On f. 218r (*left*), it marks the Greek term 'tetragrammaton' with a horizontal line above (col. 2, line 19) and divides another unfamiliar term into syllables, marking them with superscript letters indicating how they should be pronounced (col. 2, line 34), recalling rabbinic practice and that of late Roman schoolrooms; f. 219r (*right*) contains some Greek in col. 1, line 10. It also resembles the hand of the St Cuthbert Gospel.

Matthew's Gospel to mark the Messianic prophecies (f. 803r–v) and on 809v, 829r, 839v, 855r, 895v–896r, 906v, 940r and 999v, for example. The passage marked is the first part of the Ten Commandments (ESV):

> 2 'I am the Lord your God, who brought you out of the land of Egypt, out of the house of slavery.
> 3 You shall have no other gods before me.
> 4 You shall not make for yourself a carved image, or any likeness of anything that is in heaven above, or that is in the earth beneath, or that is in the water under the earth.
> 5 You shall not bow down to them or serve them, for I the Lord your God am a jealous God, visiting the iniquity of the fathers on the children to the third and the fourth generation of those who hate me,
> 6 but showing steadfast love to thousands of those who love me and keep my commandments.
> 7 You shall not take the name of the Lord your God in vain, for the Lord will not hold him guiltless who takes his name in vain.
> 8 Remember the Sabbath day, to keep it holy.'

The palaeographical details of these letters (such as the minuscule e with its closed bow, the B with its fluid, rustic capital strokes, the uncial a with its rounded bow) are similar to the hand that writes the running heads (the titles of the biblical books, so that the reader can see where they are) and the rubricated rustic capital titles on f. 110v and f. 111v, for example. The other commandments are marked in a similar way on f. 101v and the entire ten are marked in Deuteronomy on f. 151r.

This hand was also responsible for the titles and the text on f. 218r column 2 to f. 221r column 1 (the preface to the Book of

Kings). This includes a line containing Greek (f. 219r column 1 line 10) and which marks Greek terms (for example, *tetragrammaton*, f. 218r, column 2, line 19) with a line above them (features also found on ff. 174r, 329v col. 2–330r col. 1, 633r–634r, 730v) and separates out *chaph mem nun phe sade*, Hebrew letters transliterated into Latin (f. 218r column 2 line 34), writing superscript letters above the start of each syllable to indicate how they should be pronounced. This recalls the schoolroom practice of teaching how to read out loud, syllabically, in late Roman schoolrooms and also rabbinic practice in providing guidance on pronunciation when reading from Scripture, in the form of the Masoretic marginal annotations.

From ff. 407v until 417r there are a number of psalms for which this hand has labelled the verses in the inner margin, either with sequences of roman numerals or the names in Latin of the letters of the Hebrew alphabet (aleph, beth, gemel, deleth and so on). It does the same on f. 436v, at the end of the Book of Proverbs, and on ff. 586r–589v.

The hand is a neat, compact little uncial, exhibiting plenty of character and fluidity, and a willingness to depart from the canonical form and mix letter-forms and features, all betokening confidence and experience in writing. The line endings in passages written by this hand show a tendency to slip into minuscule script (notably a rather casual tall s, sometimes in ligature) and the mixture of rustic capital, uncial, half uncial and minuscule letter-forms indicates a scribe who had mastered the entire range of Insular scripts, but who was less formal and wedded to a house style that consciously emulated the details of the uncial script of Gregory the Great's Rome than one that was comfortable in a range of local hands and was willing to mix features. This hand also resembles that of the St Cuthbert Gospel. These features and an evident concern with the comprehension and correct pronunciation of Greek and Hebrew terms, plus marginal reference annotations, all speak of the interests and practices of Bede, the teacher. However, the evidence is circumstantial. There may have been others at Wearmouth-Jarrow who knew Greek and were academically interested in Hebrew and its correct pronunciation and who were also pioneering marginal annotation systems and using graphic devices to highlight such features, as Bede is known to have done, and who were using teaching practices derived from Roman schoolrooms. But we know that Bede was. We also know from his own admission that he was 'author, notary and scribe' and would have mastered the gamut of the Insular system of scripts, as this hand had. On f. 221r, column 1, is a calligraphic final passage in which the final word – *labore* ('work') – is divided syllabically across three lines, marked by the distinctive lightning flash marks that Bede used to highlight quotations. This would be a fitting colophon for Bede's own contribution to this great endeavour, devoted as he was to *opus Dei* and study (it takes a different form to the 'Ora pro me' – 'Pray for me' – colophons at the end of a section of work at f. 146r and at the very end of the book on f. 1029v). Following it, in the same hand (now using rustic capitals), is the incipit to the Book of Kings, to which it adds 'Qui Hebraice appellatur Samuhel' (which is called, in Hebrew, Samuel), the prophet-priest with whom Bede felt a particular affinity. I suggest that we are indeed seeing Bede's own hand here.

The hand occurs elsewhere (including writing much of the Book of Leviticus), for example on ff. 86r and 86v (with Greek characters in the rubric). It will require a separate piece of work to identify all its occurrences and to assess its overall role in the project, but this seems to be one of responsibility for stints of work, for prefatory matter, for rubrication and headings, some quire numeration and correction and an engagement with linguistics and pronunciation. This may imply something of an academic and supervisory capacity as well as collective scribal participation.

Another famous Wearmouth-Jarrow uncial manuscript is the little copy of St John's Gospel found inside St Cuthbert's coffin, thought to have been presented to his shrine in 698 (see illus. 28 and 29).[11] It is bound using 'Coptic sewing' and tooled in Eastern fashion, reflecting Eastern influences on the Insular world.[12] Bede seems to have had a special relationship with St John's Gospel, of which he has left us the first English translation, made on his deathbed, and he would have been well aware of its importance to Sts Cuthbert and Boisil, who had studied it together. It is therefore tempting to wonder whether he might have been entrusted with penning the St Cuthbert Gospel. If this was made to be placed in the coffin at the time of the translation of Cuthbert's relics in 698, Bede would have been around 27 years of age and would not yet have been priested, which may argue against him being entrusted with such an important task at that early stage in his life, though he had been made a deacon at the young age of nineteen and was responsible for carrying and reading the Gospels during the liturgy.

An example of the Continental uncial books that served as models in such work survives in the Bodleian Library (Laud Gr. 35)[13] – the Codex Laudianus, a sixth-century Greek and Latin copy of Acts from Sardinia, which, judging from its close textual correspondences, may be that used by Bede when working on his *Commentary on Acts*. The Latin Creed in uncial (f. 226v) was probably added at Wearmouth-Jarrow. It has sometimes been suggested that this might be in Bede's hand, but the aspect of the script is erratic and rather spidery and lacks the distinctive features of Wearmouth-Jarrow uncial, which emulates details found in the uncial practised in the Rome of Gregory the Great. It might conceivably be in the hand of one of Bede's early-stage pupils, or a later member of the community, but it is unlikely to be that of an experienced scribe such as Bede.

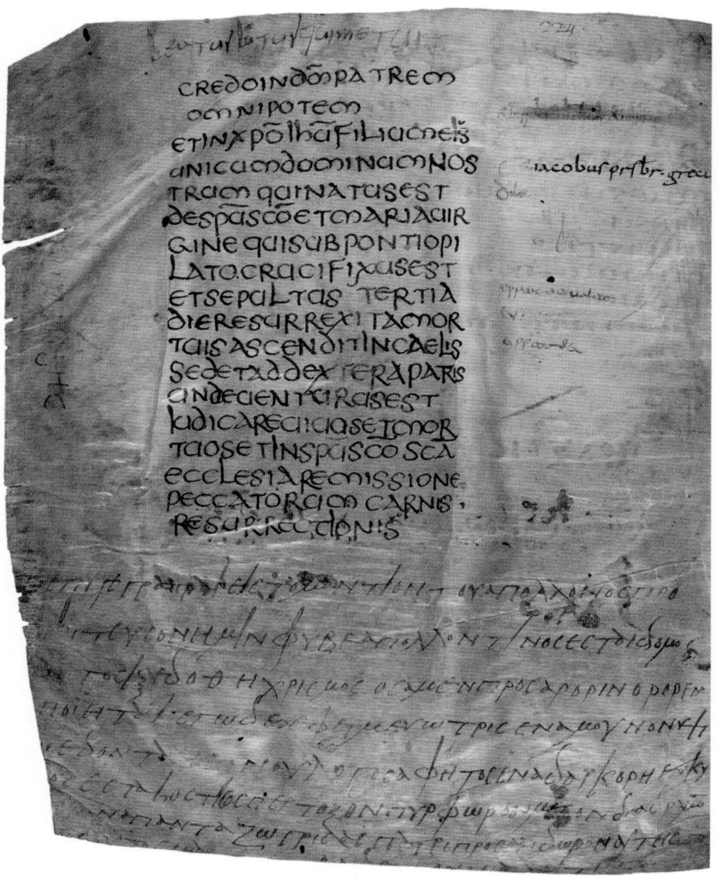

40 Codex Laudianus (Bodleian Library, Oxford, MS Laud Gr. 35), a 6th-century Greek and Latin copy of Acts from Sardinia which, judging from its close textual correspondences, may be that used by Bede when working on his *Commentary on Acts*. The Latin Creed in uncial seen here (in the black ink) was probably added at Wearmouth-Jarrow, perhaps by a student of Bede's.

Another possible candidate as an example of Bede's handwriting is Durham Cathedral MS A.II.16 (see illus. 30), a Gospel book thought to have come from Wearmouth-Jarrow and is possibly the Gospel book referred to in the cathedral's 1392 Spendement inventory as 'de manu Bede' (in the hand of Bede), which

Alan Piper suggests may have been removed from the shrine after Bede's relics were translated from there to the Galilee Chapel in 1370.[14] A fourteenth-century ascription of this sort cannot, of course, be taken at face value. It might merely indicate that the book was thought to be among the properties of Wearmouth-Jarrow that came to the community of St Cuthbert after the Viking raids, but there is always the possibility that the inscription preserves a piece of earlier information about the book that once formed part of the lore of the community. The style of script and decoration of the manuscript would certainly be consistent with a Wearmouth-Jarrow origin during Bede's lifetime, as I have previously suggested.[15]

Renowned palaeographer Elias Avery Lowe thought that he had detected Bede's hand in the colophon to one of the earliest extant copies of the *Ecclesiastical History*, the St Petersburg Bede,[16] as it refers to Bede 'the unworthy' – such humility pointing to self-deprecation by Bede himself. (Aldred also referred to himself as a miserable and unworthy priestly scribe – followed by a question mark in his own inimitable fashion – in his colophon to the gloss on the Lindisfarne Gospels, added in the mid-tenth century.)[17] However, this is now considered to be a copy made at Wearmouth-Jarrow a decade or so after Bede's death. This manuscript, along with the Moore Bede (Cambridge University Library, MS Kk.5.16), which may date to circa 737 or soon after (illus. 42),[18] and BL, Cotton MS Tiberius A XIV (illus. 43),[19] which is a little later, represents the publishing response of the Wearmouth-Jarrow scriptorium to demand, at home and abroad, for Bede's works following his death. They are written in an elegant, highly legible minuscule script and date to between 737 and the 760s.[20] A further copy (BL, Cotton MS Tiberius C II) was made in Kent in the early ninth century and has given its name to the 'Tiberius Group' of southern English manuscripts. It demonstrates the status afforded to this important work in what I have termed 'Greater Mercia', which had eclipsed Northumbria's ascendency during the eighth and early ninth centuries.[21]

The Moore Bede is written in single columns and has not been laid out as a formal presentation copy, unlike the St Petersburg Bede. It is generally thought to have been written around 737 or soon after, shortly after Bede's death in 735, so it may have been copied from his original manuscript and be in a similar hand to his. This detail shows Caedmon's hymn, in the top four lines, the earliest Old English poem to survive, and a list of recent

41 The St Petersburg Bede (formerly Leningrad Bede; National Library of Russia, St Petersburg (MS Lat. Q. v. I. 18, f. 26v)) is an early surviving illuminated manuscript of Bede's *History of the English People* written in the 740s–50s in the fine Insular minuscule (lower case) script that Wearmouth-Jarrow perfected, probably in order to publish Bede's works. It is laid out as a two-column presentation copy and is probably a little later than the single-column Moore Bede. It contains what may be the earliest historiated initial in medieval art, seen here, from the opening of Book 2, perhaps depicting Pope Gregory the Great or St Augustine of Canterbury. It may have travelled to the Continent in response to early demand for Bede's work and then to Russia during the French Revolution.

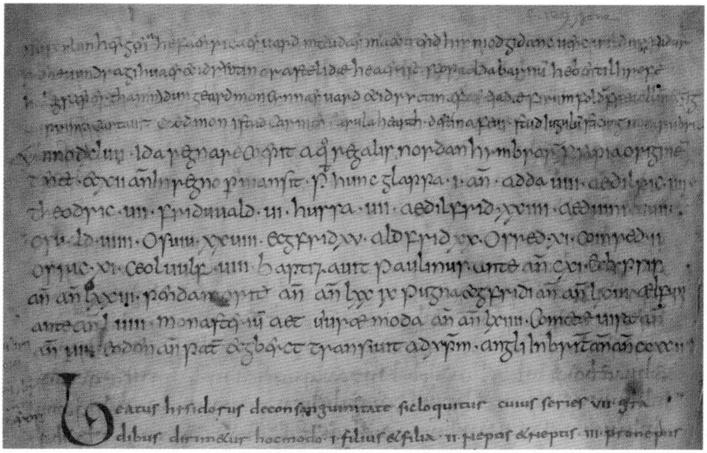

42 This copy of the *Ecclesiastical History* (the Moore Bede, Cambridge University Library, MS Kk.5.16, f. 128v) may be the earliest to have survived. It is written in Insular minuscule script of Wearmouth-Jarrow style and has not been laid out as a formal presentation copy; written c. 737, it may have been copied from Bede's original manuscript in a similar hand to his. This detail shows Caedmon's hymn, in the top four lines, the earliest Old English poem to survive, and a list of recent kings of Northumbria up to 737, written by the main scribe of the work. Below are texts of Isidore of Seville, written in caroline minuscule script, relating to marriage (consanguinity) regulations. This book was probably at Charlemagne's court at Aachen, c. 800, and was the model for many Carolingian copies.

kings of Northumbria up to 737. This is written by the main scribe of the work. Below this are texts written in caroline minuscule relating to marriage regulations. This book was in Frankia, probably at Charlemagne's court at Aachen, by 800 and may have been taken there by Alcuin of York or another English cleric. It was the model for many of the copies made in the Carolingian Empire.

We may not be able to securely identify Bede's handwriting, but it is probably present in the Codex Amiatinus and the formal uncials that he would have used for Scripture would have looked like those in the Ceolfrith Bibles and the St Cuthbert

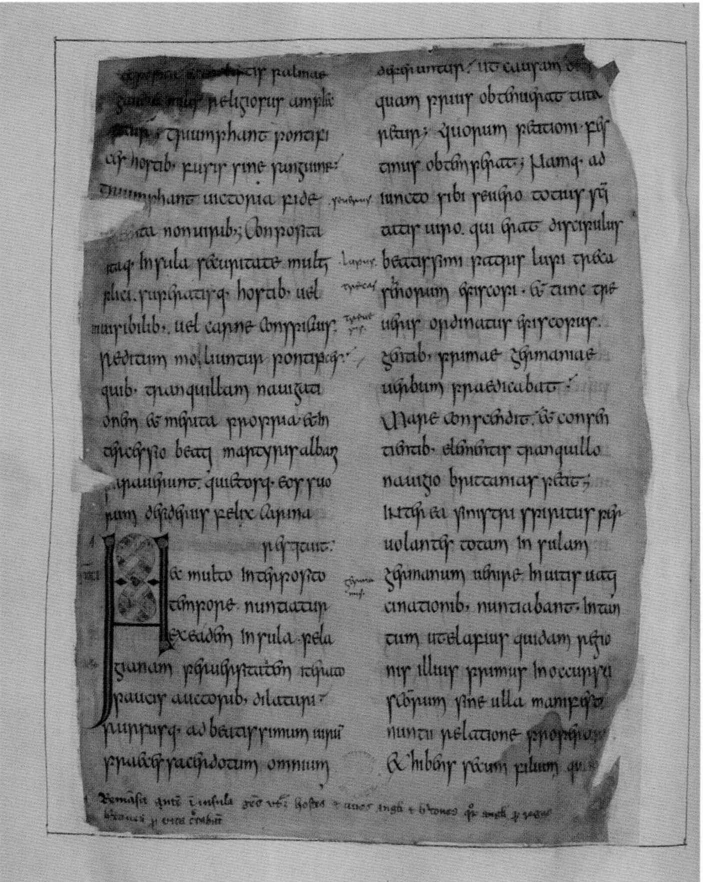

43 Bede's *Ecclesiastical History* (BL, Cotton MS Tiberius A XIV, f. 20v), copied at Wearmouth-Jarrow, c. 760s. The infill to the initial may be modelled upon the stained-glass windows of Biscop's twin foundation. The book was damaged in the Ashburnham House fire of 1731, which destroyed part of Sir Robert Cotton's former library.

Gospels, while the minuscule script that he used for other purposes would probably have looked like that in the Moore Bede, certainly in the later decades of his life.

Bede finished the *Ecclesiastical History* in 731, but a list of yearly events added by the Moore Bede scribe at the end of the

44 Bede's *Ecclesiastical History* (BL, Cotton MS Tiberius C II, f. 5v), copied at Canterbury during the first quarter of the 9th century. It gave its name to the 'Tiberius group' of Mercian manuscripts and the initial 'b' here resembles contemporary metalwork.

book on f.128v, known as the Moore annals or Moore memorandum, record that in the year 731, 'King Ceolwulf was captured, tonsured, and restored to the throne of Northumbria, and Bishop Acca fled from his see.' The political trends that had been so troubling Bede were coming to a head. Ceolwulf (to whom Bede dedicated the *Ecclesiastical History*) would take refuge with the Lindisfarne community in 737 and Acca's fall prevented his attempts to remove that community and its history from the map of the English Church. Kings 'retiring' by entering monasteries, willingly or under duress, was a practice known as kings 'in clericatu' and was practised in England and Ireland at this time.[22] This may have contributed to Bede's expression of concern at the conclusion of the *Ecclesiastical History* that so many lay people were entering monasteries rather than protecting the realm. We do not know exactly which passages from Isidore that Bede was focusing upon translating into English in the last weeks of his life, but it may be relevant that the addendum in the Moore Bede relating events that occurred between Bede completing his work on the *Ecclesiastical History* in 731 and 737 are accompanied by a citation (written in caroline minuscule script and perhaps added after the book reached Charlemagne's court at Aachen around 800) of Isidore's writings concerning the rules of consanguinity (the acceptable degrees of blood relationship within which marriage was permissable). Might this have been related in some way to the reasons given for King Ceolwulf's deposition, causing his legitimacy and that of his reign to be questioned? And might these be the difficult passages by Isidore (with their implications for dynastic succession and their possible relevance to the crisis in Northumbrian kingship) that Bede was concerned that his pupils – and others – should be clear about interpreting and which he therefore spent his last days translating, along with the Gospel of St John? If so, this may indicate that his final thoughts and provisions were very much with the future of the kingdom and its ruler, the threat posed to them and to Lindisfarne by the constitutional threat and hostility (perhaps from Bishop Acca and others perpetuating Wilfrid's agendas) and, above all, for the spiritual safety of God's people.

Another important Wearmouth-Jarrow copy of a Bedan text is Oxford, Bodleian Library, Bodl. 819, a late eighth-century copy of his *Commentary on Proverbs* (see illus. 27). It is unusual for so many early copies of an early medieval text to survive, but Bede's works, particularly the *Ecclesiastical History*, enjoyed tremendous popularity.[23] The production of these elegant books, all written in a beautifully legible pointed minuscule script (of Julian Brown's Insular Type II) represent, I consider, an extension of the publication programme for the Ceolfrith Bibles and other copies of biblical books for circulation, which was to influence that of Alcuin of York and the Tours Bibles for dissemination throughout the Carolingian Empire in the ninth century. It is appropriate that this should then have embraced the works of Wearmouth-Jarrow's home-grown patristic authority and sought-after historian and proto-scientist, Bede.

Wearmouth-Jarrow, the Ceolfrith Bibles and Their Influence

Cassiodorus was a key figure in the establishment of an approach to biblical studies founded upon the syllabus of the liberal arts, and an influential advocate of responsible copying and dissemination of texts; his textual intervention was more concerned with the form and mechanics (orthography, latinity) of the text, rather than with its actual revision. His own exegetical works take the Old Latin as their basis, his Novem Codices or nine-volume copy of this text being prepared as his own working copy. He was also responsible for producing an illustrated one-volume Bible – the Codex Grandior, a copy of which Ceolfrith brought to Wearmouth-Jarrow from Rome – the Old Testament of which was based upon Jerome's earlier Hexaplaric version, based in turn on the Septuagint. The Gospels in the Codex Grandior are thought to have been the Vulgate and the rest of the New Testament probably Old Latin. Cassiodorus also produced a smaller one-volume Bible ('pandectam . . . minutiore manu'), probably written in minuscule script and Vulgate throughout. That the pandect brought by Ceolfrith to Wearmouth-Jarrow was the Codex Grandior, rather than Cassiodorus' smaller pandect, is indicated by Bede's reference to a picture of the Tabernacle that he had seen, and which was copied in the Codex Amiatinus on ff. 2v–3r (see illus. 11), corresponding to one Cassiodorus said he had included in the Codex Grandior.

However, the editors/makers of the Codex Amiatinus did not use the Hexaplaric text (Jerome's revision of the Old Latin on the basis of the Hexaplaric Septuagint) of the Codex Grandior but substituted a primarily Vulgate version of the text. It is possible that reference was made to Cassiodorus' smaller pandect, although there is no firm evidence that there was a copy of this in Northumbria (Bede simply saying that Ceolfrith added three pandects to the one he brought from Rome), and an analysis of Amiatinus indicates that its component texts are likely to have been compiled from a variety of sources.

Its gospels relate to those in the Lindisfarne Gospels (which includes prefatory texts to each Gospel listing the readings for the feasts of particular saints who relate to Naples, indicating that the source for the gospel texts in both the Ceolfrith Bibles and the Lindisfarne Gospels originated in Naples or its vicinity). In Amiatinus the gospels are preceded by a majesty miniature, the *Novum Opus* (St Jerome's letter to Pope Damasus explaining his intention in providing a new Latin translation of Scripture), canon tables (tables which preface the Gospels and which show where each of the four gospels agree or diverge) on seven pages, then the *Plures Fuisse* (St Jerome's prologue to the gospels), the gospel prefaces (*argumenta*), partly edited to agree with early Irish versions, and *capitula lectionum* (the lection lists, which agree with those of the Lindisfarne Gospels; the lists of Neapolitan feasts are, however, omitted).

The varied textual affiliations of the Codex Amiatinus, which has, in the absence of fuller evidence, to be taken as representative of the other two Ceolfrith Bibles, indicate that, rather than undertaking a direct copy of any one of Cassiodorus' major *oeuvres*, as has often been suggested, the scriptoria of Wearmouth-Jarrow conceived of a major editorial project that would locate them within the prime lines of transmission of the sacred texts. They may have been inspired to produce uncharacteristic and ambitious single-volume Bibles in emulation of the Codex Grandior, and they may have made reference to this, and to any other of Cassiodorus' biblical works that they possessed, but as one of a number of sources. Amiatinus was not an antiquarian facsimile of an Italian pandect (such as Cassiodorus' smaller pandect), or a reworking of Cassiodorus' Novem Codices in the single-volume format of the Codex Grandior, but an active, dynamic work of scholarly compilation and emendation. The Ceolfrith Bibles were a new edition. They represented a version of the Vulgate, and indeed are still viewed as good early witnesses of such a text, but they achieved this by a complex process of excavation, compilation and interpretation, working from a number of sources in emulation of, and probably with reference to, Jerome's own process of distillation from a plethora of varying sources from different 'vulgata' traditions. It is not surprising that the Ceolfrith pandects should exhibit the influence of work undertaken on individual books by the leading scholar of the day, Bede, who was undoubtedly a driving force behind the enterprise initiated by his beloved abbot, Ceolfrith.

The famous 'Ezra' miniature in the Codex Amiatinus (f. Vr; illus. 23) should perhaps be read less as an image of Cassiodorus, adapted with reference to the great preserver of the Judaic Scriptures, Ezra the scribe, than as a homage to the continued process

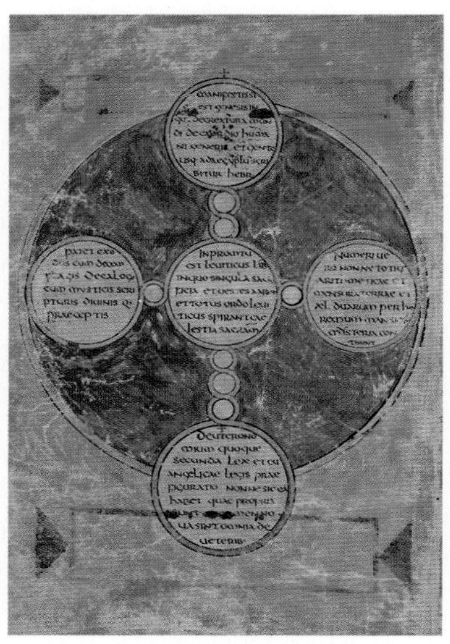

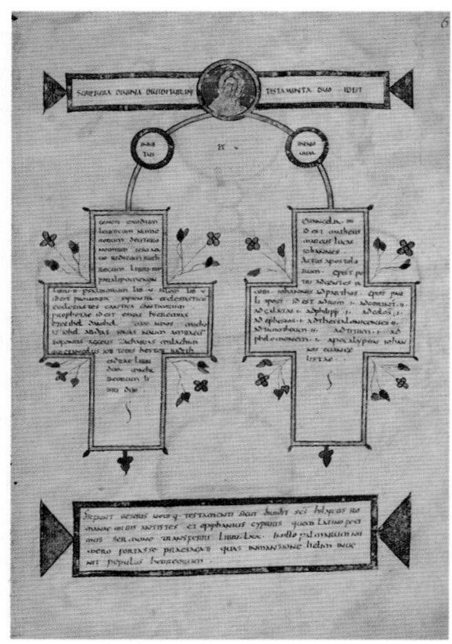

45, 46 Codex Amiatinus: diagram of the arrangement of the biblical books of the Pentateuch, designed as a Cross (*left*, f. 7v); and Christ forming a bridge between the Old and New Testaments (*right*, f. 7r). Both were designed to emphasize the reinterpretation of the Law of the Old Testament by Christ's redemptive sacrifice in the New Testament and were probably based on similar diagrams by Cassiodorus.

of rediscovery and emendation of sacred text, continually inspired by the Holy Spirit, in which the Ceolfrith Bibles played a significant role. The bookcase (*armarium*) containing its nine volumes simultaneously makes reference to Cassiodorus' work but labels them in an arrangement that does not accord with the clues given in the *Institutiones* to the organization of his actual Novem Codices. Instead, the labelling makes reference to book titles favoured by other writers, such as Augustine: the number nine symbolically represents the Novem Codices, while the labelling indicates that they were part of a fluid, living tradition. That the image of Ezra is likely to have originated at the Vivarium is reinforced by Cassiodorus' *Institutiones* (5.22, 12.3), in which he gives various lists of the sacred books and refers to an image of the Tabernacle and to diagrams of the arrangements of the biblical books, all of which are perpetuated in the Codex Amiatinus. This is a significant adjustment to perception of the image, for it indicates that both Cassiodorus and those responsible for the Ceolfrith Bibles were not attempting to provide an 'authorized' edition, but an authoritative one, drawing and improving upon the best sources they could find in order to carry forward the process of revelation and understanding of the divine Word. It would have been anathema to them to view their work as the 'last word' – the process of transmission and exploration was a divinely inspired one, which had to be perpetuated. The figure is simultaneously Ezra, the evangelists, Cassiodorus, Ceolfrith, Bede and their brethren and everyone involved in the ongoing transmission of the Word.

This is significant when we consider the relationship of the Lindisfarne Gospels to the Ceolfrith Bibles, their closest textual relatives, and to other Insular Gospel books. Is the Lindisfarne Gospels itself a 'facsimile' of the gospels component of the Ceolfrith Bibles, or of the Italian, possibly Neapolitan, gospel book which was the source for this part of their texts – forming essentially a complete sixth-century Gospel book in disguise? Should achieving close proximity to Jerome's Vulgate necessarily be considered as an evolutionary advancement against which other texts should be measured? The answer on both counts is no.

The Lindisfarne Gospels' unique arrangement and the decorative enhancement of its prefatory matter emphasized Jerome as the ultimate authority for its particular version of the Vulgate text and stressed the function of the Eusebian canon tables, which he espoused as a means of navigating and comprehending the interrelationships of the four gospels. Lindisfarne preserves the recollection of its principal textual exemplar, which was probably a southern Italian gospel book that came via Wearmouth-Jarrow or was one of their scriptoria's copies of it, including some distinctive matter relating to Italian liturgical feasts (of probable South Italian/Neapolitan character), probably retained as a means of enhancing the perceived authority of an exemplar from an early Christian centre. From changes that he made to his decorated initials, the artist-scribe did not really understand them and did not fully grasp the way in which the lections for the feasts related to their accompanying rubrics, associating the latter with the following rather than the preceding texts and having to erase the large initials he had drawn once he realized his mistake. If such features were retained despite being unfamiliar (or useful in a Northumbrian liturgical context), this suggests that it was important to retain them to signal that such an exotic exemplar had been consulted, or because its entire textual integrity was being preserved through respect.

The Lindisfarne Gospels can, therefore, be seen on one level as a conscious statement of Italian textual influence and of affiliation with Jerome's version of the Vulgate, but it is not exclusively a copy of a single source, even for its texts, let alone for its highly individual decoration, which, among other innovative features, represents the most ambitious attempt to articulate text by the ornamentation of script at text breaks that the world had seen and which was the result of innovative, original planning of layout on the part of its artist-scribe.

An appreciation of the Vulgate tradition as part of a continuing process of interaction with orality and the vernacular might have had some bearing on contemporary work to translate Scripture into English, signalled by Bede's translation work on John's gospel, which would lead eventually to Aldred's gloss. Aldred opens his colophon with a Latin synopsis of the Monarchian prologues outlining the process of transmission, which he translates into Old English. In associating himself with the names of the three makers, Aldred presents himself as the fourth evangelist, John, beloved of Christ, placing himself, and the English

47 St Matthew accompanied by his evangelist symbol, from the Lindisfarne Gospels (BL, Cotton MS Nero D IV, f. 25v), Lindisfarne, c. 715–22, which is partly modelled upon the Ezra image in the Codex Amiatinus, or its model.

language, within that direct line of transmission from the divine to humankind.

The Lindisfarne Gospels' evangelist miniatures contain Greek inscriptions, but written in Latin characters with some Latin endings, which may be a local innovation. If so, this would parallel its maker's approach to the fusing of roman capitals, Greek characters and runic features in display script in the Incipit pages

48 Ezra (or possibly Jeremiah) reads the Law, fresco from the Dura Europos synagogue, 245 CE.

(see illus. 20). There may also be an implicit intention of thereby symbolically placing the English vernacular in the tradition of transmission of Scripture from Greek, to Latin, to English. This visually conveys the babble of tongues of the Tower of Babel, reconciled and made mutually intelligible by the power of the Holy Spirit, as at Pentecost, and by the sending out of the apostles to the farthest corners of the earth (then thought to be these islands) to preach the gospel.

Bede tells us that Benedict Biscop designed the customs of Wearmouth-Jarrow by merging elements from seventeen different customaries to form a new, unified one. He had seen Benedictinism in action in Italy and had also spent two years in the monastery of Lérins from 664 until 666 (*History of the Abbots*, chs 1–2), where he would have gained an insight into the eremitic traditions of the desert fathers introduced there by John Cassian and also, closer to home, have appreciated the way that its influence had helped shape the approach of the Celtic churches. Bede may have learned much from Biscop, but he was seldom at his foundations between the time Bede joined and his own death in 690, when Bede was around seventeen. The approach that he and Ceolfrith adopted though was one of searching wide for what was good, assessing its merits and utilizing it accordingly. Neither Wearmouth-Jarrow nor Lindisfarne were in the business of 'facsimilizing' or fossilizing traditions; they were too busy contributing to a vibrant, living process.

Unusually, Ceolfrith's Bibles stressed the integral, complementary nature of the Old and New Testaments in a single monumental pandect. They were not merely facsimiles of Italian books – notably Cassiodorus' biblical editions and a gospel book from Naples – acquired by Wearmouth-Jarrow.[24] Ceolfrith, self-styled in his dedication page as 'abbot from the ends of the earth', intended Amiatinus to proclaim to Rome his people's contribution to the apostolic mission, worthy of the Church Fathers. Ceolfrith's embassy was also an *apologia* on behalf of the English, for political problems surrounded the turbulent career of Archbishop Wilfrid of York. Amiatinus served as ambassador of the English nation, proclaiming its catholic orthodoxy and unity, within a year of when the final bastion of Columban tradition, Iona, finally conformed to the Roman dating of Easter.

The Ezra miniature features among Amiatinus' sacred *figurae* (schematic, symbolic images) and symbolizes the ongoing process of transmission of Scripture and the role of the priestly scribe who, as Cassiodorus said (in his *Commentary* on Psalm 44/45:1–2 and in the *Institutiones*), could preach with the hand and 'unleash tongues with the fingers', imitating the action of the Lord who wrote the Law with his all-powerful finger.[25] Bede furthermore described Ezra the Scribe as 'typus Christi', a 'type' (Old Testament precursor) of Christ.[26]

Many of the scribes mentioned in the Bible were priests, entrusted with the preservation, interpretation and exposition of Scripture (Nehemiah 8:9, Matthew 17:10, 23:2) and gained a reputation for wisdom and learning (for example, Jonathan in 1 Chronicles 27:32). Ezra the Scribe became the epitome of these ideals and of the rabbinic sage. Their responsibilities meant that such scribes were also subjected to scrutiny, with both Jeremiah (Jeremiah 8:8) and Jesus (Matthew 23) levelling criticism at them on occasion.

In view of this biblical conceptualization of the role of the priestly scribe, it is not surprising that Bede should have focused upon Ezra and Nehemiah as suitable subjects for study and, in the process, have meditated and implicitly commented upon his own calling to that role as a man 'of great wisdom and learning' and upon the prophetic critique to which he also found himself subjected.

Emphasizing his role as a teacher, Ezra 7:6 describes Ezra as 'a scribe, skilled in the law of Moses that the Lord, the God of Israel, had given'. A fresco preserved on the West wall of the Dura Europos synagogue beside a Torah niche depicts him standing, clothed in priestly garb and reading from a scroll with a draped Torah ark at his feet, stressing his responsibility for writing, preserving and transmitting Israel's sacred scrolls of the Law.[27] Later Jewish traditions even ascribes to him the very rewriting of the Old Testament (4 Ezra 14). Likewise, Ezra 7:10 states that Ezra had set his heart to study the law of the Lord, to enact it and to teach his will and ways in Israel. Bede endeavoured to do the same.

EIGHT

Bede and Lindisfarne

A particularly good copy of Jerome's Vulgate was made in Naples, an important early Christian centre, during the sixth century. By the early eighth century this had travelled across Europe to a land that was then on the periphery of the known world – Anglo-Saxon England. There it found a home in one of the greatest libraries of the age at Wearmouth-Jarrow. Given the evidence for a relationship between Bede and the cult of St Cuthbert on Holy Island, it may have been he who ensured that Wearmouth-Jarrow's prized Neapolitan Vulgate exemplar, or a copy of it, was sent to Holy Island to serve as an exemplar for the great cult-book of St Cuthbert's shrine, the Lindisfarne Gospels (BL, Cotton MS Nero D IV).[1] The first Life of St Cuthbert had been composed by an anonymous monk of Lindisfarne sometime between 699 and 705.[2] It relates that the Irish Columban foundation of Lindisfarne had already adopted the substantially Benedictine Rule favoured at Wearmouth-Jarrow, probably thereby inaugurating closer collaboration between these centres.

Eadfrith was Bishop of Lindisfarne from 698 until 722. He had succeeded to the see on the death of his predecessor, Eadberht, who died on 6 May 698, not long after the translation he had arranged on 20 March of the body of St Cuthbert to a wooden coffin placed above ground near the high altar at Lindisfarne. Eadberht's own body was placed beneath it in

Cuthbert's former tomb. During his episcopacy, Eadfrith restored the Inner Farne hermitage, commissioned an anonymous member of the community to write the first Life of St Cuthbert around 699–705 and commissioned Bede to rewrite a second Prose Life of St Cuthbert, which was completed and dedicated to Eadfrith shortly before his death in 722.

Eadfrith promised to have Guthrith the sacrist enter Bede's name in the Lindisfarne book of life (*Liber vitae*) of those to be remembered in the community's prayers, at Bede's own request. In return, Bede promised him a copy of his earlier verse Life of St Cuthbert. The St Cuthbert Gospel of St John (BL, Add. MS 89000, formerly known as the Stonyhurst Gospel), written at Wearmouth-Jarrow, was placed in Cuthbert's coffin and was discovered therein in 1104. It has been assumed that it was put there at the translation of 698, although the coffin was opened subsequently, for example when Athelstan's gift of textiles was deposited, probably around the time of his visit to the shrine in 934, by which time Lindisfarne had absorbed the property Wearmouth-Jarrow.

In its prologue Bede dedicated his prose Life of St Cuthbert to Eadfrith, his 'most blessed lord and father' and the probable artist-scribe of the Lindisfarne Gospels; together they shaped the Cuthbertine cult to reflect, or rather bring to fruition, a new era of ecumenical unity and spiritual rejuvenation after the Paschal dispute between the Roman and Columban Churches which had culminated in the Synod of Whitby.[3]

Bede's prologue to the Life indicates that he probably visited Holy Island, to gather information and to seek the community's approbation. There he would have imbibed the ascetic spirituality of its Irish Columban founding saints, whom he so admired despite their adherence to their own traditions. He would have prayed at the shrine of St Cuthbert, newly established at the high altar of the easternmost of the two stone churches that had been built, replacing the earlier wooden oratories built by the Columban monks, following the visit of Archbishop Theodore. To the right of that altar lay the wooden coffin of St Cuthbert (which survives still at Durham Cathedral), in which lay remains that had been found to be incorrupt when they were exhumed to be moved to that place of honour in 698. Traces of pigment have been found on its sides, indicating that the figures of the evangelists, angels and the Virgin and Child (depicted in the sideways seated pose adapted in Coptic Christian art from that of Isis and Horus) were once painted there. Indeed, I would suggest that the whole arrangement of the new shrine may have been modelled upon those recently established to commemorate Egyptian bishops, such as St Bishoi, whose incorrupt remains you can still prod to ensure that his undecayed body is intact inside his vestments when you visit his shrine at the monastery named after him in the Wadi El-Natroun. When the coffin was reopened in 1104 at its translation to the shrine at the east end of the new Norman cathedral at Durham, whence the shrine had been relocated in 995, it was found to contain the saint's body in his vestments, along with relics that include an early pectoral cross, a liturgical bone comb, a portable altar, oriental silks, an embroidered stole and maniple gifted by the royal house of Wessex and the little copy of St John's Gospel, bound in Coptic fashion (see illus. 28, 29 and 32). As in some Coptic burials, the Christian book of life replaces the ancient Egyptian book of the dead.[4]

The style of fine uncial script and the purity of its Vulgate text proclaims this book – the St Cuthbert Gospel – to be a product of the Wearmouth-Jarrow scriptorium. I have proposed that the way it was constructed was designed to associate it with references in the Lives of St Cuthbert to the copy of St John's Gospel that Cuthbert had studied with his master, St Boisil, at Melrose.[5] It is conceivable that it may have been given by Bede's twin community as a gift to St Cuthbert's nascent cult and placed in his coffin during the translation of 698 or on a subsequent occasion when the coffin was opened.

This gift was probably followed by Bede's writing of the verse and prose Lives of St Cuthbert and his associated visit to Holy Island. This may also have led to a closer relationship between the Wearmouth-Jarrow and Lindisfarne communities and the gift or loan of a well-researched and reconstructed copy of St Jerome's Vulgate text of the four gospels which was used as the primary textual model for the Lindisfarne Gospels, made on Holy Island around 715–22 by Bishop Eadfrith as the main cult book of St Cuthbert's shrine. There it was displayed on its high altar to pilgrims, to be used for readings during the celebration of the principal liturgical festivals of Christmas, Easter and the Feasts of St Cuthbert.

This book was made to enshrine the values that the saint represented and was to be the most visible symbol of his authority and, more importantly, that of God. Just as Bede seems to have played a strategic role in shaping the cult of St Cuthbert through his collaboration with Bishop Eadfrith and the Lindisfarne community in writing what was to become the main version of the saint's life, might he also have played a role in shaping the form of the Lindisfarne Gospels?

The outstandingly beautiful, subtle illumination of the Lindisfarne Gospels (illus. 20, 21, 25, 47) blends Celtic, Germanic, Roman and Near Eastern elements, reflecting their formative influences upon the English Church, to visually and symbolically embody the eternal harmony for which Cuthbert, Eadfrith and Bede laboured.[6] Like the Ceolfrith Bibles, the Lindisfarne Gospels makes an informed statement of the position of the mature Insular Church in respect of age-old religious controversies such as the Monothelete controversy and proclaims international ecumenical unity in adherence to the orthodoxy of Chalcedon. There may well have been some synergy between the conceptualization and implementation of these highly symbolic big book projects.

The Significance of the Years 715–16

The years 715–16 witnessed a number of significant events, several of which are recorded by Bede. The papal librarian, a friend of Abbot Ceolfrith, who would have facilitated Bede's research requests, became Pope Gregory II. He had additional cause for celebration, for that year Sergius became Bishop of Naples, having repulsed the Arian Lombards (recently, during the late seventh century, it had also been successfully defended against Islam). The important early Christian centre of Naples was thus restored to orthodoxy. That same year Iona was also received back into Chalcedonian orthodoxy, marking the end of what many must have viewed as the schismatic tendencies of the Columban monastic federation.

It was also around 715 that the new stational liturgy of the veneration of the Cross on Good Friday, introduced in Rome at the end of the seventh century, began to appear in Roman liturgical manuscripts. Pope Gregory II had introduced stational masses for the Thursdays in Lent. These are marked by minor initials in the Lindisfarne Gospels, which also marks passages used for readings at feasts celebrated in the Columban liturgy and others which are particular to key saints' feast days in the diocese of Naples. The textual family followed by the Lindisfarne Gospels' canon tables is that of Aquileia, an important early Christian archdiocese at the head of the Adriatic where St Jerome had settled for a while, impressed by its orthodoxy, but which had subsequently descended into a state of schism, with two opposing archbishops, for several generations. This schism was also healed around 715. All of these markers of different traditions, now newly reconciled, are thus celebrated in the design of the Lindisfarne Gospels and would have been laid upon the high altar at Lindisfarne as a symbolic celebration of the unity of Christendom. This complex artistic, textual and theological programme speaks of the intellectual and spiritual fervour and intent of a mind or minds well versed in both local and international religious and secular affairs and with the ability to integrate them within the bigger picture and the philosophical framework of eternity.[7] Such were Eadfrith, Ceolfrith and Bede.

It is probably no coincidence (and one that speaks of a grand plan, as had Biscop's foundation of his second house, Jarrow, to reflect the 'two wills' dictat of the Sixth Ecumenical Council in 681 – for both were highly symbolic actions) that the following year Abbot Ceolfrith set out for Rome with the Codex Amiatinus, one of the three massive pandects made in the Wearmouth-Jarrow scriptorium, which formed part of a Cassiodoran-type publication programme to reconstruct and disseminate St Jerome's Vulgate. This programme would presumably have taken some years to plan and execute, perhaps spanning the decade preceding Ceolfrith's departure for Rome. It should be recalled that in the ninth century the Tours scriptorium could produce several such pandects per annum by throwing a lot of human and other resources at the project. This was conceived by Alcuin in order to disseminate standardized text and script versions to other scriptoria throughout the diverse territories incorporated into the Carolingian empire as exemplars for further copies, which would discourage the perpetuation of local traditions and regional separatism. I have proposed that the Lindisfarne Gospels, with its close relationship to the Codex Amiatinus, was also conceived during this time and that its programme was then finalized and implemented around 715–22, incorporating visual and textual allusions to the Codex Amiatinus and to a conjunction of key international events appertaining to orthodox unity that clustered around 715.

Bishop Eadfrith may have made the Lindisfarne Gospels with his own hands, in accordance with Columban tradition, having spent some time planning the project as a cult focus and a celebration of different traditions and their reconciliation in ecumenical orthodoxy, led in the West by Rome. The book's complex blend of iconic and aniconic artistic solutions and responses to the issues of the day still display sensitivity to Eastern sensibilities in a way that would shortly change with the onset of iconoclasm.

Thus, on the very eve of Byzantium's iconoclast controversy (which erupted in 720 and led to a period of desecration of images of the Divine and avoidance of their use, for fear of idolatry), the maker of the Lindisfarne Gospels was experimenting with sophisticated iconic, aniconic and oblique iconographic solutions to depicting the divine. These were to form a distinctive aspect of the Insular approach to imagery in the service of complex international theological debate. Its sensitivity to the iconoclast debate and to unease concerning idolatry suggests that it pre-dates Pope Gregory II's reassertion of anti-iconoclastic figural imagery from 727 as part of the Western Orthodox Church's rebuttal of absolutist subjugation to Emperor Leo the Iconoclast. Eadfrith's death in 722 sits within this chronological margin.

The visual fusion of cultural motifs and styles that characterizes the great cult book of St Cuthbert would therefore have formed a fitting contribution to the shrine of the saint, which in some ways recalls the princely burials of Sutton Hoo and Prittlewell, which contain Germanic, Celtic, Frankish, Coptic and Byzantine artefacts as a means of indicating the breadth of economic and cultural contacts enjoyed by the deceased and their peoples. Like such secular monuments, the decorated display pages of the Lindisfarne Gospels reflect the agendas, aspirations and wide-ranging affiliations of the leaders of a new age and the historical context in which these were conceived.[8]

Creating the Cult of St Cuthbert: A Rallying Point for Reconciliation in the North

The translation of St Cuthbert's relics to the high altar of Lindisfarne in 698, eleven years after his death, marked the beginning of the creation of a cult that was to serve as a rallying point for the emerging identity of the north – and which survives to this day. In the post-Whitby period there was a need for reconciliation between the various peoples and traditions that had prevailed and it was under Bishop Eadfrith, who came into office later that year, that the work of elevating Cuthbert as a social and spiritual role model began. During the 23 years of Eadfrith's leadership three lives of St Cuthbert were written – one by an anonymous monk of Lindisfarne and two by Bede – and the shrine on Holy Island became a focus for pilgrimage, featuring Stations of the Cross (a practice recently introduced from Rome) marked by stone crosses at key points on the island and the saint's coffin – resembling a painted Egyptian sarcophagus of the sort in which the desert fathers might be enshrined – set adjacent to the high altar in the main church, upon which liturgical metalwork and relics were probably displayed, alongside the Word of God in the form of a gospel book. Eadfrith himself was probably responsible for conceiving and undertaking the work of producing a particularly fine example – the Lindisfarne Gospels – perhaps to replace an earlier volume, which might rival the purple codex at St Wilfrid's shrine in Ripon. Lindisfarne's great book, however, was to bring together not only elements from Rome and the Mediterranean but visual motifs redolent of the range of local cultures and of the Christian Orient.

Why was St Cuthbert deemed suitable for elevation in this way? He was Northumbrian by birth, served as Bishop of Lindisfarne from 685–7 and was one of those early figures who won sainthood by popular acclaim, by virtue of their living out of

Christ's teachings. His early Lives present him as an eloquent teacher and preacher; a canny politician who would have been guided by Christ's injunction to his disciples to be 'wise as serpents and gentle as doves'; a risk-taker who carried humanitarian aid and an eternal message of hope into the most poverty-striken war zones of the day; and a hermit who did battle with his demons on the rock of the isle of Inner Farne (only a stone's throw from the ramparts of the citadel of Bamburgh, wherein dwelt one of the most dangerous despots of his age, the Christian ruler King Ecgfrith, whose plans for territorial expansion led him to turn the blind eye of the 'political realist' to a little genocide or invasion of other civilizations) also of the Christian faith. One of the responsibilities of Columban church leaders was to remind secular authorities of the responsibility attendant upon wealth and power. Each time Ecgfrith and his courtiers looked out of their windows they would have seen the little island cell with 'walls so high that even if all I could see was the sky, I would still be afraid that the love of money and the cares of the world might steal me away' (Bede's prose Life of St Cuthbert), wherein dwelt the emaciated, vulnerable, indomitable, Gandhi-like holy man. His shrine soon became one of the most significant pilgrimage sites of medieval Britain.

Cuthbert was presumably well acquainted with Irish legal practice, which dictated that if one could not receive natural justice, one shamed the perpetrator of injustice by fasting against them, outside their door. Attuned to the natural environment in which he left the light footprint of his physical life, he was probably also familiar with the teachings of monastic founding fathers, such as Columbanus, who wrote that 'Nature is a second Scripture, in which we behold God.'

The popular image of 'Celtic Christianity' that has emerged in recent years needs to be modified by more informed study of the sources for the period and ethos that it purports to embrace.

Nonetheless, there is much that this formative period of early Christianity in the watery western 'deserts' of these islands can still offer us in the way of challenge and inspiration today. Spiritual ideals, political realities and the issues facing humanity and the environment merge in the Lindisfarne Gospels into a complex web of words and images – a painted labyrinth of prayer and praise.

Between circa 715 and 731 Bede was working simultaneously on his commentaries on the Tabernacle and the Temple, on Ezra and Nehemiah and on the *Ecclesiastical History of the English People*. Scott DeGregorio has referred to this as 'a massive exegetical-historical project on a set of interrelated themes which he deemed particularly pressing'.[9] Noteworthy here is his concern for unity-in-diversity, for according to Bede, 'the Holy Church universal is built from many elect persons, from many churches throughout the world, and from flowers of diverse virtues' (*On the Tabernacle*). These are compared to the many shades of purple in which the curtains of the Temple were dyed, which also represent, for Bede, the journey of the just soul. These shades are replicated in the subtle range of colours from red to blue made from the lichen orchil (with the addition of alkaline or acidic substances) by the maker of the Lindisfarne Gospels.

For Bede the process of conversion related in the Acts of the Apostles was being brought to its conclusion in that of the various peoples inhabiting the islands of Britain and Ireland, on the farthest edge of the then known world. The key figures in that process – the latter-day equivalents of the apostles – are lauded by Bede in the *Ecclesiastical History*, which relates the progress of their mission, for the completion of the Apostolic age would herald the Second Coming of Christ. Among them are Columba, Aidan, Cuthbert, Gregory the Great, Augustine and his followers, Theodore of Tarsus and Abbot Hadrian, Hild,

Aethelfrith, Wilfrid, Boniface, various Celtic missionaries and certain bishops from Gaul. As Iona, the final bastion of Columban practices, had conformed to those of international orthodoxy in 715, Bede felt able, however, to give full credit to the crucial contribution of the Columban monastic federation to the conversion process. He felt no such impulse towards the British Church, which remained in a schismatic state (with Cornwall being the last to conform in the tenth century), and he directed strong criticism (much of it unwarranted) at it for not playing its part in the missionary endeavour to convert the Germanic settlers.

Bede would only have been about fifteen years old when St Cuthbert died, but he would have heard many tales of his exploits and ministry, sowing the seeds of the creation of a Christian hero-figure to outstrip the stories of secular heroes heard during his childhood. Likewise mighty St Columba, who had defeated the Loch Ness Monster, and St Aidan, who had refused the king's gift of a fine horse, preferring to walk in God's service as a sign of humility and to align himself with the poor.

Gone are the days when scholars viewed Lindisfarne as a bastion of 'Celtic' monasticism and Wearmouth-Jarrow of *romanitas*. It is now widely accepted that they interacted and even collaborated somewhat in their ministry to the people of Northumbria and beyond. But this was not necessarily the case elsewhere.

St Wilfrid (*c.* 633–709/710) emerges from the pages of the *Ecclesiastical History* as a powerful protagonist in the affairs of both Church and State and frequently found himself in conflict with his peers. Ironically, his vocation began on Holy Island, whose monks granted him permission to travel to study in Canterbury, Gaul and Rome. Of noble birth, Wilfrid was to aspire to become a prince of the Church and would later travel with a large retinue and live ostentatiously, constructing fine abbeys in the Roman fashion at Ripon and Hexham, the crypts of which he filled with relics collected during his travels abroad. He converted parts of Sussex by the sword and was a political player and an eloquent debater. His career trajectory left a wake of ousted colleagues, such as St Chad of Holy Island, who was appointed Bishop of Northumbria but displaced by Wilfrid (and given the bishopric of Lichfield instead by Archbishop Theodore). Wilfrid subsequently quarrelled with King Ecgfrith of Northumbria, who expelled him from the kingdom. Despite interventions by Wilfrid's powerful friends, the Pope and Archbishop Theodore, both Ecgfrith and his successor, King Aldfrith, persisted in exiling this particularly 'troublesome priest'. Cuthbert was Ecgfrith's appointment as Bishop of Lindisfarne, which would hardly have recommended him to Wilfrid. In 687–8, following Cuthbert's death, Wilfrid administered the see of Lindisfarne himself, engendering a period of bitterness of which Bede can scarcely bring himself to speak.[10]

The pope once again intervened to restore Ripon and Hexham to Wilfrid after the Council of Austerfield in 702 tried to confiscate all of Wilfrid's possessions, and after his death in 709 or 710 his followers sought to establish his cult at Ripon, focusing upon the crypt. He was soon venerated as a saint and Stephen of Ripon composed a Life of St Wilfrid. I have suggested that this cult was intended to compete with the nascent cult of St Cuthbert on Holy Island (which would compete with it, in turn) and it is surely no coincidence that the composition of the anonymous first Life of St Cuthbert (probably by one of the Lindisfarne monks) should have been followed fairly quickly by the Life of Wilfrid, written soon after his death by one of his followers at Ripon at the behest of Acca, who was to succeed Wilfrid as Bishop of Hexham. The Life of Wilfrid copies some lines from the anonymous Life of St Cuthbert, and Clare Stancliffe has proposed that the Anonymous Life and Bede's verse Life, which was indebted to it and was composed between 705 and 716, were subject to criticism by Acca and the pro-Wilfridian camp and were used by them to disparage St Cuthbert's ministry and the churchmanship practised at Lindisfarne.[11] She suggests that this caused Bede to write a second Life of St Cuthbert in prose around 721, at the behest of Bishop Eadfrith of Lindisfarne, to refute such criticism and to cast Cuthbert as a rallying point for reconciliation and social justice – the prophetic priest and pastoral leader. Bede then went on to write on the Tabernacle, the Temple and Ezra and Nehemiah and to cast the English Church and those who had constructed it in the guise of their counterparts, with their deeds recounted and their cohesive identity asserted in the *Ecclesiastical History*.

Bishop Acca is often presented as a patron and friend of Bede, but Bede evidently had to tread carefully where his championing of the Lindisfarne cause and approach were concerned. The questions raised concerning Bede's 'heretical' tendencies had come from the circle of Wilfrid, and Acca had subsequently had to urge Bede to defend himself from further slurs in respect of his exegesis on the evangelists and their symbols. This may have been a warning shot, for Acca was apparently intent upon regularizing the Northumbrian episcopacy and placing Hexham at its head. There was no place in this hierarchical structure for the anomalous bishop-monks of Lindisfarne and its daughter houses, or for the ascetic, eremitic form of monasticism that Aidan had introduced there and that Cuthbert had reasserted. The power of this model of Christian life, which had inspired the respect of kings and people alike, and the supra-territorial networking that it fostered through monastic federations of houses descending from the same founder figure, posed a threat to the hierarchical diocesan and parochial structure and its integration with secular governance. The Carolingian rulers would later refer to such Insular traveller-monks as 'gyrovagues' whose ministries could not be controlled by the state. Another big issue was that at Lindisfarne, like Iona, there was an abbot and a bishop and the latter, as a monk, was subject to the authority of the abbot. This did not sit well with most bishops.

Shortly before his death, Cuthbert had warned the Lindisfarne community of the dangers, spiritual and material, of too close a relationship with the ways of the world and cautioned against the wealth attendant upon them. He also urged them to live in charity with one another and with the other servants of God. By the end of the eighth century Lindisfarne would fall prey to the Vikings, attracted by the treasures bestowed upon the shrine and by kings who sought refuge from political situations within its walls. From the luxury of the Carolingian court circle Alcuin of York wrote a letter of condolence to one of the Lindisfarne monks, named Cuthbert, commiserating but pointing out that it was its departure from the asceticism of its founding fathers that had called down such tragedy upon the community. The Celtic eremitic tradition was evidently still held up as an ideal among churchmen who had learned to reach a compromise with the world.

Much of the episcopal reputation of Wilfrid and Acca resided in their restoration, construction and adornment of major churches (York, Ripon and Hexham) and their engagement with ecclesiastical process and clerical provision – what we equate today with 'establishment men'. Bede comments, 'Other popes applied themselves to the tasks of building churches and adorning them with gold and silver, but he [Gregory the Great] devoted himself entirely to winning souls' (*Ecclesiastical History* II.1). This may have been overstating the case, but one can see why, holding this view, Bede was drawn in the local orbit to figures such as Aidan and Cuthbert as embodiments of monastic humility in the service of God in tending the bodies and souls of his people.

The final words that Bede ascribes to Cuthbert in the prose Life (ch. 39) were: 'I know that, although I seemed contemptible to some while I lived, yet, after my death, you will see what I was and how my teaching is not to be despised.' Together, Eadfrith and Bede ensured that this would be so.

The Temple that Bede's later writings presents, housing the holy of holies of the Tabernacle, and tended by committed priestly leaders, is constructed for the new Israelites (whom Bede characterizes as the English) by a host of kings, priests and prophets, among whom those associated with Lindisfarne and Wearmouth-Jarrow played important roles. Following Bishop Eadfrith's death in 722, the future of Lindisfarne seems to have entered into question as Hexham and the followers of Wilfrid were increasingly in ascendancy. Hexham was also courting the new king, Osric (718–29), by promoting the cult of his great-uncle King Oswald and his victory over the pagans at Heavenfield which he claimed was gained in the sign of the cross, like Emperor Constantine's victory at the Milvian Bridge, events both perhaps recalled in the 'in the sign of the cross' carvings among the early sculptures at both Monkwearmouth and Jarrow (see illus. 10). Bede's Letter to Bishop Ecgbert of York in 734 expresses the urgency of his concern at the declining standards of leadership in Church and State and particularly on the part of the bishops who were supposed to lead and tend to their flocks. Such concerns still occupy the churches today.

Bede's fears at the implications of such church politics were justified. Acca's ambition to construct a single Bernician see under Hexham would lead to his expulsion from the latter in 731 and in 750 King Eadberht imprisoned the bishop of Lindisfarne for having honoured the right of claiming sanctuary at St Cuthbert's shrine, when it was claimed by a son of a former king, Aldfrith. As a result, Hexham was given the administration of Lindisfarne's see. Both parties had lost out to secular strategies and dynastic competition.

By contrast, the ultimate goal of Cuthbert and his community, to which Bede also subscribed, had been to create a unified Church which would form an integrated part of the international Christian oecumen, adhering to the practices of orthodoxy as expressed by the Council of Chalcedon and conforming to the dictates of more recent key councils such as the Sixth Ecumenical Council of 681 and its rulings on the Monothelete controversy. Schisms, heresies and the disruptive ambitions of the powerful were Bede's particular bêtes noirs, for they disrupted this longed-for unity.

Whereas the focal point of Wilfrid's cult at Ripon was a purple gospel codex penned in gold and silver inks, the epitome of ecclesiastical visible consumption of wealth in the praise of God, that of Cuthbert's shrine was a theologically complex and visually harmonious expression of the various peoples and traditions, stretching from the deserts of the Holy Land to the Atlantic seaboard of the West – a visual tower of Babel: the Lindisfarne Gospels. Within it, the cultural legacies of the peoples of Britain and Ireland were designed to interact with those of the international past and present in vision of an eternal harmony in which the flora and fauna of Creation were sustained and made whole by the Word – Logos.

In the *Ecclesiastical History* Bede likewise adopts what Clare Stancliffe has termed an 'eirenic synthesis',[12] balancing the contributions of the Roman, Columban, Cuthbertine and Wilfridian missions (and others) to show how, together, they contributed to the formation of the English Church and people, who could then take their place as part of the communion that is the body of Christ.

Bede, the historian and monastic priest, was also prepared to put his labour, his reputation and the benefits of patronage on the line to defend these principles against revisionism and the power of the establishment, where he perceived its lack of vision to endanger them. For Bede's was a prophetic voice, grounded in an appreciation of long time and space and the interconnectivity of all things. Within the confines of the extent of human knowledge in his day, his thinking encapsulated a theory of everything.

NINE

Bede and His Legacy

The tale of Bede's own death is best left to the eyewitness account of those who were with him:

From a Letter on the Death of the Venerable Bede by his amanuensis, Cuthbert, to Cuthwin[1]

To his fellow-lector, Cuthwin, beloved in Christ, Cuthbert, his fellow-student, greeting and salvation for ever in the Lord. I have very gladly received the gift which thou sentest to me, and with much joy have read thy devout and learned letter, wherein I found that which I greatly desired, to wit, that masses and holy prayers are diligently offered by you for our father and master Bede, beloved of God. Wherefore I rejoice, rather for love of him than from confidence in my own power, to relate in few words after what manner he departed out of this world, understanding also that thou hast desired and asked this of me. He was troubled with weakness and chiefly with difficulty in breathing, yet almost without pain, for about a fortnight before the day of our Lord's Resurrection; and thus he afterwards passed his time, cheerful and rejoicing, giving thanks to Almighty God every day and night, nay, every hour, till the day of our Lord's Ascension, to wit, the twenty-sixth day of May, and daily gave lessons to us, his disciples; and whatsoever remained of the day he spent in singing psalms, as far as he was able; he also strove to pass all the night joyfully in prayer and thanksgiving to God, save only when a short sleep prevented it; and then he no sooner awoke than he straightway began again to repeat the well-known sacred songs, and ceased not to give thanks to God with uplifted hands. I declare with truth that I have never seen with my eyes, or heard with my ears, any man so earnest in giving thanks to the living God. O truly blessed man! He repeated the words of St. Paul the Apostle, 'It is a fearful thing to fall into the hands of the living God,' and much more out of Holy Scripture; wherein also he admonished us to think of our last hour, and to arise out of the sleep of the soul; and being learned in our native poetry, he said also in our tongue, concerning the dread parting of souls from the body:

Fore then neidfaerae
naenig uiuurthit
thonc suotturra
than him tharf sie
to ymb hycggannae
aer his hin iongae
huaet his gastae
godaes aeththa yflaes
aefter deothdaege
doemid uueorthae.

Facing Death, that inescapable journey,
who can be wiser than he

who reflects, while breath yet remains,
on whether his life brought others happiness, or pains,
since his soul may yet win delight's or night's way
after his death-day.[2]

He also sang antiphons for our comfort and his own. One of these is, 'O King of Glory, Lord of all power, Who, triumphing this day, didst ascend above all the heavens, leave us not comfortless, but send to us the promise of the Father, even the Spirit of Truth – Hallelujah.' And when he came to the words, 'leave us not comfortless,' he burst into tears and wept much. And an hour after, he fell to repeating what he had begun. And this he did the whole day, and we, hearing it, mourned with him and wept. Now we read and now we lamented, nay, we wept even as we read. In such rapture we passed the fifty days' festival till the aforesaid day; and he rejoiced greatly and gave God thanks, because he had been accounted worthy to suffer such weakness. And he often said, 'God scourgeth every son whom He receiveth'; and the words of St. Ambrose, 'I have not so lived as to be ashamed to live among you; but neither do I fear to die, because we have a merciful Lord.' And during those days, besides the lessons we had daily from him, and the singing of the Psalms, there were two memorable works, which he strove to finish; to wit, his translation of the Gospel of St. John, from the beginning, as far as the words, 'But what are they among so many?' into our own tongue, for the benefit of the Church of God; and some selections from the books of Bishop Isidore, saying, 'I would not have my boys read a lie, nor labour herein without profit after my death.'

On Tuesday before the feast of the Ascension, Bede's breathing became laboured and a slight swelling appeared in his legs. Nevertheless, he gave us instruction all day long and dictated cheerfully the whole time. It seemed to us, however, that he knew very well that his end was near, and so he spent the whole night giving thanks to God.

At daybreak on Wednesday he told us to finish the writing we had begun. We worked until nine o'clock, when we went in procession with the relics as the custom of the day required. But one of our community, a boy named Wilbert, stayed with him and said to him, 'Dear master, there is still one more chapter to finish in that book you were dictating. Do you think it would be too hard for you to answer any more questions?' Bede replied: 'Not at all; it will be easy. Take up your pen and ink, and write quickly,' and he did so.

At three o'clock, Bede said to me, 'I have a few treasures in my private chest, some pepper, napkins, and a little incense. Run quickly and bring the priest of our monastery, and I will distribute among them these little presents that God has given me.'

When the priests arrived he spoke to them and asked each one to offer Masses and prayers for him regularly. They gladly promised to do so. The priests were sad, however, and they all wept, especially because Bede had said that he thought they would not see his face much longer in this world. Yet they rejoiced when he said, 'If it so please my Maker, it is time for me to return to him who created me and formed me out of nothing when I did not exist. I have lived a long time, and the righteous Judge has taken good care of me during my whole life. The time has come for my departure, and I long to die and be with Christ. My soul yearns to see Christ, my King, in all his glory.' He said many other things which profited us greatly, and so he passed the day joyfully till evening.

When evening came, young Wilbert said to Bede, 'Dear master, there is still one sentence that we have not written down.' Bede said, 'Quick, write it down.' In a little while, Wilbert said, 'There; now it is written down.' Bede said, 'Good. You have spoken the truth; it is finished. Hold my head in your hands, for I really enjoy sitting opposite the holy place where I used to pray; I can call upon my Father as I sit there.'

And so Bede, as he lay upon the floor of his cell, sang, 'Glory be to the Father, and to the Son and to the Holy Spirit.' And when he had named the Holy Spirit, he breathed his last breath. We believe most firmly that Bede has now entered into the joy of the heaven he longed for, since his labours here on earth were always dedicated to the glory of God.

Thus died Bede, humble and working to share with others to the last, with the song of his beloved Scripture on his lips. A good death, and an exemplary one, of the sort he had so lauded in others.

There was evidently an immediate demand for Bede's work, to judge by the unusually high survival rate of copies of the *Ecclesiastical History of the English People* made at Wearmouth-Jarrow in the decades following his death in 735. The Moore Bede (Cambridge University Library, MS Kk.5.16) and the St Petersburg Bede (National Library of Russia, St Petersburg, MS lat. Q. v. I. 18) were deemed by Malcolm Parkes to have been made as early as the 740s–50s (see illus. 41 and 42) and British Library, Cotton MS Tiberius A XIV (illus. 43), also from Wearmouth-Jarrow, is not much later (although David Dumville places the start of production of the group in the 760s). Another copy in the British Library (Cotton MS Tiberius C II) was made in Canterbury in the early ninth century (illus. 44).

By the end of the century Emperor Charlemagne is known to have obtained a copy of his own.

Bede's popularity on the Continent was assured by the mission of St Boniface to the Germans and the scholarly work of Alcuin of York, who was head-hunted by Charlemagne in the late eighth century to help lead the Carolingian reformation of religious and cultural life and learning. Boniface wrote repeatedly back to England requesting copies of Bede's theological works. Charlemagne and the Carolingian educators greatly valued Bede's work and one of the most prominent of them, Alcuin, was taught at the school established in York by one of Bede's pupils, Bishop Ecgbert. The publishing drive formulated by Wearmouth-Jarrow to disseminate the Bible, which was extended to circulate Bede's works, was a major influence behind Alcuin's publication of his own edition of the Bible, copied at his monastery of Tours and distributed to other scriptoria throughout the Carolingian Empire for copying and distribution. His edition went on to form the mainstay of the theology syllabus of the medieval universities. But it was the Ceolfrith Bibles, and before them the Codex Grandior of Cassiodorus, that formed the inspiration for the great Touronian single-volume bibles and Alcuin at one point quotes an inscription accompanying the image of Ezra the Scribe in the Codex Amiatinus (see illus. 23), indicating that he may have seen it, or one of its two counterparts. Alcuin also praised Bede as an exemplar for monks and was instrumental in disseminating Bede's works within his circle.[3]

Bede became known as Venerable (*Beda Venerabilis*) by popular acclaim by the ninth century. Legend relates that the epithet was miraculously bestowed upon him by angels to complete his unfinished epitaph. Bede was grouped with others termed 'venerable' at two ecclesiastical councils held at Aachen in 816 and 836 and was the title was formalized at the Council of Aachen in 853. Paul the Deacon, an eighth-century Benedictine monk, scribe and historian of the Lombards, consistently used this title when referring to Bede and by the twelfth century this had become commonplace.

Bede's cult became prominent in England during the tenth-century monastic revival and by the fourteenth century his feast was celebrated in many English cathedrals. Wulfstan, Bishop of Worcester (*c.* 1008–1095), was a particular devotee of Bede's, dedicating a church to him in 1062 immediately after his consecration as bishop. Bede's body was translated from Jarrow to Durham Cathedral around 1020 and placed in St Cuthbert's tomb, alongside one of his own spiritual role models.

Bishop Eadfrith also rapidly achieved saintly status within the community. Symeon of Durham tells us that his bones, along with those of Cuthbert, Æthilwald and Eadberht, all of them bishops of Lindisfarne, were taken with the community when they left Holy Island in 875. They may even, like Eadberht's, have been deposited in Cuthbert's tomb. They were certainly reported to have joined Cuthbert in his coffin by 1104. A custodian of the shrine, Alfred Westou, who was active under Bishop Eadmund (1020–41) and into the time of Bishop Æthelwine (1056–71), acquired the bones of Billfrith the Anchorite (who is said to have made the treasure binding for the Lindisfarne Gospels) for Durham, along with those of Bede and Cuthbert's teacher, St Boisil of Melrose, as stated in a list of relics composed between 1104 and the mid-twelfth century.

Bede's relics were later moved to a shrine in the Galilee Chapel at Durham Cathedral in 1370. The shrine was destroyed in 1541 during the Reformation, but the bones were reburied in the chapel. In 1831 they were again dug up and Bede's were interred in a new tomb, imposing but elegant, which remains there to this day. Other of his relics were claimed by York, Glastonbury and Boniface's foundation of Fulda. What might Bede have thought of his earthly remains, which he had devoted to

xxxiii·cap·Quom·tpr mortalitatis moriente
puerum matri sanum restituerit.

49 St Cuthbert healing a child held by its mother, folio from a late 12th-century Durham copy of Bede's *Prose Life of St Cuthbert* (BL, Yates Thompson MS 26, f. 62v).

the labours of monastic humility, being enshrined in a place of high honour in the cathedral of the community of St Cuthbert, in whose book of life he had asked to be remembered? Cuthbert's shrine, the heart of the cult that Bede had assisted Bishop Eadfrith and the Lindisfarne community in creating, presides over the eastern end of the great cathedral, while Bede's watches over the western end, to which access for women, children and the humbler pilgrims was restricted within the cathedral. Bede surely would not mind this, for this was the very ministry for which he commended Cuthbert – and Christ.

Bede had died on the feast day of St Augustine of Canterbury and so, when he was venerated in England, he was either commemorated after Augustine on that day (26 May) or his feast was moved to 25 or 27 May. His scholarship and importance to Catholicism were recognized in 1899 when he was declared a Doctor of the Church – the only Englishman to have gained this honour. He is also the only Englishman in Dante's *Paradise* (x.130), where he is mentioned among theologians and Doctors of the Church in the same canto as Isidore of Seville and the Scotsman Richard of St Victor.

His feast day was included in the General Roman Calendar in 1899, for celebration on 27 May rather than on 26 May, which was by then the feast day of Pope Gregory VII. He is now venerated in both the Anglican and Catholic Church on 25 May and in the Eastern Orthodox Church on 27 May.

Bede's reputation as a historian remains prominent; he is celebrated with the annual Jarrow Lecture, which has been held at St Paul's Church, Jarrow, since 1958. English Heritage (with the driving passion of Professor Rosemary Cramp and others) created Bede's World (now part of Jarrow Hall Museum), a museum and Anglo-Saxon village/farm reconstruction celebrating Bede and his age, next to the site of that half of the twin monastery where he spent so much of his life. Architectural remains, sculpture, glass, manuscript facsimiles and other artefacts of Bede's age can be seen there and at St Peter's Monkwearmouth.

Bede's long-term legacy lies not only in creating a distinct identity for Northumbria and the 'English', or in bestowing order upon the fragmented narrative of the period when Roman Britain crumbled and its aftermath. It resides in his academic rigour in researching and ordering large bodies of data and his ability to combine deep thinking in the realm of the spiritual and scriptural and a fine literary and poetic style (in both Latin and Old English) with a scientific, mathematically based rigour and an experimental, enquiring approach to the world around him. He took the long view and is both remarkably joined up and nuanced in his thinking.

As he himself taught, there may be a literal meaning of a thing, but to understand its nature you need to peel away the layers and engage in multivalent interpretation. An onion may look like an onion, but you do not know what an onion is until you bite it and you do not understand it until you fathom its propensities, be it as a foodstuff, a flavouring, a medicinal aid preventing headache and hair loss, or a pigment for creating colour and beauty. If your mental reference library contains the necessary data, you will know that it was traditionally considered a powerful amulet for warding off disease, serpents and evil and as a historian you might know that the onion bulb was worshipped in ancient Egypt as a symbol of eternity, owing to its concentric rings. If you were of a poetic literary bent, you might also be aware of its humorous propensities (as in the ribald Riddle 25 of the Exeter Book).

Bede's love of literary pursuits and interest in the arts – underpinned by his belief in spirituality, pastoral ministry, social justice and good government – also led him to make a substantial contribution to the formation of the Cuthbertine cult, the making of its visual focus – the Lindisfarne Gospels – and the Ceolfrith Bibles, the supreme statement of the maturity of the early English

Church and its culture. His prime motivation behind these endeavours was, ultimately, the desire to attract others to the Christian faith by setting before them beautiful and uplifting models of the Gospel and what it means to live it. He was unafraid to raise his voice in protest and concern at injustice, abuse or misdirection of power and self-interest at the expense of others. To Bede we also owe the earliest translation of the gospels into a Western vernacular language – English – and the earliest extant written poetry in the English language: Caedmon's Hymn and his own deathbed elegy.

By the early tenth century a skilful abridgement of Bede's *Ecclesiastical History*, translated into the vernacular and known as the Old English Bede, had been made and was in circulation quite widely. It seems designed to instruct those who were not well educated enough to deal with Bede's elegant Latin and is in the Mercian dialect, indicating that it pre-dated the Alfredian revival of learning in the late ninth century, although it may well have been promoted and used by it, then and subsequently, in the creation of a unified England of the sort that Bede had first envisaged.[4]

Well may we imagine Bede, standing beneath moon and stars between the monastery and the glistening silver waters of Jarrow Slake, the light diffused from the small stained-glass windows of its two churches and the glow of tallow candles and domestic fires to his back, gazing up at the canopy of the heavens, picking out the constellations – Ursus Minor, Orion, the pulsating Pleiades – spotting Jupiter or Venus and assessing the Moon's waxing or waning state (not yet favourable tides for the ship's departure to Lindisfarne). Only an hour to go until daybreak and the singing of the divine office of lauds . . . What a union of the scholar-scientist's mind and the poet's heart would have occurred and what a thrilling chord of praise would have reverberated through his soul, perfectly in unison and union with

50 James Doyle Penrose, *The Last Chapter*, c. 1902, oil on canvas.

Creation. Aware of the triumphs and follies of history and fully committed to playing his part in addressing and repenting of them, he would surely have taken comfort in this vision of their littleness, and his, in the bigger picture of eternity, of which he was part, secure in the perpetual love of Logos. Bede may have looked 'through a glass darkly', but he saw further than most.

So let us leave the final words of wisdom to Brother Bede:

Bede's Death Song

Facing Death, that inescapable journey,
who can be wiser than he
who reflects, while breath yet remains,
on whether his life brought others happiness, or pains,
since his soul may yet win delight's or night's way
after his death-day.[5]

The original Old English text:

> Fore ðæm nedfere nænig wiorðe
> ðonc snottora ðon him ðearf siæ
> to ymbhycgenne ær his hinionge
> hwæt his gastæ godes oððe yfles
> æfter deað dæge doemed wiorðe.

APPENDIX: BEDE'S CV

Bede's list of his works

Bede wrote some forty works (or sixty, including others that have been ascribed to him by scholars from the Middle Ages to the present), most of which are still known, and he lists most of them – rather in the manner of a modern CV – in his autobiographical note at the end of the *Ecclesiastical History of the English People*. Some of the works listed have not survived and some that certainly seem to be by him are omitted, since some were completed after the *Ecclesiastical History*. It is unusual for such a list to be composed by an author at this date and likewise his autobiographical note. They are in keeping, however, with Bede's working methods and his intellectual rigour and they set out his credentials and his qualifications for his work.

The following is a translation of Bede's autobiographical note from the end of the *Ecclesiastical History*, V.24; this version is taken from A. M. Sellar, ed., *Bede's Ecclesiastical History of England* (London: George Bell and Sons, 1907), and can be found on the Project Gutenberg site at www.gutenberg.org. The original Latin titles are given in a separate list at the end.

> Thus much of the Ecclesiastical History of Britain, and more especially of the English nation, as far as I could learn either from the writings of the ancients, or the tradition of our forefathers, or of my own knowledge, with the help of the Lord, I, Bede, the servant of Christ, and priest of the monastery of the blessed Apostles, Peter and Paul, which is at Wearmouth and Jarrow, have set forth. Having been born in the territory of that same monastery, I was given, by the care of kinsmen, at seven years of age, to be educated by the most reverend Abbot Benedict, and afterwards by Ceolfrid, and spending all the remaining time of my life a dweller in that monastery, I wholly applied myself to the study of Scripture; and amidst the observance of monastic rule, and the daily charge of singing in the church, I always took delight in learning, or teaching, or writing. In the nineteenth year of my age, I received deacon's orders; in the thirtieth, those of the priesthood, both of them by the ministry of the most reverend Bishop John, and at the bidding of the Abbot Ceolfrid. From the time when

I received priest's orders, till the fifty-ninth year of my age, I have made it my business, for my own needs and those of my brethren, to compile out of the works of the venerable Fathers, the following brief notes on the Holy Scriptures, and also to make some additions after the manner of the meaning and interpretation given by them:

On the Beginning of Genesis, to the birth of Isaac and the casting out of Ishmael, four books.

Concerning the Tabernacle and its Vessels, and of the Vestments of the Priests, three books.

On the first part of Samuel, to the Death of Saul, three books.

Concerning the Building of the Temple, of Allegorical Exposition, and other matters, two books.

Likewise on the Book of Kings, thirty Questions.

On the Proverbs of Solomon, three books.

On the Song of Songs, seven books.

On Isaiah, Daniel, the twelve Prophets, and Part of Jeremiah, Divisions of Chapters, collected from the Treatise of the blessed Jerome.

On Ezra and Nehemiah, three books.

On the song of Habakkuk, one book.

On the Book of the blessed Father Tobias, one Book of Allegorical Explanation concerning Christ and the Church.

Also, Chapters of Readings on the Pentateuch of Moses, Joshua, and Judges.

On the Books of Kings and Chronicles.

On the Book of the blessed Father Job.

On the Proverbs, Ecclesiastes, and the Song of Songs.

On the Prophets Isaiah, Ezra, and Nehemiah.

On the Gospel of Mark, four books.

On the Gospel of Luke, six books.

Of Homilies on the Gospel, two books.

On the Apostle, whatsoever I have found in the works of St. Augustine I have taken heed to transcribe in order.

On the Acts of the Apostles, two books.

On the seven Catholic Epistles, a book on each.

On the Revelation of St. John, three books.

Likewise, Chapters of Lessons on all the New Testament, except the Gospel.

Likewise a book of Epistles to divers Persons, of which one is of the Six Ages of the world; one of the Halting-places of the Children of Israel; one on the words of Isaiah, 'And they shall be shut up in the prison, and after many days shall they be visited'; one of the Reason of Leap-Year, and one of the Equinox, according to Anatolius.

Likewise concerning the Histories of Saints: I translated the Book of the Life and Passion of St. Felix, Confessor, from the metrical work of Paulinus, into prose; the Book of the Life and Passion of St. Anastasius, which was ill translated from the Greek, and worse amended by some ignorant person, I have corrected as to the sense as far as I could; I have written the Life of the Holy Father Cuthbert, who was both monk and bishop, first in heroic verse, and afterwards in prose.

The History of the Abbots of this monastery, in which I rejoice to serve the Divine Goodness, to wit, Benedict, Ceolfrid, and Huaetbert, in two books.

The Ecclesiastical History of our Island and Nation, in five books.

The Martyrology of the Festivals of the Holy Martyrs, in which I have carefully endeavoured to set down all whom I could find, and not only on what day, but also by what sort of combat, and under what judge they overcame the world.

A Book of Hymns in divers sorts of metre, or rhythm.

A Book of Epigrams in heroic or elegiac verse.

Of the Nature of Things, and of the Times, one book of each; likewise, of the Times, one larger book.

A book of Orthography arranged in Alphabetical Order.

Likewise a Book of the Art of Poetry, and to it I have added another little Book of Figures of Speech or Tropes; that is, of the Figures and Modes of Speech in which the Holy Scriptures are written.

And I beseech Thee, good Jesus, that to whom Thou hast graciously granted sweetly to drink in the words of Thy knowledge, Thou wilt also vouchsafe in Thy loving-kindness that he may one day come to Thee, the Fountain of all wisdom, and appear for ever before Thy face.

Bede's list of his works, as cited by him in Latin in his autobiographical note, along with English translations in verbatim and modern short forms

In principium Genesis, usque ad natiuitatem Isaac et eiectionem Ismahelis, libros III

On the beginning of Genesis, to the nativity of Isaac, and the reprobation of Ismael, three books. (*Commentary on Genesis*)

De tabernaculo et uasis eius, ac uestibus sacerdotum, libros III.
Of the tabernacle and its vessels, and of the priestly vestments, three books. (*On the Tabernacle*)

In primam partem Samuelis, id est usque ad mortem Saulis, libros III.
On the first part of Samuel, to the death of Saul, four books. (*Commentary on Samuel*)

De aedificatione templi, allegoricae expositionis, sicut et cetera, libros II.
Of the building of the temple, of allegorical exposition, like the rest, two books. (*On the Temple*)

Item, in Regum librum XXX quaestionum.
Item, on the book of Kings, thirty questions. (*Thirty Questions*)

In Proverbia salomonis libros III.
On Solomon's Proverbs, three books. (*Commentary on Proverbs*)

In Cantica canticorum libros VII.
On the Canticles, seven books. (*Commentary on the Song of Songs*)

In Isaiam, Danihelem, XII prophetas, et partem Hieremiae, distinctiones capitulorum ex tractatu beati Hieronimi excerptas.
On Isaiah, Daniel, the twelve prophets, and part of Jeremiah, distinction of chapters, collected out of St Jerome's treatise (no manuscript survives)

In Ezram et Neemiam libros III.
On Esdras and Nehemiah, three books. (*Commentary on Ezra and Nehemiah*)

In Canticum Habacum librum I.
On the song of Habakkuk, one book. (*Commentary on the Prayer of Habakkuk*)

In librum beati patris Tobiae explanationis allegoricae de Christo et ecclesia librum I.
On the book of the blessed father Tobias, one book of allegorical exposition concerning Christ and the Church. (*Commentary on Tobias*)

Item, Capitula lectionum in Pentateucum Mosi, Iosue, Iudicum
Also, chapters of readings on Moses's Pentateuch, Joshua, and Judges (no manuscript survives)

In libros Regum et Uerba dierum
On the books of Kings and Chronicles (no manuscript survives)

In librum beati patris Iob
On the book of the blessed father Job (no manuscript survives)

In Parabolas, Ecclesiasten, et Cantica canticorum
On the parables, Ecclesiastes, and canticles (no manuscript survives)

In Isaiam prophetam, Ezram quoque et Neemiam
On the prophets Isaiah, Esdras, and Nehemiah (no manuscript survives)

In euangelium Marci libros IIII.
On the gospel of Mark, four books. (*Commentary on Mark*)

In euangelium Lucae libros VI.
On the gospel of Luke, six books. (*Commentary on Luke*)

Omeliarum euangelii libros II.
Of homilies on the gospel, two books. (*The Homilies*)

In apostolum quaecumque in opusculis sancti Augustini exposita inveni, cuncta per ordinem transscribere curavi.
On the Apostle, I have carefully transcribed in order all that I have found in St Augustine's works. (*Collectaneum on the Pauline Epistles*)

In Actus apostolorum libros II.
On the Acts of the Apostles, two books. (*Commentary on Acts and Retractation*)

In Epistolas VII catholicas libros singulos.
On the seven catholic epistles, a book on each. (*Commentary on the Catholic Epistles*)

In Apocalypsin sancti Iohannis libros III.
On the Revelation of St. John, three books. (*Commentary on the Apocalypse*)

Item, Capitula lectionum in totum nouum testamentum, excepto euangelio.
Also, chapters of readings on all the New Testament, except the Gospel (no manuscript survives)

Item librum epistularum ad diuersos: quarum de sex aetatibus saeculi una est; de mansionibus filiorum Israel una; una de eo, quod ait Isaias: 'Et claudentur ibi in carcerem, et post dies multos uisitabantur;' de ratione bissexti una; de aequinoctio iuxta Anatolium una.
Also a book of epistles to different persons, of which one is of the six ages of the world; one of the mansions of the children of Israel; one on the works of Isaiah, 'And they shall be shut up in the prison, and after many days shall they be visited'; one of the reasons of the bissextile or leap-year; and of the equinox, according to Anatolius. (Letter to Plegwin; Letter to Acca 'de mansionibus filiorum Israhel'; Letter to Acca 'de eo quod ait Isaias'; Letter to Helmwald; Letter to Wicthede)

Item de historiis sanctorum: librum uitae et passionis sancti Felicis confessoris de metrico Paulini opere in prosam transtuli
Also, of the histories of saints. I translated the book of the life and passion of St Felix, Confessor, from Paulinus's work in metre, into prose. (Life of St Felix)

Librum uitae et passionis sancti Anastasii, male de Greco translatum, et peius a quodam inperito emendatum, prout potui, ad sensum correxi
The book of the life and passion of St Anastasius, which was ill translated from the Greek, and worse amended by some unskilful person, I have corrected as to the sense. (Life of St Anastasius)

Uitam sancti patris monachi simul et antistitis Cudbercti, et prius heroico metro et postmodum plano sermone, descripsi.
I have written the life of the holy father Cuthbert, who was both monk and prelate, first in heroic verse, and then in prose. (verse Life of St Cuthbert and prose Life of St Cuthbert)

Historiam abbatum monasterii huius, in quo supernae pietati deseruire gaudeo, Benedicti, Ceolfridi, et Huaetbercti in libellis duobus.
The history of the Abbots of this monastery, in which I rejoice to serve the divine goodness, viz. Benedict, Ceolfrith, and Hwaetberht, in two books. (*History of the Abbots of Wearmouth and Jarrow*)

Historiam ecclesiasticam nostrae insulae ac gentis in libris v.
The ecclesiastical history of our island and nation, in five books. (*The Ecclesiastical History of the English People*)

Martyrologium de nataliciis sanctorum martyrum diebus; in quo omnes, quos inuenire potui, non-solum qua die, uerum etiam quo genere certaminis, uel sub quo iudice mundum uicerint, diligenter adnotare studui.
The martyrology of the birth-days of the holy martyrs, in which I have carefully endeavoured to set down all that I could find, and not only on what day, but also by what sort of combat, or under what judge they overcame the world. (*The Martyrology*)

Librum hymnorum diuerso metro siue rhythmo.
A book of hymns in several sorts of metre or rhyme. (*The Book of Hymns*)

Librum epigrammatum heroico metro, siue elegiaco.
A book of epigrams in heroic or elegiac verse. (*Book of Epigrams*)

De natura rerum, et de temporibus libros singulos
Of the nature of things, and of the times, one book of each. (*On the Nature of Things* and *On Times*)

Item de temporibus librum I maiorem
Also, of the times, one larger book. (*On the Reckoning of Time*)

Librum de orthographia, alfabeti ordine distinctum
A book of orthography digested in alphabetical order. (*Book of Orthography*)

Item librum de metrica arte, et huic adiectum alium de schematibus siue tropis libellum, hoc est de figuris modisque locutionum, quibus scriptura sancta contexta est.
Also a book of the art of poetry, and to it I have added another little book of tropes and figures; that is, of the figures and manners of speaking in which the holy scriptures are written. (*The Art of Poetry* and *On Tropes and Figures*)

The ascribed works, which are not mentioned by Bede, include:

On the Holy Places
Letter to Albinus
Letter to Bishop Ecgbert
De die iudicii (On Judgement Day)
A poem in thirteen couplets
Paenitentiale Bedae (Bede's Penitential)

REFERENCES

Introduction

1 Bede, *Ecclesiastical History of the English People*, ed. L. Sherley-Price, revd R. Latham and D. H. Farmer (Harmondsworth, 1990), p. 329.
2 A. Mann, 'What Is the Theory of Everything?', *Space* (29 August 2019), at www.space.com.
3 This is a device previously employed by another eminent historian of the post-Roman period, Gregory of Tours.
4 The conception of Christ, celebrated on 25 March, rather than the Nativity. Bede was building on a system introduced by Dionysius Exiguus in the sixth century.

1 Boyhood and Background

1 J. Insley, 'Portesmutha', in *Reallexikon der Germanischen Altertumskunde*, vol. XXIII (Berlin and Boston, MA, 2003), p. 29.
2 N. J. Higham, *(Re-)Reading Bede: The Historia Ecclesiastica in Context* (London and New York, 2006), pp. 8–9.
3 M. Lapidge and B. Bishchoff, *Biblical Commentaries from the Canterbury School of Theodore and Hadrian* (Cambridge, 1994); M. Lapidge, ed., *Archbishop Theodore: Commemorative Studies on His Life and Influence* (Cambridge, 1995). See also D. Howlett, 'Hellenic Learning in Insular Latin: An Essay on Supported Claims', *Peritia*, 12 (1998), pp. 54–78, W. Berschin, *Griechisch-Lateinisches Mittelalter* (Berne, 1980), and M. C. Bodden, 'Evidence for the Knowledge of Greek in Anglo-Saxon England', *Anglo-Saxon England*, XVII (1988), pp. 217–46.
4 M. P. Brown, 'Reading the Lindisfarne Gospels: Text, Image, Context', in *From Holy Island to Durham: The Contexts and Meanings of the Lindisfarne Gospels*, ed. R. G. Gameson (London, 2013), pp. 84–95.
5 R. J. Cramp, *Wearmouth and Jarrow Monastic Sites*, vol. I (London, 2005) and vol. II (London, 2006).
6 'Monkwearmouth Anglo-Saxon Monastery and Medieval Priory', https://historicengland.org.uk, accessed 19 December 2022.

7 See S. DeGregorio, ed., *The Cambridge Companion to Bede* (Cambridge, 2010), pp. 136–7.
8 See D. Ayerst and A.S.T. Fisher, *Records of Christianity*, vol. II: *Christendom* (Oxford, 1977), pp. 101–2; C. Chazelle, 'Pictures, Books and the Illiterate: Pope Gregory I's Letters to Serenus of Marseilles', *Word and Image*, VI/2 (1990), pp. 138–53. See also M. P. Brown, 'Images to Be Read and Words to Be Seen: The Iconic Role of the Early Medieval Book', in *Iconic Books and Texts*, ed. J. W. Watts (Sheffield and Bristol, CT, 2013), pp. 93–108, and 'The Image in Its Place: Forms and Functions of Illumination', in *La Fisonomía del Libro Medieval y Moderno*, ed. M.J.P. Gracia, C. S. Oliveira and A. G. Gonzalo (Zaragoza, 2019), pp. 39–58.
9 Bede, *Lives of the Abbots*, in D. H. Farmer, ed., *The Age of Bede*, revd edn (Harmondsworth, 1998), p. 188.
10 Bede, *Lives of the Abbots*, ch. 15; Farmer, *Age of Bede*, p. 201.
11 Tomás Ó Carragáin, *Churches in Early Medieval Ireland: Architecture, Ritual and Memory* (New Haven, CT, and London, 2010) and *Churches in the Irish Landscape, AD 400–1100* (Cork, 2021).
12 J. O'Sullivan and Tomás Ó Carragáin, *Inishmurray: Monks and Pilgrims in an Atlantic Landscape*, vol. I: *Archaeological Survey and Excavations, 1997–2000* (Cork, 2008).
13 Bede, *On 1 Samuel*, preface to Book IV, Corpus Christianorum Series Latina 119.

2 Bede the Monk and Priest

1 G. H. Brown, *Bede the Educator*, Jarrow Lecture 1996 (Newcastle upon Tyne, 1996).
2 Sister Benedicta Ward argues that these passages are Bede employing a rhetorical device, in *The Venerable Bede: Outstanding Christian Thinkers* (London and Harrisburg, PA, 1990), p. 57.
3 M. P. Brown, 'Imagining, Imaging and Experiencing the East in Insular and Anglo-Saxon Cultures: New Evidence for Contact', in *Anglo-Saxon England and the Visual Imagination, ISAS 6, Proceedings of the ISAS Conference, Madison, 2012*, ed. J. D. Niles, S. Klein and J. Wilcox (Tempe, AZ, 2016), pp. 49–84. M. P. Brown, 'The Bridge in the Desert: Towards Establishing an Historical Context for the Newly Discovered Latin Manuscripts of St Catherine's Sinai', in *Palaeography Between East and West*, ed. A. d'Ottone Rambach, *Rivista degli studi orientali*, New Series Supplement no. 1 (2018), pp. 73–98. M. P. Brown, *The Latin Manuscripts of the Holy Monastery*

of St Catherine, Sinai: A New Reading of Early East-West Relations (forthcoming).

4 A. G. Holder, 'Bede and the New Testament', in S. DeGregorio, *The Cambridge Companion to Bede* (Cambridge, 2010), pp. 142–55, at p. 146.

3 Bede the Scholar and Scientist: Cosmos and Logos

1 On this subject, see E. Ahern, *Bede and the Cosmos: Theology and Nature in the Eighth Century* (London and New York, 2020). See also the excellent overview by F. Wallis, 'Bede and Science', in *The Cambridge Companion to Bede*, ed. S. DeGregorio (Cambridge, 2010), pp. 113–26, at p. 120.

2 *Adomnán, De locis sanctis*, ed. D. Meehan, *Scriptores Latini Hiberniae* 3, 3 vols (Dublin, 1958); Bede, *Liber de locis sanctis*, ed. P. Geyer, CSEL 39 (1898); T. O'Loughlin, *Adomnán and the Holy Places: The Perceptions of an Insular Monk on the Location of the Biblical Drama* (London, 2007); J. R. Macpherson, trans., *The Pilgrimage of Arculfus in the Holy Land, about the Year* AD 670, Palestine Pilgrims' Text Society 3 (London, 1895).

3 M. P. Brown, 'Imagining, Imaging and Experiencing the East in Insular and Anglo-Saxon Cultures: New Evidence for Contact', in *Anglo-Saxon England and the Visual Imagination*, ISAS 6, *Proceedings of the* ISAS *Conference, Madison, 2012*, ed. J. D. Niles, S. Klein and J. Wilcox (Tempe, AZ, 2016), pp. 49–84; M. P. Brown, 'The Bridge in the Desert: Towards Establishing an Historical Context for the Newly Discovered Latin Manuscripts of St Catherine's Sinai', in *Palaeography Between East and West*, ed. A. d'Ottone Rambach, *Rivista degli studi orientali*, New Series Supplement no. 1 (2018).

4 R. Love, 'The Library of the Venerable Bede', in *The History of the Book in Britain*, vol. I: *c.* 400–1100, ed. R. G. Gameson (Cambridge, 2011), pp. 606–32; M. Lapidge, *The Anglo-Saxon Library* (Oxford, 2006), p. 37; G. H. Brown, *Bede the Educator*, Jarrow Lecture 1996 (Newcastle upon Tyne, 1996), p. 3.

5 Brown, 'The Bridge in the Desert', pp. 73–98.

6 Brown, 'Imagining, Imaging and Experiencing the East in Insular and Anglo-Saxon Cultures'.

7 C. W. Jones, 'The "Lost" Sirmond Manuscript of Bede's Computus', *English Historical Review*, LII/206 (1937), pp. 204–19. On the Irish background to Bedan computes, see D. Ó Cróinin, 'The Irish Provenance of Bede's Computus', *Peritia*, 2 (1983), pp. 238–42,

and D. Ó Cróinin, ed., *Early Irish History and Chronology* (Dublin, 2003).

8 H. Härke, 'Astronomical and Atmospheric Observations in the Anglo-Saxon Chronicle and in Bede', *Antiquarian Astronomer: Journal of the Society for the History of Astronomy*, VI (January 2012), pp. 34–43.

9 Ibid.

10 M. P. Brown, 'Reading the Lindisfarne Gospels: Text, Image, Context', in *From Holy Island to Durham: The Contexts and Meanings of The Lindisfarne Gospels*, ed. R. G. Gameson (London, 2013), pp. 84–95. On computus and context, see M. MacCarron, *Bede and Time: Computus, Theology and History in the Early Medieval World* (London and New York, 2020).

11 L. Holford-Strevens, *The History of Time: A Very Short Introduction* (Oxford, 2005), pp. 49–51; G. Declercq, *Anno Domini: The Origins of the Christian Era* (Turnhout, 2000), pp. 152–3; A. A. Mosshammer, *The Easter Computus and the Origins of the Christian Era* (Oxford, 2009), pp. 254, 270, 328.

12 R. Landes, 'Lest the Millennium Be Fulfilled: Apocalyptic Expectations and the Pattern of Western Chronography, 100–800 CE', in *The Use and Abuse of Eschatology in the Middle Ages*, ed. W. Verbeke, C. Verhelst and A. Welkenhuysen (Leuven, 1988), pp. 137–209.

13 F. Wallis, 'Bede and Science', in *The Cambridge Companion to Bede*, ed. S. DeGregorio (Cambridge, 2010), pp. 113–26, at p. 120.

14 From *Cuthbert's Letter on the Death of Bede*, in B. Colgrave and R. Mynors, eds, *Oxford Medieval Texts: Bede's Ecclesiastical History of the English People* (Oxford, 1969), pp. 582–3. There may be another meaning implicit here though, for Bede had earlier, in his *On the Nature of Things*, conducted a critique and reworking of Isidore's work of the same name, using Pliny's work as a corrective. Might he have been translating those excerpts that, at the end of his life, he considered to be the useful filleted core of Isidore's contribution in this area, for the use of his students, that they might not expend effort on grappling with passages he considered unprofitable? – a teacher to the last!

15 D. Hurst, ed., *Bede, Expositio in Lucam*, CCSL 120, prol. 93–115; M. Stansbury, 'Early Medieval Biblical Commentaries, Their Writers and Readers', in *Frümittelalterliche Studien, Herausgegeben von H. Keller und C. Meier*, ed. K. Hauck (Berlin and New York, 1999), pp. 50–82, at p. 72. For discussions of the depiction of the

evangelists in Insular art, see, for example, M. P. Brown, *The Book of Cerne: Prayer, Patronage and Power in Ninth-Century England* (London and Toronto, 1996), pp. 82–114, and J. O'Reilly, 'Patristic and Insular Traditions of the Evangelists: Exegesis and Iconography', in *Le Isole Britanniche e Roma in Età Romanobarbarica*, ed. A. M. Luiselli and E. O Carragáin (Rome, 1998), pp. 49–94; M. P. Brown, 'Embodying Exegesis: Depictions of the Evangelists in Insular Manuscripts', in A. M. Luiselli and E. O Carragàin, eds, *Quadrini di Romania Barbarica* (Rome, 1999).

16 D. Howlett, *The Celtic Latin Tradition of Biblical Style* (Dublin, 1995) and 'The Start of the Anglo-Latin Tradition', in *Latin in Medieval Britain*, ed. Richard Ashdowne and Carolinne White (London, 2017).

17 M.L.W. Laistner, 'The Library of the Venerable Bede', in *Bede: His Life, Times and Writings*, ed. A. H. Thompson (Oxford, 1935; reissued New York, 1966), pp. 237–66, at pp. 263–6. See also Love, 'The Library of the Venerable Bede'.

18 M. Smyth, *Understanding the Universe in Seventh-Century Ireland* (Woodbridge, 1996), see index, under Bede.

19 L. Webster, *Franks Casket* (London, 2012).

20 *Encyclopaedia Judaica* (2008); L. M. Surhone, M. T. Timpledon and S. F. Marseken, eds, *Pardes (Jewish Exegesis)* (Beau Bassin, 2010).

21 C. A. Farr, *The Book of Kells and Its Audience* (London and Toronto, 1997). See also Brown, *The Book of Cerne*.

22 M. P. Brown, 'The Image in Its Place: Forms and Functions of Illumination', in *La Fisonomía del Libro Medieval y Moderno*, ed. M.J.P. Gracia, C. S. Oliveira and A. G. Gonzalo (Zaragoza, 2019), pp. 39–58.

23 P. W. Conner, *Anglo-Saxon Exeter: A Tenth-Century Cultural History*, Studies in Anglo-Saxon History (Woodbridge, 1993).

24 G. P. Krapp and E. Van Kirk Dobbie, eds, *The Exeter Book*, *The Anglo-Saxon Poetic Records* (New York, 1936), vol. III, p. 193.

25 Gregory the Great, *Moralia in Iob*, 2 vols, *Corpus Christianorum Series Latina*, 143, I.3.110–115 4.

26 Brown, 'Reading the Lindisfarne Gospels', pp. 79–90.

4 Bede, Poetry and the Origins of Written English

1 C. B. Kendall, 'Bede and Education', in *The Cambridge Companion to Bede*, ed. S. DeGregorio (Cambridge, 2010), pp. 99–112, at p. 107.

2 J. A. Giles, *Venerabilis Bedae Opera*, vol. VI (London, 1843); see https://sourcebooks.fordham.edu/basis/bede-cuthbert.asp, accessed 7 February 2022.

3 C. Stancliffe, 'Disputed Episcopacy: Bede, Acca and the Relationship Between Stephen's *Life of St Wilfrid* and the Early Prose Lives of St Cuthbert', *Anglo-Saxon England*, XLI (2013), pp. 7–39.

4 Kendall, 'Bede and Education', p. 112.

5 From the Moore Bede, *Ecclesiastical History*, Cambridge University Library, MS Kk.5.16.

6 See D. R. Howlett, 'The Structure of "The Dream of the Rood"', *Studia Neophilologica*, XLVIII/2 (1976), pp. 301–6, and É. Ó Carragáin, *Ritual and the Rood: Liturgical Images and the Old English Poems of the Dream of the Rood Tradition* (London and Toronto, 2005).

7 *The Dream of the Rood*, trans. Richard Hamer, in *A Choice of Anglo-Saxon Verse* (London, 1970).

8 M. P. Brown, *The Lindisfarne Gospels: Society, Spirituality and the Scribe* (London, Lucerne and Toronto, 2003); M. P. Brown, '"A good woman's son": Aspects of Aldred's Agenda in Glossing the Lindisfarne Gospels', in *The Old English Gloss to the Lindisfarne Gospels* (ANGB 51), ed. Julia Fernández Cuesta and Sara M. Pons-Sanz (Berlin and Boston, 2016), pp. 13–36.

9 Julia Fernández-Cuesta and Nieves Rodríguez-Ledesma, 'Reduced Forms in the Nominal Morphology of the Lindisfarne Gospel Gloss: A Case of Accusative/Dative Syncretism?', *Folia Linguistica Historica*, XLI/1 (2020), pp. 37–65, at pp. 60–61.

10 W.J.P. Boyd, *Aldred's Marginalia: Explanatory Comments in the Lindisfarne Gospels* (Exeter, 1975).

11 See A.S.C. Ross, 'A Connection between Bede and the Anglo-Saxon Gloss to the Lindisfarne Gospels?', *Journal of Theological Studies*, XX/2 (1969), pp. 482–94, and 'Supplementary Note to "A Connection between Bede and the Anglo-Saxon Gloss to the Lindisfarne Gospels?"', *Journal of Theological Studies*, XXIV/2 (1973), pp. 519–21.

5 Bede the English Patristic

1 A.S.C. Ross, 'A Connection between Bede and the Anglo-Saxon Gloss to the Lindisfarne Gospels?', *Journal of Theological Studies*, XX/2 (1969), pp. 482–94; 'Supplementary Note to "A Connection between Bede and the Anglo-Saxon Gloss to the Lindisfarne Gospels?"', *Journal of Theological Studies*, XXIV/2 (1973), pp. 519–21.

2 S. DeGregorio, 'Bede and the Old Testament', in *The Cambridge Companion to Bede*, ed. S. DeGregorio (Cambridge, 2010), pp. 127–41; and A. G. Holder, 'Bede and the New Testament', in *The Cambridge Companion to Bede*, ed. DeGregorio, pp. 142–55.
3 T. J. Brown, ed., *The Stonyhurst Gospel of Saint John* (Oxford, 1969); C. Breay and B. Meehan, eds, *The St Cuthbert Gospel: Studies on the Insular Manuscript of the Gospel of John* (London, 2015).
4 M. P. Brown, 'House-Style in the Scriptorium: Scribal Reality and Scholarly Myth', in *Anglo-Saxon Styles*, ed. G. Brown and C. Karkov (New York, 2003), pp. 131–50.
5 For an online version of Bede's prose Life of St Cuthbert, see https://sourcebooks.fordham.edu/basis/bede-cuthbert.asp, accessed 7 February 2022.
6 Sister B. Ward, '"In medium duorum animalium": Bede and Jerome on the Canticle of Habakkuk', *Studia Patristica*, XXV (1993), pp. 189–93. It was earlier discussed in John Gill's *Exposition of the Bible*: see www.biblestudytools.com, accessed May 2022. Gill (1697–1771) was an English Baptist pastor and theologian.
7 For an online version of Bede's prose Life of St Cuthbert, see https://sourcebooks.fordham.edu/basis/bede-cuthbert.asp.
8 L. T. Martin, 'Bede and Preaching', in *The Cambridge Companion to Bede*, ed. DeGregorio, pp. 156–69, at p. 168.
9 Ibid., at p. 162.
10 *Bede: On the Song of Songs and Other Spiritual Writings*, trans. A. Holder, Classics of Western Spirituality (New York, 2011), p. 251; see DeGregorio, 'Bede and the Old Testament', p. 130.
11 M.L.W. Laistner and H. H. King, *A Hand-List of Bede Manuscripts* (Ithaca, NY, 1943), p. 87.
12 Ibid., p. 62.
13 M. P. Brown, *The Book of Cerne: Prayer, Patronage and Power in Ninth-Century England* (London and Toronto, 1996).
14 See Bede, *On Ezra and Nehemiah*, trans. S. DeGregorio (Liverpool, 2006), pp. 138–9.
15 DeGregorio, 'Bede and the Old Testament', pp. 127–41.

6 Bede the Historian and Reformer

1 J. H. Wallace-Hadrill, 'Gregory of Tours and Bede: Their Views on the Personal Qualities of Kings', *Frühmittelalterliche Studien*, II/1 (1968), pp. 31–44.

2 C. Stancliffe, 'Disputed Episcopacy: Bede, Acca and the Relationship Between Stephen's *Life of St Wilfrid* and the Early Prose Lives of St Cuthbert', *Anglo-Saxon England*, XLI (2013), pp. 7–39.
3 M. P. Brown and L. Webster, eds, *The Transformation of the Roman World* (London, 1997).
4 M. P. Brown, *The British Library Guide to Writing and Scripts: History and Techniques* (London and Toronto, 1998).
5 M. P. Brown, 'Mercian Manuscripts: The Implications of the Staffordshire Hoard, Other Recent Discoveries, and the "New Materiality"', Inaugural Lecture to the Chair of Medieval Manuscript Studies, School of Advanced Study, University of London, 22 June 2010, in *Writing in Context: Insular Manuscript Culture, 500–1200*, ed. E. Kwakkel (Leiden, 2013), pp. 23–66.

7 Bede the 'Scribe of Scripture' and the Making of the Ceolfrith Bibles

1 C. de Hamel, *Meetings with Remarkable Manuscripts* (London, 2016).
2 G. B. de Rossi, *La Bibbia offerta da Ceolfrido Abbate al Sepolchro di S. Pietro. Al Sommo Pontefice Leone XIII omaggio giubilare della Biblioteca Vaticana* (Vatican City, 1888), pp. 1–22. For a summary of the issue, see R. Bruce-Mitford, *The Art of the Codex Amiatinus*, Jarrow Lecture (Newcastle upon Tyne, 1967), and P. J. Nordhagen, *The Codex Amiatinus and the Byzantine Element in the Northumbrian Renaissance*, Jarrow Lecture (Newcastle upon Tyne, 1977).
3 C. Chazelle, 'Ceolfrid's Gift to St Peter: The First Quire of the Codex Amiatinus and the Evidence of Its Roman Destination', *Early Medieval Europe*, XII/2 (2003), pp. 129–57; C. Chazelle, 'Christ and the Vision of God: The Biblical Diagrams of the Codex Amiatinus', in *The Mind's Eye: Art and Theological Argument in the Middle Ages*, ed. J. F. Hamburger and A.-M. Bouché (Princeton, NJ, 2006), pp. 84–111; K. Corsano, 'The First Quire of the Codex Amiatinus and the Institutiones of Cassiodorus', *Scriptorium*, XLI/1 (1987), pp. 3–34; P. Meyvaert, 'Bede, Cassiodorus, and the Codex Amiatinus', *Speculum*, LXXI/4 (1996), pp. 827–83; P. Meyvaert, 'The Date of Bede's *In Ezram* and His Image of Ezra in the Codex Amiatinus', *Speculum*, LXXX/4 (2005), pp. 1087–133.
4 For the Codex Amiatinus, see J.J.G. Alexander, *Insular Manuscripts, 6th to the 9th Century* (London, 1978), no. 7. For a brief discussion of the surviving remnants of the Ceolfrith Bibles and the Worcester

connection, see L. Webster and J. M. Backhouse, eds, *The Making of England: Anglo-Saxon Art and Culture*, exh. cat. British Museum (London, 1991), pp. 122–3, and, especially for the Offa connection, see M. P. Brown, *The Book of Cerne: Prayer, Patronage and Power in Ninth-Century England* (London and Toronto, 1996), p. 166. On Ceolfrith's commission, see I. Wood, *The Most Holy Abbot, Ceolfrid*, Jarrow Lecture (Newcastle upon Tyne, 1995).

5 W. Davies, *An Early Welsh Microcosm: Studies in the Llandaff Charters* (London, 1978).

6 J. O'Reilly, 'The Library of Scripture: Views from the Vivarium and Wearmouth-Jarrow', in *New Offerings, Ancient Treasures: Essays in Medieval Art for George Henderson*, ed. P. Binski and W. G. Noel (Stroud, 2001). See also M. Walsh and D. O Cróinín, eds, *Cummian's Letter De controversia Paschali* (Toronto, 1988), pp. 15–18, 57–9.

7 M. P. Brown, '"In the Beginning was the Word": Books and Faith in the Age of Bede', Jarrow Lecture, 2000 (Newcastle upon Tyne, 2000).

8 Ibid.; M. P. Brown, *The Lindisfarne Gospels: Society, Spirituality and the Scribe* (London, Lucerne and Toronto, 2003); and M. P. Brown, 'Reading the Lindisfarne Gospels: Text, Image, Context', in *From Holy Island to Durham: The Contexts and Meanings of The Lindisfarne Gospels*, ed. R. G. Gameson (London, 2013), pp. 84–95.

9 Brown, '"In the Beginning was the Word"'.

10 D. H. Farmer, ed., *The Age of Bede* (Harmondsworth, 1983; revd edn 1998), p. 35; E. A. Lowe, *English Uncial* (Oxford, 1960); M. P. Brown, 'Writing in the Insular World', in *The History of the Book in Britain*, vol. I: *c*. 400–1100, ed. R. G. Gameson (Cambridge, 2011).

11 The St Cuthbert Gospel (formerly known as the Stonyhurst Gospel), now BL, Add. MS 89000; see T. J. Brown et al., *The Stonyhurst Gospel of St John* (Oxford, 1969) and C. Breay and B. Meehan, eds, *The St Cuthbert Gospel: Studies on the Insular Manuscript of the Gospel of John* (London, 2015).

12 M. P. Brown, 'The Eastwardness of Things: Relationships between the Christian Cultures of the Middle East and the Insular World', in *The Genesis of Books: Studies in the Interactions of Words, Text, and Print in Honor of A. N. Doane*, ed. M. Hussey and J. D. Niles (Turnhout, 2011); M. P. Brown, 'Concealed and Revealed: Insular Visualisations of the Word', in *Clothing Sacred Scriptures*, ed. D. Ganz and B. Schellewald (Berlin and Boston, MA, 2018), pp. 69–80.

13 E. A. Lowe, *Codices Latini Antiquiores* (11 vols and suppl., Oxford, 1934–72), 2.251.

14 A. J. Piper, 'The First Generations of Durham Monks and the Cult of St Cuthbert', in *St. Cuthbert, His Cult and His Community to AD 1200*, ed. G. Bonner, D. Rollason and C. Stancliffe (Woodbridge, 1989), pp. 437–46.

15 M. P. Brown, 'House-Style in the Scriptorium: Scribal Reality and Scholarly Myth', in *Anglo-Saxon Styles*, ed. G. Brown and C. Karkov (New York, 2003), pp. 131–50.

16 National Library of Russia, St Petersburg, MS Lat. Q. v. I. 18, see J.J.G. Alexander, *Insular Manuscripts* (London, 1978), no. 19; Lowe, *Codices Latini Antiquiores*, 11.1621. This manuscript contains one of the earliest examples of a historiated (storytelling) initial depicting a nimbed saint, thought to be Augustine of Canterbury or, more likely, Gregory the Great.

17 E. A. Lowe, 'An Autograph of the Venerable Bede', *Revue Bénédictine*, 68 (1958), pp. 199–202.

18 Cambridge University Library, MS Kk.5.16; Lowe, *Codices Latini Antiquiores*, 2.139.

19 E. A. Lowe, *Codices Latini Antiquiores*, Suppl. 1703. The initials in this and the St Petersburg manuscript have coloured panelled infills recalling the stained glass of Wearmouth-Jarrow.

20 There is debate among scholars as to the palaeographical dating, Parkes favouring a dating of c. 746 for the St Petersburg copy, with the Moore Bede following soon after and Tiberius A.xiv a decade or so later: see M. B. Parkes, *The Scriptorium of Wearmouth-Jarrow*, Jarrow Lecture, 1982 (Newcastle upon Tyne, 1982). Dumville, however, has argued for a later dating of the group commencing in the 760s: see D. N. Dumville, 'The Two Earliest Manuscripts of Bede's Ecclesiastical History', *Anglo-Saxon*, 1 (2007), pp. 55–108. The earlier dating would tie in better with the context of the scriptorium's activity in the field of uncial book production during the late seventh and early eighth centuries, and with its relationship with Holy Island around the time of the making of the Lindisfarne Gospels, c. 715–22: see M. P. Brown, *The Lindisfarne Gospels* (London, Lucerne and Toronto, 2003).

21 For an introduction to the manuscript culture of the Insular age, see M. P. Brown, *Manuscripts from the Anglo-Saxon Age* (London and Toronto, 2008).

22 E. Bhreathnach, 'Abbesses, Minor Dynasties and Kings In Clericatu: Perspectives of Ireland, 700–850', in *Mercia, an Anglo-Saxon Kingdom in Europe*, ed. M. P. Brown and C. A. Farr (Woodbridge, 2001), pp. 113–25.

23 See Lowe, *Codices Latini Antiquiores*, 2.235.
24 M. P. Brown, '"In the Beginning was the Word"'; Wood, *The Most Holy Abbot, Ceolfrid*; Brown, 'House-Style in the Scriptorium'; Brown, 'Writing in the Insular World'.
25 Cassiodorus' Commentary on Psalm 44/45:1–2 and *De institutione divinarum litterarum*, ch. 30; see Fridh, *Magni Aurelii*, CCSL 96; J. P. Migne, *Patrologiae cursus completus*, 70 (Paris, 1847), cols 1144–5; D. Ayerst and A.S.T. Fisher, *Records of Christianity*, vol. II: *Christendom* (Oxford, 1977), p. 14.
26 O'Reilly, 'Library of Scripture'.
27 C. Kraeling, *The Synagogue [The Excavations at Dura-Europos Conducted by Yale University and the French Academy of Inscriptions and Letters: Final Report VIII, Part I]* (New Haven, CT, 1979), pp. 232–9; L. Lee Levine, *Visual Judaism in Late Antiquity: Historical Contexts of Jewish Art* (New Haven, CT, 2012), p. 144; A. Saldarini, 'Scribes', in *The Anchor Yale Bible Dictionary*, ed. D. Freedman (New York, 2008), pp. 1012–16.

8 Bede and Lindisfarne

1 M. P. Brown, *The Lindisfarne Gospels: Society, Spirituality and the Scribe* (London, Lucerne and Toronto, 2003).
2 W. Berschin, '*Opus deliberatum ac perfectum*: Why Did the Venerable Bede Write a Second Prose Life of St Cuthbert?', in *St. Cuthbert, His Cult and His Community to AD 1200*, ed. G. Bonner, D. Rollason and C. Stancliffe (Woodbridge, 1989), pp. 95–102; M. Lapidge, 'Bede's Metrical *Vita S. Cuthberti*', in *St Cuthbert*, ed. Bonner et al., pp. 77–93.
3 Brown, *Lindisfarne Gospels*; A. Thacker, 'Lindisfarne and the Origins of the Cult of St Cuthbert', in *St Cuthbert*, ed. Bonner et al., pp. 103–22, at p. 116.
4 M. P. Brown, 'Concealed and Revealed: Insular Visualisations of the Word', in *Clothing Sacred Scriptures*, ed. D. Ganz and B. Schellewald (Berlin and Boston, MA, 2018), pp. 69–80.
5 M. P. Brown, 'Uncial', in 'Writing in the Insular World', in *A History of the Book in Britain*, vol. I: *From the Romans to the Normans*, ed. R. G. Gameson (Cambridge, 2011); M. P. Brown, 'The Insular System of Scripts', in *The Oxford Handbook of Palaeography*, ed. F. Coulson and R. Babcock (Oxford, 2020).
6 Brown, *Lindisfarne Gospels*; M. P. Brown, 'Reading the Lindisfarne Gospels: Text, Image, Context', in *From Holy Island to Durham:*

The Contexts and Meanings of The Lindisfarne Gospels, ed. R. G. Gameson (London, 2013), pp. 84–95.

7 Brown, 'Reading the Lindisfarne Gospels: Text, Image, Context', pp. 84–95.

8 Ibid., and Brown, *Lindisfarne Gospels*.

9 S. DeGregorio, 'Bede and the Old Testament', in *The Cambridge Companion to Bede*, ed. S. DeGregorio (Cambridge, 2010), pp. 127–41, at pp. 136–7.

10 A. Thacker, 'Lindisfarne and the Origins of the Cult of St Cuthbert', p. 116.

11 C. Stancliffe, 'Disputed Episcopacy: Bede, Acca and the Relationship between Stephen's *Life of St Wilfrid* and the Early Prose Lives of St Cuthbert', *Anglo-Saxon England*, XLI (2013), pp. 7–39.

12 Ibid., p. 39.

9 Bede and His Legacy

1 Cuthbert to Cuthwin (the *Epistola Cuthberti de obitu Bedae*), Nn. 4–6: J. P. Migne, *Patrologia Latina* (Paris, 1841–65), vol. XC, col. 62–6, English translation based upon that by A. M. Sellar, ed., *Bede's Ecclesiastical History of England* (London, 1907), which can be found on the Project Gutenberg site at www.gutenberg.org.

2 A modern English translation by Michael R. Burch, see www.thehypertexts.com, accessed 19 December 2022.

3 J. P. McGowan, review of M. Lapidge, ed. and trans., *Bede's Latin Poetry*, Oxford Medieval Texts (Oxford, 2019), in *Medieval Review* (4 April 2021), pp. 1–6.

4 M. MacCarron, *Bede and Time: Computus, Theology and History in the Early Medieval World* (London and New York, 2020); D. Ó Cróinin, 'The Irish Provenance of Bede's Computus', *Peritia*, II (1983), pp. 238–42.

5 A modern English translation by Michael R. Burch, see www.thehypertexts.com, accessed 19 December 2022.

BIBLIOGRAPHY

PRIMARY SOURCES

Standard Editions

Bede's Ecclesiastical History of the English People, ed. B. Colgrave and R.A.B. Mynors (Oxford, 1969)

For an online translation of Bede's Prose Life of St Cuthbert, see https://sourcebooks.fordham.edu/basis/bede-cuthbert.asp

In cantica canticorum, ed. D. Hurst, CCL 119B (Turnhout, 1983), pp. 175–375

Expostio Actvvm Apostolorvm, ed. M.L.W. Laistner, CCL 121 (Turnhout, 1960), pp. 3–99

In Ezram et Neemiam, ed. D. Hurst, CCL 119A (Turnhout, 1969)

In Habacvc, ed. J. E. Hudson, CCL 119B (Turnhout, 1972), pp. 379–409

Homiliae euangelii, ed. D. Hurst, CCL 122 (Turnhout, 1965)

Liber quatuor in principivm Genesis usque ad nativitatem Isaac et eiectionem Ismahelis adnotationum, ed. C. W. Jones, CCL 118A (Turnhout, 1967)

In Lucae evangelium expositio, ed. D. Hurst, CCL 120 (Turnhout, 1960)

In Marci evangelium expositio, ed. D. Hurst, CCL 120 (Turnhout, 1960)

In primam partem Samvhelis libri IIII, ed. D. Hurst, CCL 119 (Turnhout, 1962)

In regum librum XXX quaestiones, ed. D. Hurst, CCL 119 (Turnhout, 1972), pp. 289–322

De tabernaculo, ed. D. Hurst, CCL 119A (Turnhout, 1969), pp. 1–139

De templo, ed. D. Hurst, CCL 119A (Turnhout, 1969), pp. 1–234

Opera didascalica. Pars I, ed. C. W. Jones, CCL 123A (Turnhout, 1975)

Opera didascalica. Pars II, ed. C. W. Jones, CCL 123A (Turnhout, 1977)

Opera didascalica. Pars III, ed. C. W. Jones, ed. CCL 123C (Turnhout, 1980)

Two Lives of Saint Cuthbert, ed. and trans. B. Colgrave, 1st paperback edn (Cambridge, 1985)

Other Works and Early Copies

Baedae Historia ecclesiastica gentis anglorum, in Venerabilis Baedae opera historica, ed. C. Plummer, 2 vols (Oxford, 1896)

Bedae opera de temporibus, ed. C. W. Jones (Cambridge, MA, 1943)
Bedas metrische Vita Sancti Cuthberti, in Palaestra 198, ed. W. Jaager (Leipzig, 1935)
Bede, De arte metrica, ed. H. Keil, *Grammatici Latini*, vol. VII (Lipsiae, 1880)
Bede, De schematibus et tropis, ed. C. Halm, *Rhetores Latini minores* (Leipzig, 1863)
Martyrologium Bedae, in Les martyrologes historiques du moyen âge, ed. H. Quentin (Paris, 1908)
Patrologia Latina, ed. J. Migne, vols XC–XCIV (Paris, 1861–2)
The Leningrad Bede, Early English Manuscripts in Facsimile, ed. O Arngart (Copenhagen, 1952)
The Moore Bede, Early English Manuscripts in Facsimile, ed. Peter Hunter Blair (Copenhagen, 1959)
Venerabilis Bedae opera quae supersunt, ed. J. A. Giles, 12 vols (London, 1843–4)

Translations

Bede: A Biblical Miscellany, trans. W. Trent Foley and A. G. Holder, Translated Texts for Historians, 28 (Liverpool, 1999)
Bede: Celtic and Roman Christianity in Britain, ed. R. Van de Weyer (Berkhamsted, 1997) (selections from Bede's *Ecclesiastical History*)
Bede: Commentary on Revelation, trans. F. Wallis (Liverpool, 2013)
Bede, Excerpts from the Works of Saint Augustine on Letters of St. Paul the Apostle, Cistercian Studies Series (Kalamazoo, MI, 1989)
Bede: Homilies on the Gospels: Lent to the Dedication of the Church (Book Two), trans. L. T. Martin and D. Hurst, 2 vols, Cistercian Studies Series, 110–11 (Kalamazoo, MI, 1991)
Bede: On Genesis, ed. C. B. Kendall (Liverpool, 2008)
Bede: On Ezra and Nehemiah, trans. S. DeGregorio (Liverpool, 2006)
Bede: On the Nature of Things and On Times, ed. C. B. Kendall and F. Wallis, Translated Texts for Historians 56 (Liverpool, 2010)
Bede: The Reckoning of Time, trans. F. Wallis (Liverpool, 1999)
Bede: On the Song of Songs and Other Spiritual Writings, trans. A. Holder, Classics of Western Spirituality (New York, 2011)
Bede: On the Tabernacle, trans. A. Holder, Translated Texts for Historians, 18 (Liverpool, 1994)
Bede: On the Temple, trans. S. Connolly, with an introduction by J. O'Reilly, Translated Texts for Historians Series, 21 (Liverpool, 1995)

Bede: On Tobias and On the Canticle of Habakkuk, trans. S. Connolly (Dublin, 1997)

Bede's Ecclesiastical History of England: A Revised Translation with Introduction, Life, and Notes, A. M. Sellar, ed. (London, 1907). For an online translation of this edition of Bede's *Ecclesiastical History*, see www.gutenberg.org.

Commentary on the Acts of the Apostles, trans. L. Martin, Cistercian Studies Series, 117 (Kalamazoo, MI, 1989)

Commentary on the Seven Catholic Epistles, trans. Dom D. Hurst, Cistercian Studies Series, 82 (Kalamazoo, MI, 1985)

Ecclesiastical History of the English People, trans. L. Sherley-Price (London, 1955)

Ecclesiastical History of the English People, trans. M. MacLagan (Oxford, 1949)

The Ecclesiastical History of the English People, The Greater Chronicle, Bede's Letter to Egbert, trans. B. Colgrave, ed. J. McClure and R. Collins (Oxford, 1994)

The Illustrated Bede, ed. J. Marsden and trans. J. Gregory (London, 1989)

Libri II de Arte Metrica et de Schematibus et Tropis / The Art of Poetry and Rhetoric: The Latin Text with an English Translation, Introduction and Notes, ed. and trans. C. B. Kendall, Bibliotheca Germanica: Series Nova, vol. II (Saarbrücken, 1991)

The Old English Version of Bede's Ecclesiastical History of the English People, ed. and trans. T. Miller, EETS O.S. 95, 96, 110, 111 (1890)

Browne, G., ed., *The Abbreviated Psalter of the Venerable Bede* (Grand Rapids, MI, 2001)

Farmer, D. H., ed., *The Age of Bede: Revised Edition* (London, 1998)

Tannenhaus, G. H., 'Bede's "De schematibus et tropis": A Translation', in *Readings in Medieval Rhetoric*, ed. J. M. Miller, M. H. Prosser and T. W. Benson (Bloomington, IN, 1973), pp. 96–122, rptd *Quarterly Journal of Speech*, XLVIII/3 (1962), pp. 237–53

Trent Foley, W., and A. G. Holder, trans., 'Thirty Questions on the Book of Kings', in *Bede: A Biblical Miscellany* (Liverpool, 1999), pp. 89–138

GENERAL

Ahern, E., *Bede and the Cosmos: Theology and Nature in the Eighth Century* (London and New York, 2020)

Alcock, L., 'Fenestrae Obliquae: A Contribution to Literate Archaeology', *Antiquity*, XLVIII/190 (1974), pp. 141–3

Allen, M. I., 'Bede and Freculf at Medieval St Gallen', in *Beda Venerabilis*, ed. L.A.J.R. Houwen and A. A. MacDonald

Anderson, R., 'Passing the Harp in Bede's Story of Caedmon', *English Language Notes*, 15 (1977), pp. 1–4

Armstrong, J. III, 'The Old Welsh Computus Fragment and Bede's *Pagina regularis*', *Proceedings of the Harvard Celtic Colloquuim*, 2 (1982), pp. 187–273

Arngart, O. S., 'On the Dating of Early Bede Manuscripts', *Studia Neophilologica*, XLV (1973), pp. 47–52

Babcock, R. G., 'The 'proverbium antiquum' in Acca's Letter to Bede', *Mittellateinisches Jarbuch*, XXII (1989), pp. 53–5

Baker, M., 'Medieval Illustrations of Bede's Life of St Cuthbert', *Warburg and Courtauld Institute*, 41 (1978), pp. 16 and 40

Barnard, L. W., 'Bede and Eusebius as Church Historians', in *Famulus Christi*, ed. Bonner, pp. 354–72

Bassett, S., ed., *The Origins of the Anglo-Saxon Kingdoms* (Oxford, 1989)

Bately, J., 'Bede and the Anglo-Saxon Chronicle', in *Saints, Scholars, and Heroes*, ed. King and Stevens

Benedikz, B. S., 'Bede in the Uttermost North', in *Famulus Christi*, ed. Bonner, pp. 334–43

Benison, L., 'Early Medieval Science: The Evidence of Bede', *Endeavour*, XXIV/3 (2000), pp. 111–16

Bieler, L., 'Ireland's Contribution to the Culture of Northumbria', in *Famulus Christi*, ed. Bonner, pp. 210–28

Bischoff, B., 'Zur Kritik der Heerwagenschen Ausgabe von Bedas Werken (Basel 1563)', in B. Bischoff, *Mittelaleterliche Studien* I (Stuttgart, 1966–81), pp. 112–17

Bolton, W. F., 'A Bede Bibliography, 1935–1960', *Traditio*, 10 (1962), pp. 436–45

Bonner, G., 'Bede and Medieval Civilization', ASE, 2 (1973), pp. 71–90

—, 'Bedan Studies in 1973', *Clergy Review*, 58 (1973), pp. 689–96

—, ed., *Famulus Christi: Essays in Commemoration of the Thirteenth Century of the Birth of the Venerable Bede* (London, 1976)

—, 'Ireland and Rome: The Double Inheritance of Northumbria', in *Saints, Scholars, and Heroes*, ed. M. H. King and W. M. Stevens, pp. 299–309

Boyd, W.J.P., *Aldred's Marginalia: Explanatory Comments in the Lindisfarne Gospels* (Exeter, 1975)

Breay, C., and B. Meehan, eds, *The St Cuthbert Gospel: Studies on the Insular Manuscript of the Gospel of John* (London, 2015)

—, and J. Story, eds, *Anglo-Saxon Kingdoms: Art, Word, War*, exh. cat., British Library (London, 2018)

Bridbury, A. R., *The English Economy from Bede to the Reformation* (Woodbridge, 1992)

Brown, A., 'Bede: A Hisperic Etymology and Early Sea Poetry', *Medieval Studies*, xxxvii (1975), pp. 419–32

Brown, G. H., *A Companion to Bede*, Anglo-Saxon Studies, 12 (Woodbridge, 2009)

—, *Bede the Educator*, Jarrow Lecture 1996 (Newcastle upon Tyne, 1996)

—, *Bede the Venerable*, Twayne's English Authors series 443 (Boston, 1987)

—, 'The Meanings of *interpres* in Aldhelm and Bede', in *Interpretation: Medieval and Modern*, ed. P. Boiatni and A. Torti (Cambridge, 1993), pp. 43–65

—, 'The Preservation and Transmission of Northumbrian Culture: Alcuin's Debt to Bede', in *The Preservation and Transmission of Anglo-Saxon Culture: Selected Papers from the 1991 Meeting of the International Society of Anglo-Saxonists*, ed. P. E. Szarmach and J. T. Rosenthal (Kalamazoo, MI, 1997), pp. 405–30

Brown, M. P., *Art of the Islands: Celtic, Pictish, Anglo-Saxon and Viking Visual Culture, c. 450–1050* (Oxford, 2016)

—, 'Bede's Life in Context: Materiality and Spirituality', in *The Cambridge Companion to Bede*, ed. DeGregorio, pp. 3–24

—, *The British Library Guide to Writing and Scripts: History and Techniques* (London and Toronto, 1998)

—, 'House-Style in the Scriptorium: Scribal Reality and Scholarly Myth', in *Anglo-Saxon Styles*, ed. G. Brown and C. Karkov (New York, 2003), pp. 131–50

—, *How Christianity Came to Britain and Ireland* (Oxford, 2006)

—, 'Imagining, Imaging and Experiencing the East in Insular and Anglo-Saxon Cultures: New Evidence for Contact', in *Anglo-Saxon England and the Visual Imagination, ISAS 6, Proceedings of the ISAS conference, Madison, 2012*, ed. J. D. Niles, S. Klein and J. Wilcox (Tempe, AZ, 2016), pp. 49–84

—, '"In the Beginning was the Word": Books and Faith in the Age of Bede', Jarrow Lecture 2000 (Newcastle upon Tyne, 2000)

—, M. P. Brown, 'The Bridge in the Desert: Towards Establishing an Historical Context for the Newly Discovered Latin Manuscripts of St Catherine's Sinai', in *Palaeography Between East and West*, ed. Arianna d'Ottone Rambach, *Rivista degli Studi Orientali*, New Series Supplement no. 1 (2018), pp. 73–98

—, *The Lindisfarne Gospels: Society, Spirituality and the Scribe* (London, Lucerne and Toronto, 2003)
—, 'Mercian Manuscripts: The Implications of the Staffordshire Hoard, Other Recent Discoveries, and the "New Materiality"', Inaugural Lecture to the Chair of Medieval Manuscript Studies, School of Advanced Study, University of London, 22 June 2010, in *Writing in Context: Insular Manuscript Culture, 500–1200*, ed. E. Kwakkel (Leiden, 2013), pp. 23–66
—, 'Reading the Lindisfarne Gospels: Text, Image, Context', in *From Holy Island to Durham: The Contexts and Meanings of the Lindisfarne Gospels*, ed. R. G. Gameson (London, 2013), pp. 84–95
—, 'Starcraeft and the Interface between Faith and Science in Anglo-Saxon England, from Bede to Byrhtferth . . . and Beyond', in a Festschrift for Kevin Kiernan, ed. D. Johnson (forthcoming)
—, and L. Webster, eds, *The Transformation of the Roman World* (London, 1997)
Brown, T. J., 'An Historical Introduction to the Use of Classical Latin Authors in the British Isles from the Fifth Century to the Eleventh Century', in *La cultura antica nell'Occidente Latino dal VII all'XI secolo*, Settimane di studio del Centro italiano di studi sull'alto Medioevo, 22 (1974), pp. 237–93
—, ed., *The Stonyhurst Gospel of Saint John* (Oxford, 1969)
Bruce-Mitford, R., *The Art of the Codex Amiatinus*, Jarrow Lecture 1967 (Newcastle upon Tyne, 1967)
Campbell, J., 'Bede I', in *Latin Historians*, ed. T. A. Dorey (London, 1966)
—, 'Bede II', in *Essays in Anglo-Saxon History*, ed. J. Campbell (London, 1986)
—, 'Bede, the First Century of Christianity in England', *Ampleforth Journal*, LXXVI (1971), pp. 12–29
—, 'Bede's Words for Places', in *Names, Words and Graves: Early Medieval Settlements*, ed. P. H. Sawyer (Leeds, 1979), pp. 34–5
Cedrini, L. B., 'Annotozioni lessicali considetto Beda (mss. from 1747 della Biblioteca Nazionale de Parigi), a margine delle Lexikalische Untersuchungen zu Girart de Roussillon di M. Pfister', *Cultura Neolatina*, 36 (1978), pp. 33–59
Chadwick, H., *The Origin of the English Nation* (Washington, DC, 1983)
Chazelle, C., 'Ceolfrid's Gift to St Peter: The First Quire of the Codex Amiatinus and the Evidence of Its Roman Destination', *Early Medieval Europe*, XII/2 (2003), pp. 129–57
—, 'Christ and the Vision of God: The Biblical Diagrams of the Codex Amiatinus', in *The Mind's Eye: Art and Theological Argument in the*

Middle Ages, ed. J. F. Hamburger and A.-M. Bouché (Princeton, NJ, 2006), pp. 84–111

—, 'Pictures, Books and the Illiterate: Pope Gregory I's Letters to Serenus of Marseilles', *Word and Image*, VI/2 (1990), pp. 138–53

—, *The Codex Amiatinus and Its Sister Bibles: Scripture, Liturgy, and Art in the Milieu of the Venerable Bede* (Leiden and Boston, MA, 2019)

Christie, Y., 'Ap. IV-VII, I: de Bède à Bruno de Segni', in *Études de Civilisation Médiévale (IXe - XIIe siècles)*, CESCM (Poitiers, 1974), pp. 145–51

Coates, S., 'Bede, the Miraculous and Episcopal Authority in Early Anglo-Saxon England', *Downside Review*, CXIII/392 (1995), pp. 219–32

—, 'The Bishop as Pastor and Solitary: Bede and the Spiritual Authority of the Monk-Bishop', *Journal of Ecclesiastical History*, XLVII/4 (1996), pp. 601–19

Commemorative Supplement on Bede, Northumbria: Northern Echo (24 May 1973, to mark the 1,300th anniversary of his birth)

Conner, P., 'Bede's Monastery Museum', *Illustrated London News*, 267 (August 1979), p. 44

Corsano, K., 'The First Quire of the Codex Amiatinus and the Institutiones of Cassiodorus', *Scriptorium*, XLI/1 (1987), pp. 3–34

Cosmos, S., 'Oral Tradition and Literary Convention in Bede's Life of St. Aidan', *Classical Folia*, 31 (1977), pp. 47–63

Cowdrey, H.E.J., 'Bede and the "English People"', *Journal of Religious History*, XI/4 (1980–81), pp. 501–23

Cramp, R. J., 'Monkwearmouth and Jarrow: The Archaeological Evidence', in *Famulus Christi*, ed. Bonner, pp. 5–18

Creider, L. S., 'Bede's Understanding of the Miraculous', PhD thesis, Yale University, 1979

Crépin, A., 'Bede and the Vernacular', in *Famulus Christi*, ed. Bonner, pp. 170–92

Cross, J. E., 'Bede's Influence at Home and Abroad', in *Beda Venerabilis*, ed. Houwen and MacDonald

Darby, P., 'Bede, Iconoclasm and the Temple of Solomon', *Early Medieval Europe*, XXI/4 (2013), pp. 390–421

—, and F. Wallis, *Bede and the Future* (London and New York, 2020)

Davidse, J., 'On Bede as Christian Historian', in *Beda Venerabilis*, ed. Houwen and MacDonald

—, 'The Sense of History in the Works of the Venerable Bede', *Studi Medievali*, 23 (1982), pp. 647–95

Davies, W., *An Early Welsh Microcosm: Studies in the Llandaff Charters* (London, 1978)

Davis, R.H.C., 'Bede after Bede', *Studies in Medieval History Presented to R. Allen Brown*, ed. C. Harper-Bill et al. (Woodbridge, 1989)
DeGregorio, S., *Innovation and Tradition in the Writings of the Venerable Bede* (Morgantown, WV, 2006)
—, ed., *The Cambridge Companion to Bede* (Cambridge, 2010)
Dickerson III, W. W., 'Bede as Literary Architect of the Church: Another Look at Bede's Use of Hagiography in the Historia Ecclesiastica', *American Benedictine Review*, XLV/1 (1994), pp. 93–105
Dillon, M., 'The Vienna Glosses on Bede', *Celtica*, 3 (1956), pp. 865–72
Dionisotti, A. C., 'On Bede, Grammar, and Greek', *Revue Bénédictine*, XCII (1982), pp. 111–41
Dumville, D. N., 'New Chronicle-Fragment of Early English History', *English Historical Review*, LXXXVIII/347 (1973), pp. 312–14
Echlin, E., 'Bede and the Church', *Irish Theological Quarterly*, XL/4 (1973), pp. 351–63
Eckenrode, T., 'A Case for the Venerable Bede: More Attentive Inclusion of an Eighth Century Monk's Pedagogical Values in the History of Education Textbooks', *Dialogue*, 9 (1975), pp. 21–4
—, 'The Growth of a Scientific Mind: Bede's Early and Late Scientific Writings', *Downside Review*, XCIV/316 (1976), pp. 197–212
—, *Original Aspects in Venerable Bede's Tidal Theories with Relation to Prior Tidal Observations* (Ann Arbor, MI, 1970)
—, 'The Venerable Bede: A Bibliographical Essay, 1970–81', *American Benedictine Review*, 36 (1985), pp. 172–94
—, 'The Venerable Bede: A Humanist Educator of the Early Middle Ages', *Dialogue*, 10 (1976), pp. 21–31
—, 'The Venerable Bede as an Educator', *History of Education*, 6 (1977), pp. 159–68
—, 'Venerable Bede as Scientist', *American Benedictine Review*, 22 (1971), pp. 486–507
—, 'Venerable Bede's Theories of Ocean Tides', *American Benedictine Review*, 25 (1974), pp. 56–74
Englische, B., 'Realitä'tsorientierte Wissenschaft oder paxisferne Traditionwissen? Inhalte und Probleme mittelalterlicher Wissenschaftsvorstellungen am Beispiel von De temporum ratione des Beda Venerabilis', in *Dilettanten und Wissenschaft. Zur Geschichte und Aktualität eines wechselvollen Verhältnisses*, ed. E. Strauss (Amsterdam, 1996), pp. 11–34
Fairless, P. J., *Northumbria's Golden Age: The Kingdom of Northumbria, AD 547–735* (York, 1994)

Fanning, S., 'Bede, Imperium, and the Bretwaldas', *Speculum*, LXVI/1 (1991), pp. 1–26

Farrell, R. T., ed., *Bede and Anglo-Saxon England: Papers in Honour of the 1300th Anniversary of the Birth of Bede, Given at Cornell University in 1973 and 1974* (Oxford, 1978)

Fischer, B., 'Bedae de titulus psalmorum liber', in *Festschrift Bernhard Bischoff zu seinen 65. Geburstag dargebracht von Freunden, Kollegen und Schüern*, ed. J. Autenrieth und F. Brunholzl (Stuttgart, 1971), pp. 90–110

Folkerts, M., 'Pseudo-Beda: De Arithmeticis propositionibus: eine mathematische Schrift aus der Karolingerzeit', *Sudhoffs Archiv Zeitschrift für Wissenschaftgeschichte*, 56 (1972), pp. 22–43

Foot, S., 'The Making of *Angelcynn*: English Identity Before the Norman Conquest', *Transactions of the Royal Historical Society*, VI (1996), pp. 25–49

Fordyce, C. J., 'A Rhythmical Version of Bede's *De Ratione Temporum*', *Archivum latinitatis medii aevi*, 3 (1927), pp. 59–73, 129–41

Fraser, V., 'The Influence of the Venerable Bede on the Fourteenth-Century Occitan Treatise Las Leys d'Amors', *Rhetorica*, II/1 (1993), pp. 7–26

Frich, H. I., '"Even the Sea Served Him . . .": The Soldiers of Christ and the Restoration of Nature in Some Works of the Venerable Bede', in *Quest of the Kingdom*, ed. A. Härdelin (Stockholm, 1991), pp. 65–77

Fry, D. K., 'The Art of Bede: Edwin's Council', *Old English Newsletter*, 11 (1977), pp. 4–5

—, 'Two Bede Bibliographies: A Progressive Report', *Old English Newsletter*, XXV/1 (1991), pp. 34–6

Gewalt, D., 'Der entstummte Bettler. Zu Beda Venerabilis, Historia Ecclesiastica Gentis Venerabilis V, 2', *Linguistica Biblica*, 54 (1983), pp. 53–60

Gleason, M., 'Bede and His Fathers', *Classica et Mediaevalia*, 45 (1994), pp. 223–38

Godfrey, J., 'The Place of the Double Monastery', in *Famulus Christi*, ed. Bonner, pp. 344–50

Goffart, W., *The Narrators of Barbarian History (AD 550–800): Jordanes, Gregory of Tours, Bede, and Paul the Deacon* (Princeton, NJ, 1988)

Gòmez Pallarès, J., 'Los excerpta de Beda (De temporum ratione, 23–25) en el MA.ACA, Ripoll 225', *Emerita*, 59 (1991), pp. 101–22

Gorman, M., 'Bede's VIII Quaestiones and Carolingian Biblical Scholarship', *Revue Bénédictine*, CIX (1999), pp. 32–7

Grant, R. J., 'Lawrence Nowell's Transcript of BM Cotton Otho. B. xi', *Anglo Saxon England*, 3 (1973), pp. 111–24

Gribomont, J., 'Saint Bède et ses dictionnaires grecs', *Revue Bénédictine*, 89 (1979), pp. 271–80

Gunn, V., *Bede's Historiae: Genre, Rhetoric and the Construction of Anglo-Saxon Church History* (Woodbridge, 2009)

Härke, H., 'Astronomical and Atmospheric Observations in the Anglo-Saxon Chronicle and in Bede', *Antiquarian Astronomer: Journal of the Society for the History of Astronomy*, 6 (2012), pp. 34–43

Harris, S. J., 'Bede, Social Practice, and the Problem with Foreigners', *Essays in Medieval Studies*, XIII (1996), pp. 97–109

Harrison, K., 'The Beginning of the Year in England *c*. 500–900', *ASE*, 2 (1963), pp. 51–70

Hawkes, J., and S. Mills, eds, *Northumbria's Golden Age* (Stroud, 1999)

Heidenreich, H. B., 'Beda Venerabilis in Spain', *MLN*, LXXXV/2 (1970), pp. 120–37

Higgitt, J., and M. Spearman, eds, *The Age of Migrating Ideas, Early Medieval Art in Northern Britain and Ireland* (Stroud, 1984)

Higham, N. J., *The Convert Kings: Power and Religious Affiliation in Early Anglo-Saxon England* (Manchester, 1997)

—, *An English Empire: Bede and the Early Anglo-Saxon Kings* (Manchester, 1995)

—, *The Kingdom of Northumbria A.D. 350–1100* (Dover, NH, 1993)

Hill, R., 'Bede and the Boors', in *Famulus Christi*, ed. Bonner, pp. 93–105

Hines, J., 'Britain after Rome: Between Multiculturalism and Monoculturalism', in *Cultural Identity and Archaeology: The Construction of European Communities*, ed. P. Graves-Brown, S. Jones and C. Gamble (London, 1996)

Holtz, L., 'A l école de Donate, de sainte Augustin à Bède', *Latomus*, 36 (1977), pp. 522–38

Houwen, L.A.J.R., and A. A. MacDonald, eds, *Beda Venerabilis: Historian, Monk and Northumbrian* (Groningen, 1996)

Howlett, D. R., *The Celtic Latin Tradition of Biblical Style* (Dublin 1995)

—, *The Start of the Anglo-Latin Tradition* (London, 2017)

—, 'The Structure of "The Dream of the Rood"', *Studia Neophilologica*, XLVIII/2 (1976), pp. 301–6

Hudson, K., 'Enterprise in Jarrow: The Bede Gallery', *Illustrated London News*, 268 (December 1980), p. 83

Humphreys, K. W., and A.S.C. Ross, 'Further Manuscripts of Bede's *Historia Ecclesiastica*, of the Epistola Cuthberti de Obitu Bedae, and further Anglo-Saxon texts of Caedmon's Hymn and Bede's Death Song', *Notes and Queries*, XXII/2 (1975), pp. 50–55

Hunter Blair, P., 'From Bede to Alcuin', in *Famulus Christi*, ed. Bonner, pp. 239–60

—, 'The Historical Writings of Bede', *La Storiographia Altomedievale. Settimane di Studi del Centro Italiano di Studi sull' Alto Medioevo*, 17 (1970), pp. 197–221

—, *Northumbria in the Days of Bede* (London, 1976)

—, *Venerable Bede*, Lecture Delivered in the Monk's Dormitory at Durham, 2 June 1979 (Chester-le-Street, 1979), pp. 261–85

—, *The World of Bede* (Cambridge, 1990; reissue of the 1970 edition, with a foreword and bibliographical addenda by M. Lapidge)

Huws, D., 'A Welsh Manuscript of Bede's *De Natura Rerum*', *Bulletin of the Board of Celtic Studies*, 27 (1978), pp. 491–504

Isola, A., 'De Schematibus et topis di Beda in rapporto al De Doctrina Christiana di Agostino', *Romanobarbarica*, 1 (1976), pp. 31–82

Jones, C. W., 'Bede', in *Dictionary of Scientific Biography*, ed. C. C. Gillispie (New York, 1970), pp. 564–6

—, 'Bede as Early Medieval Historian', *Mediaevalia et Humanistica*, IV (1946), pp. 26–36

—, 'Bede and Vegetius', *Classical Review*, 46 (1932), pp. 248–9

Jones, C. W., 'Bede's Place in Medieval Schools', in *Famulus Christi*, ed. Bonner

—, 'Bede, the Schools, and the "Computus"', in *Collected Studies*, 436, ed. W. M. Stevens (Brookfield, VT, 1994)

—, *A Concordance to the Historia Ecclesiastica of the Venerable Bede* (Cambridge, MA, 1929)

Kelly, J. F., 'On the Brink: Bede', *Journal of Early Christian Studies*, V/1 (1997), pp. 85–103

Kendall, C. B., 'Bede's Historia Ecclesiastica: The Rhetoric of Faith', in *Medieval Eloquence: Studies in the Theory and Practice of Medieval Rhetoric*, ed. J. J. Murphy (Berkeley, CA, 1978), pp. 145–72

—, 'Imitation and Bede's "Historia Ecclesiastica"', in *Saints, Scholars, and Heroes*, ed. King and Stevens, pp. 161–90

—, and F. Wallis, *Bede: On the Nature of Things and On Times* (Liverpool, 2010)

Killion, S. B., 'Bedan Historiography in the Irish Annals', *Medieval Perspectives*, 6 (1991), pp. 20–36

King, M. H., '"Grammatica mystica": A Study of Bede's Grammatical Curriculum', in *Saints, Scholars, and Heroes*, ed. King and Stevens, pp. 145–60

—, and W. Stevens, eds, *Saints, Scholars, and Heroes: Studies in Medieval Culture in Honour of Charles W. Jones* (Collegeville, MN, 1979)

King, V., 'An Unreported Early Use of Bede's *De natura rerum*', *Anglo-Saxon England*, XXII (1993), pp. 85–91

Kirby, D. P., 'Bede and the Pictish Church', *Innes Review*, XXIV/1 (1973), pp. 6–25

—, *Bede's Historia Ecclesiastica Gentis Anglorum: Its Contemporary Setting*, Jarrow Lecture 1992 (Newcastle upon Tyne, 1992)

—, 'Per universitas Pictorum provincias', in *Famulus Christi*, ed. Bonner, pp. 286–324

Knibbs, E., 'The Manuscript Evidence for the *de octo questionibus* Ascribed to Bede', *Traditio*, LXIII/1 (2008), pp. 129–83

Kottje, R., 'Ein bisher unbekanntes Fragment der Historia Ecclesiastica Gentis Anglorum Bedas', *Revue Bénédictine*, LXXXIII/3–4 (1973), pp. 429–32

Lagorio, V. M., 'Bede's *De Orthographia* in Codex Vat. Ottob. Lat. 687', *Classical Philology*, LXX/3 (1975), pp. 206–8

—, 'An Unreported Manuscript of Bede's *De Orthographia* in Codex Vaticanus Reginensis Latinus 1587', *Manuscripta*, XIX/2 (1975), pp. 98–106

Laistner, M.L.W., *A Handlist of Bede Manuscripts* (Ithaca, NY, 1943)

—, 'The Library of the Venerable Bede', in *Bede: His Life, Times and Writings*, ed. A. Hamilton (New York, 1966)

Lapidge, M., *Bede and His World: The Jarrow Lectures 1958–1993*, 2 vols (Brookfield, VT, 1994)

—, *Bede the Poet*, Jarrow Lecture 1993 (Newcastle upon Tyne, 1993)

—, 'Some Remnants of Bede's Lost *Liber Epigrammatum*', *English Historical Review*, XC/357 (1975), pp. 798–820

Lawrence-Mathers, A., 'Bede, St Cuthbert and the Science of Miracles', *Reading Medieval Studies*, XLV (2019), pp. 3–28, available at https://centaur.reading.ac.uk

Lees, C., and G. Overing, 'Birthing Bishops and Fathering Poets: Bede, Hild, and the Relations of Cultural Production', *Exemplaria*, VI/1 (1994), pp. 35–65

Leonardi, C., 'Il venerabile Beda e la cultura del secolo VIII', *I problemi dell' occidente nel secolo VII*, I (1963), pp. 603–58

Lerer, S., 'Literary Authority in Bede's Story of Imma', in *Literacy, Politics, and Artistic Innovation in the Early Medieval West*, ed. C. M. Chazelle (Lanham, MD, 1992), pp. 19–47

Levison, W., 'Bede as Historian', in *Bede: His Life, Times and Writings*, ed. Thompson

Leyser, H., *Beda: A Journey to the Seven Kingdoms at the Time of Bede* (London, 2015)

Lipp, F. R., 'The Carolingian Commentaries on Bede's *De Natura Rerum*', PhD thesis, Yale University, 1961

Lofstedt, B., 'Cauma bei Pseudo-Beda', *Eranos*, 89 (1991), pp. 61–2

Loomis, C. G., 'The Miracle Traditions of the Venerable Bede', *Speculum*, XXI/4 (1946), pp. 404–18

Love, R., 'The Library of the Venerable Bede', in *The History of the Book in Britain*, vol. I, ed. R. G. Gameson (Cambridge, 2011), pp. 606–32

Lowe, E. A., 'A New Manuscript Fragment of Bede's Historia Ecclesiastica' (1926) and 'A Key to Bede's Scriptorium: Some Observations on the Leningrad Manuscript of the Historia Ecclesiastica Gentis Anglorum' (1958), in *Paleographical Papers, 1907–1965*, ed. L. Bieler (Oxford, 1972), pp. 221–3 and 441–9

Lucas, P. J., 'Old English Christian Poetry', in *Famulus Christi*, ed. Bonner, pp. 193–209

Lynch, K., 'Evidences of a Knowledge of Greek in England and Ireland during the Age of Bede', PhD thesis, Duquesne University, 1976

MacCarron, M., *Bede and Time: Computus, Theology and History in the Early Medieval World* (London and New York, 2020)

McClure, J., 'Bede and the Life of St Ceolfrid', *Peritia*, 3 (1984), pp. 71–84

—, 'Bede's Old Testament Kings', in *Ideal and Reality in Frankish and Anglo-Saxon Society*, ed. Wormald

McCready, W. D., 'Bede and the Isidorian Legacy', *Mediaeval Studies*, LVII (1995), pp. 41–73

McKinney, W. A., 'Creating a *gens Anglorum*: Social and Ethnic Identity in Anglo-Saxon England through the Lens of Bede's Historia Ecclesiastica', PhD thesis, University of York, Centre for Medieval Studies, 2011

McNamara, J., 'Bede's Role in Circulating Legend in the Historia Ecclesiastica', *Anglo-Saxon Studies in Archeology and History*, 9 (1994), pp. 61–9

Magallon, G., and I. Ana, 'Evolucion del genero de Orthographia hasta Beda', in *Actas i congresso nacional de latin medieval*, ed. M. P. Gonzalez (León, 1995), pp. 293–9

Marin, R., 'Los verbos de 'dar' en la Historia Ecclesiastica Gentis Anglorum', in *Actas i congresso nacional de látin medieval*, ed. M. P. Gonzalez (León, 1995), pp. 587–93

Markus, R. A., 'Bede and the Tradition of Ecclesiastical Historiography', in *The Jarrow Lecture* (Jarrow, 1975)

—, 'The Chronology of the Gregorian Mission to England: Bede's Narrative and Gregory's Correspondence', in *From Augustine to Gregory the Great*

Marsden, R., 'Manus Bedae: Bede's Contribution to Ceolfrith's Bibles', *Anglo-Saxon England*, XXVII (1998), pp. 65–85

Martin, K., 'The Adventus Saxonum', *Latomus*, 33 (1974), pp. 608–39

Martin, L., 'Bede as Linguistic Scholar', *American Benedictine Review*, XXXV (1984), pp. 204–17

Mayr-Harting, H., 'Bede's Patristic Thinking as Historian', in *Historiographie im frühen Mittelalter*, ed. A. Scharer and G. Scheibelreiter (Vienna, 1994), pp. 367–74

—, *The Coming of Christianity to Anglo-Saxon England* (London, 1972)

Meaney, A. L., 'Bede and Anglo-Saxon Paganism', *Parergon*, 3 (1985), pp. 1–29

Meyvaert, P., *The Art of Words: Bede and Theodulf* (London and New York, 2008)

—, 'Bede's Capitula Lectionum for the Old and New Testaments', *Revue Bénédictine*, CV/3–4 (1995), pp. 348–80

—, 'Bede, Cassiodorus, and the Codex Amiatinus', *Speculum*, LXXI/4 (1996), pp. 827–83

—, 'Bede and the Church Paintings of Wearmouth-Jarrow', ASE, 8 (1979), pp. 63–77

—, 'Bede the Scholar', in *Famulus Christi*, ed. Bonner, pp. 40–69

—, 'Bede's Text of the Libellus Responsionumof Gregory the Great to Augustine of Canterbury', in *Studies in Primary Sources Presented to Dorothy Whitelock* (Cambridge University Press, 1971), pp. 15–33

—, 'The Date of Bede's *In Ezram* and His Image of Ezra in the Codex Amiatinus', *Speculum*, LXXX/4 (2005), pp. 1087–133

—, 'The Registrum of Gregory the Great and Bede', *Revue Bénédictine*, LXXX/1–2 (1970), pp. 162–6

Miller, M., 'Bede's Roman Dates', *Classica et Mediaevalia*, 31 (1976), pp. 239–52

—, 'Bede's Use of Gildas', *English Historical Review*, XC (1975), pp. 241–61

—, 'Starting to Write History: Gildas, Bede, and Nennius', *Welsh History Review*, 8 (1977), pp. 456–65

Miller, T., ed. and trans., *The Old English Version of Bede's Ecclesiastical History of the English People*, EETS OS 95, 96, 110, 111 (London, 1898)

Mitchell, B., 'Bede's Account of the Poet Caedmon: Two Notes', in *Iceland and the Medieval World: Studies in Honour of Ian Maxwell*, ed. G. Turville-Petre and J. S. Martin (Melbourne, 1974), pp. 126–31

Molyneaux, G., 'The Old English Bede: English Ideology or Christian Instruction?', *English Historical Review*, CXXIV/511 (December 2009), pp. 1289–323

Moreton, J., '"Doubts about the Calendar": Bede and the Eclipse of 664', *Isis*, LXXXIX/1 (1998), pp. 50–65

Morris, J., 'The Chronicle of Eusebius: Irish Fragments', *Institute of Classical Studies Bulletin*, XIX/1 (1972), pp. 80–93

Musca, G., 'Dante e Beda', in *Storici in onore di Ottorino Bertolini* (Pisa, 1972), pp. 498–524

Myers, J.N.L., 'The Adventus Saxonum', in *Aspects of Archaeology in Britain and Beyond*, ed. W. F. Grimes and H. W. Edwards (London, 1951), pp. 221–41

—, 'The Angles, the Saxons, and the Jutes' (The Raleigh Lecture on History), *British Academy Proceedings*, 56 (1970), pp. 145–74

Nicholson, J., 'Feminae gloriosae: Women in the Age of Bede', in *Medieval Women: Dedicated and Presented to Professor Rosalind M. T. Hill on the Occasion of Her Seventieth Birthday*, ed. D. Baker (Oxford, 1978), pp. 15–29

Nordhagen, P. J., *The Codex Amiatinus and the Byzantine Element in the Northumbrian Renaissance*, Jarrow Lecture 1977 (Newcastle upon Tyne, 1977)

O'Brien, C., *Bede's Temple: An Image and Its Interpretation* (Oxford and New York, 2015)

Ó Carragáin, É., *Ritual and the Rood: Liturgical Images and the Old English Poems of the Dream of the Rood Tradition* (London and Toronto, 2005)

Ó Cróinin, D., 'The Irish Provenance of Bede's Computus', *Peritia*, 2 (1983), pp. 238–42

—, and M. Walsh, eds, *Cummian's Letter De controversia paschali* (Toronto, 1988)

O'Hare, C., 'The Story of Cædmon: Bede's Account of the First Old English Poet', *American Benedictine Review*, 43 (1992), pp. 345–57

Olsen, G., 'Bede as Historian: The Evidence from His Observations on the Life of the First Christian Community at Jerusalem', *Journal of Ecclesiastical History*, XXXIII/4 (1982), pp. 519–30

O'Reilly, J., 'The Library of Scripture: Views from the Vivarium and Wearmouth-Jarrow', in *New Offerings, Ancient Treasures: Essays in Medieval Art for George Henderson*, ed. P. Binski and W. G. Noel (Stroud, 2001)

—, 'St Paul and the Sign of Jonah: Theology and Scripture in Bede's *Historia Ecclesiastica*', Jarrow Lecture 2014 (Newcastle upon Tyne, 2014)

—, Carol Farr and Elizabeth Mullins, eds, *Early Medieval Text and Image: The Codex Amiatinus, the Book of Kells and Anglo-Saxon Art* (London and New York, 2019)

—, D. Scully and M. MacCarron, eds, *History, Hagiography and Biblical Exegesis: Essays on Bede, Adomnán and Thomas Becket* (London and New York, 2019)

Petersohn, J., 'Neue Bedafragmente in Northumbrisher Unziale Saec. VIII', *Scriptorium*, 20 (1966), pp. 215–47

Pfaff, R. W., 'Bede among the Fathers? The Evidence from Liturgical Commemoration', *Studia Patristica*, XXVIII (1993), pp. 225–9

Ray, R. D., 'Bede and Cicero', *Anglo-Saxon England*, XVI (1987), pp. 1–15

—, 'Bede, the Exegete, as Historian', in *Famulus Christi*, ed. Bonner, pp. 125–40

—, 'Bede's Vera Lex Historiæ', *Speculum*, LV/1 (1980), pp. 1–21

Rector, H. J., 'The Influence of St Augustine's Philosophy of History on the Venerable Bede in the Ecclesiastical History of the English People', PhD thesis, Duke University, 1975

Renna, T., 'Bernard and Bede', *American Benedictine Review*, 44 (1993), pp. 223–35

Reynolds, S., 'What Do We Mean by "Anglo-Saxon" and "Anglo-Saxons"?', *Journal of British Studies*, XXIV/4 (1985), pp. 395–414

Riché, P., *Education and Culture in the Barbarian West: From the Sixth Century through the Eighth*, vol. III, trans. J. J. Contreni (Columbia, SC, 1976)

Richter, M., 'Bede's Angli: Angles or English?', *Peritia*, 3 (1984), pp. 99–114

Riley, S. M., 'Bede, Beowulf and the Law: Some Evidence for Dating the Poem', *Old English Newsletter*, 11 (1978), pp. 4–5

Rosenthal, J. T., 'Bede's Ecclesiastical History and the Material Conditions of Anglo-Saxon Life', *Journal of British Studies*, XIX/1 (1979), pp. 1–17

—, 'Bede's Use of Miracles in the Ecclesiastical History', *Traditio*, XXXI (1975), pp. 328–35

Ross, A.S.C., 'A Connection between Bede and the Anglo-Saxon Gloss to the Lindisfarne Gospels?', *Journal of Theological Studies*, XX/2 (1969), pp. 482–94

—, 'Supplementary Note to "A Connection between Bede and the Anglo-Saxon Gloss to the Lindisfarne Gospels?"', *Journal of Theological Studies*, xxiv/2 (1973), pp. 519–21

Rowley, S. M., 'Bede and the Northern Kingdoms', in *The Cambridge History of Early Medieval English Literature*, ed. C. Lees (Cambridge, 2012), pp. 158–82

Rozier, C. C., *Writing History in the Community of St Cuthbert, c. 700–1130: From Bede to Symeon of Durham* (York, 2022)

Saltman, A., 'Pseudo-Jerome in the Commentary of Andrew of St Victor on Samuel', *Harvard Theological Review*, LXVII/3 (1976), pp. 197–212

Santosuosso, A. C., 'Music in Bede's *De Tempore Ratione*: An 11th-Century Addition to MS London, British Library, Cotton Vespasian B. VI', *Scriptorium*, 43 (1989), pp. 255–9

Schaller, D., 'Der verleumdete David: Zum Schubkapitel von Bedas 'Epistola ad Pleguinam', in *Literatur und Sprache in Europäischen Mittelalter: Festschrift für Karl Langoosch zum 70. Geburstag*, ed. A Önnerfors, J. Rathover and F. Wagner (Darmstadt, 1973), pp. 39–43

Schneiders, M., 'Zur Datierung und Herkunft des Karlsruher Beda (Aug. CLXVII)', *Scriptorium*, 43 (1989), pp. 247–52

Scott, P. D., 'Rhetorical and Symbolic Ambiguity', in *Saints, Scholars, and Heroes*, ed. King and Stevens

Shapiro, M., 'The Decoration of the Leningrad manuscript of Bede', in *Late Antique, Early Christian and Medieval Art: Selected Papers*, ed. M. Shapiro (London, 1980), rptd from *Scriptorium*, 12 (1958), pp. 199–224

Silvestre, H., 'Emprunts non repérés à Jerome et à Bède dans l'In Johannen de Rupert de Duetz', *Revue Bénédictine*, 84 (1974), pp. 372–82

Simonetti, G., 'Osservatione sul testo di alcuni passi della 'Historia ecclesiastica' di Beda', *Siculorum Gymnasium*, 29 (1978), pp. 403–11

Sims-William, P., 'The Settlement of England in Bede and the *Chronicle*', *Anglo-Saxon England*, XII (1983), pp. 1–41

Siniscalco, P., 'Le eta' del mondo in Beda', *Romanobarbarica*, 3 (1978), pp. 297–332

Smith, C., 'Romano-British Place Names in Bede', *British Archaeological Reports*, British Series 72 (1979), pp. 1–19

Southern, R. W., 'Bede', in *Medieval Humanism and Other Studies* (Oxford, 1970), pp. 1–8

Speed, D., 'Bede's Creation of a Nation in His *Ecclesiastical History*', *Parergon*, x/2 (1992), pp. 139–15

Stancliffe, C., 'British and Irish Contexts', in *The Cambridge Companion to Bede*, ed. S. DeGregorio (Cambridge, 2010), pp. 69–83

—, '"Charity with Peace": Adomnan and the Easter Question', in *Adomnan of Iona: Theologian, Lawmaker, Peacemaker*, ed. J. Wooding (Dublin, 2010), pp. 51–68

—, 'Christianity amongst the Britons, Dalriadan Irish, and the Picts', in *The New Cambridge Medieval History*, vol. I: *c.* 500–*c.* 700, ed. P. Fouracre (Cambridge, 2005), pp. 426–61

—, 'Cuthbert and the Polarity between Pastor and Solitary', in *St Cuthbert, His Cult and His Community to* AD *1200*, ed. G. Bonner, D. W. Rollason and C. Stancliffe (Woodbridge, 1989), pp. 21–44

—, 'Disputed Episcopacy: Bede, Acca and the Relationship between Stephen's *Life of St Wilfrid* and the Early Prose Lives of St Cuthbert', *Anglo-Saxon England*, XLI (2013), pp. 7–39

—, 'The Irish Tradition in Northumbria after the Synod of Whitby', in *The Lindisfarne Gospels: New Perspectives*, ed. R. G. Gameson (Leiden, 2017), pp. 19–42

—, 'The Riddle of the Ruthwell Cross: Audience, Intention and Originator Reconsidered', in *Crossing Boundaries: Interdisciplinary Approaches to the Art, Material Culture, Language and Literature of the Early Medieval World. Essays Presented to Professor Emeritus Richard N. Bailey*, ed. E. Cambridge and J. Hawkes (Oxford, 2017), pp. 3–14

Staub, K. H., 'Ein beda-Fragment des 8. Jahrhunderts in der Hessischen Landes- und Hochschulbibliotek Darmstadt', *Bibliothek und Wissenschaft*, 17 (1983), pp. 1–7

Steadman, J. M., 'April-Aphrodite in Bede's DTR', *Notes and Queries*, XX/11 (1973), p. 409

Stephens, J. N., 'Bede's Ecclesiastical History', *History*, LXII/204 (1977), pp. 1–14

Stevens, W., *Bede's Scientific Achievement*, Jarrow Lecture 1985 (Newcastle upon Tyne, 1985)

Stock, B., and E. A. Synan, 'A Tenth Century Preface to Bede's *De temporum ratione*', *Manuscripta*, XXIII/2 (1979), pp. 113–15

Strachan, J., 'The Vienna Fragments of Bede', *Revue Celtique*, 23 (1902), pp. 40–49

Stranks, C. J., *The Venerable Bede* (London, 1974)

Sulowski, J., 'Bedy (672/3–735) 'De loquela digitorum' – sredniowieczny sposób pokazywania palcami liczb oras liter', *Studia z historia semiotyke*, 2 (1973), pp. 185–205

Symeonis Dunelmensis, 'De Primo Saxonum Adventu', in *Symeonis Dunelmensis Opera et Collecanea*, ed. H. Hinde (Durham, 1868)

Taylor, H. M., 'Splayed Windows', *Antiquity*, L/198 (1974), pp. 131–2

Thacker, A., 'Bede's Ideal of Reform', in *Ideal and Reality in Frankish and Anglo-Saxon Society*, ed. P. Wormald (Oxford, 1983), pp. 130–53

Thompson, A. H., ed., *Bede: His Life, Times and Writings* (New York, 1966)

Viereck, W., 'Beda in Bamburg', in *Einheit in der Vielfalt: Festschrift für Peter Lang zum 60. Geburtstag*, ed. G. Quast (Bern, 1988), pp. 556–69

Wallace-Hadrill, J. M., *Bede's Ecclesiastical History of the English People: A Historical Commentary* (Oxford, 1988)

—, 'Bede and Plummer', in *Famulus Christi*, ed. Bonner, pp. 366–85

—, 'Gregory of Tours and Bede: Their Views on the Personal Qualities of Kings', *Frühmittelalterliche Studien*, II/1 (1968), pp. 31–44

Wallach, L., 'The Urbana Anglo-Saxon Sylloge of Latin Inscriptions: Containing Inter Alia, a Poem Attributed to Bede', in *Poetry and Politics from Ancient Greece to the Renaissance: Studies in Honor of James Hutton*, ed. G. M. Kirkwood (Ithaca, NY, 1975), pp. 134–51

Wallis, F., 'Bede and Science', in *The Cambridge Companion to Bede*, ed. DeGregorio, pp. 113–26

—, 'Si Naturam Quæras: Reframing Bede's Science', in *Innovation and Tradition in the Writings of the Venerable Bede*, ed. S. DeGregorio (Morgantown, WV, 2006), pp. 65–99

—, and P. Darby, eds, *Bede and the Future* (Burlington, VT, 2014)

Ward, B., *Bede and the Psalter*, Jarrow Lecture 1992 (Newcastle upon Tyne, 1992)

—, 'Miracles and History', in *Famulus Christi*, ed. Bonner, pp. 70–76

—, 'Preface', in *Bede: A Biblical Miscellany*, trans. W. T. Foley and A. G. Holder (Liverpool, 1999), pp. xi–xvi.

—, *The Venerable Bede: Outstanding Christian Thinkers* (London and Harrisburg, PA, 1990)

Webster, L., and J. M. Backhouse, eds, *The Making of England: Anglo-Saxon Art and Culture*, exh. cat., British Museum (London, 1991

West, P., 'Ruminations in Bede's Account of Caedmon', *Monastic Studies*, 12 (1976), pp. 217–36

Wetherbee, W., 'Some Implications of Bede's Latin Style', *British Archaeological Reports*, 46 (1978), pp. 23–31

Wetzel, G., *Die Chronicen des Baeda Venerabilis* (Halle, 1878)

Whitbread, L., 'Bede's Verses on Doomsday: A Supplementary Note', *Philological Quarterly*, LI/2 (1972), pp. 485–6

—, 'Judgement Day II and Its Latin Source', *Philological Quarterly*, XL/2 (1966), pp. 635–56

Whitelock, D. H., 'Bede the Scholar', in *Famulus Christi*, ed. Bonner, pp. 19–39
—, 'The List of Chapter headings in the Old English Bede', in *Old English Studies in Honor of John C. Pope*, ed. R. G. Burlin and E. B. Irving Jr (Toronto, 1974), pp. 263–84
—, 'The Old English Bede', *Procedings of the British Academy*, 48 (1963), pp. 57–90
Wildhaber, R., 'Beda Venerabilis and the Snakes', in *Folklore Today: A Festschrift for Richard M. Dorson*, ed. L. Dégh, H. Glassie and F. Oinas (Notre Dame, IN, 1976), pp. 497–506
Wilson, D. M., 'The Art and Archaeology of Bedan Northumbria', *British Archaeological Reports*, 46 (1978), pp. 1–22
Wormald, P., 'Bede, 'Bede and Benedict Biscop', in *Famulus Christi*, ed. Bonner, pp. 141–69
—, "Beowulf" and the Conversion of the Anglo-Saxon Aristocracy', *British Archaeological Reports*, 46 (1978), pp. 32–95
—, 'Bede, the Bretwaldas and the Origins of the Gens Anglorum', in *Ideal and Reality in Frankish and Anglo-Saxon Society*, ed. P. Wormald (Oxford, 1983), pp. 99–129
Zaffagno, E., 'La dottrina ortografica di Beda', *Romanobarbarica*, 1 (1976), pp. 325–9

Homilies and Commentaries

Callahan, D. F., 'Ademar of Chabannes and His Insertions into Bede's Expositio Actuum Apostolorum', *Analecta Bollandiana*, 111 (1993), pp. 385–400
Douglas, I. M., 'Bede's "De Templo" and the Commentary on Samuel and Kings', in *Famulus Christi*, ed. Bonner, pp. 325–33
Gorman, M., 'The Commentary on the Pentateuch Attributed to Bede in PL 91.189–108', *Revue Bénédictine*, 106 (1996), pp. 61–108
—, 'Jacobus Pamelius (1536–1587) and a St Victor Manuscript Used for the 1563 Edition of Bede: Paris lat. 14489', *Scriptorium*, 52 (1998), pp. 321–30, pls 48–51
Hart-Hasler, J. N., 'Bede's Use of Patristic Sources: The Transfiguration', *Studia Patristica*, 28 (1993), pp. 197–204
Henderson, G., 'Cassiodorus and Eadfrith Once Again', in *The Age of Migrating Ideas*, ed. M. Spearman and J. Higgitt (Edinburgh, 1993), pp. 82–91
Holder, A. G., 'Allegory and History in Bede's Interpretation of Sacred Architecture', *American Benedictine Review*, XL/2 (1989), pp. 115–31

—, 'Bede and the Tradition of Patristic Exegesis', *Anglican Theological Review*, LXXII (1990), pp. 399–411

—, 'New Treasures for Old in Bede's "De Tabernaculo" and "De Templo"', *Revue Bénédictine*, XCIX/3–4 (1989), pp. 237–49

—, 'The Venerable Bede on the Mysteries of Our Salvation', *American Benedictine Review*, 42 (1991), pp. 140–62

Italiani, G., 'Il "De templo Salomonis" di Beda e il commento ai re di Claudio di Torino', *Immagini del Medioevo: saggi di cultura mediolatina*, ed. S. Bruni (Biblioteca del 'Centro per il collegamente degli studi medievali e umanistici in Umbria' 13) (Spoleto, 1994), pp. 179–90

Kelly, J. F., 'Bede's Exegesis of Luke's Infancy Narrative', *Mediaevalia*, XV (1993), pp. 59–70

Martin, L., 'Bede's Structural Use of Wordplay as a Way to Truth', in *From Cloister to Classroom: Monastic and Scholastic Approaches to Truth*, ed. E. Rozanne Elder (Kalamazoo, MI, 1986), pp. 27–46

—, 'The Two Worlds in Bede's Homilies: The Biblical Event and the Listener's Experience', in *De Ore Domini: Preacher and Word in the Middle Ages*, ed. T. L. Amos, E. A. Green and B. Mayne Kienzle (Kalamazoo, MI, 1989), pp. 27–40

Meyvaert, P., 'Bede's "Capitula Lectionum" for the Old and New Testaments', *Revue Bénédictine*, CV/3–4 (1995), pp. 348–80

—, 'Bede, Cassiodorus, and the Codex Amiatinus', *Speculum*, LXXI/4 (1996), pp. 827–83

Ray, R., 'What Do We Know about Bede's Commentaries?', *Recherches de théologie ancienne et médiévale*, 49 (1982), pp. 5–20

Robinson, B., 'The Venerable Bede as Exegete', *Downside Review*, CXII/388 (1994), pp. 201–26

Ward, B., '"In medium duorum animalium": Bede and Jerome on the Canticle of Habakkuk', *Studia Patristica*, XXV (1993), pp. 189–93

Hagiography

Abraham, L., 'Bede's Life of Cuthbert: A Reassessment', *Proceedings of the Patristic, Medieval, and Renaissance Conference*, 1 (1976), pp. 23–32

Baker, M., 'Medieval Illustrations of Bede's *Life of S. Cuthbert*', *Warburg and Courtauld Institute*, XLI/1 (1978), pp. 16 and 40

Berschin, W., '*Opus deliberatum ac perfectum*: Why Did the Venerable Bede Write a Second Prose Life of St Cuthbert', in *St Cuthbert, His Cult and His Community to AD 1200*, ed. G. Bonner, D. Rollason and C. Stancliffe (Woodbridge, 1989), pp. 95–102

Bolton, W. F., 'Epistola Cuthberti de obitu Bedae: A Caveat', *Medievalia et Humanistica*, 1 (1970), pp. 127–39

Bonner, G., 'The Christian Life in the Thought of the Venerable Bede', *Durham University Journal*, 63 (1970), pp. 37–55

Brinkworth, G., 'The English Mystic and the English Scholar', *L'Osseruatore Romano*, 25 (1973), p. 273

Chickering, H. D., 'Some Contexts for Bede's Death-Song', PMLA, XCI/1 (1976), pp. 91–100

Dickerson, W. W. III, 'Bede as Literary Architect of the English Church: Another Look at Bede's Use of Hagiography in the *HE*', *American Benedictine Review*, 45 (1994), pp. 93–105

Eby, J. C., 'Bringing the Vita to Life: Bede's Symbolic Structure of the Life of St Cuthbert', *American Benedictine Review*, 48 (1997), pp. 316–38

Eckenrode, T. R., 'The Venerable Bede and the Pastoral Affirmation of the Christian Message in Anglo-Saxon England', *Downside Review*, XCIX/337 (1981), pp. 258–78

Foley, W. T., 'Suffering and Sanctity in Bede's Prose Life of St Cuthbert', *Journal of Theological Studies*, L/1 (1999), pp. 102–16

Jones, C. W., 'Some Introductory Remarks on Bede's Commentary on Genesis', *Sacris Erudiri*, XIX (1970), pp. 115–98

Kirby, D. P., 'The Genesis of a Cult: Cuthbert of Farne and Ecclesiastical Politics in Northumbria in the Late Seventh and Early Eighth Centuries', *Journal of Ecclesiastical History*, XLVII/3 (1995), pp. 383–97

Lapidge, M., 'Bede's Metrical *Vita S. Cuthberti*', in *St Cuthbert, His Cult and His Community to AD 1200*, ed. G. Bonner, D. Rollason and C. Stancliffe (Woodbridge, 1989), pp. 77–93

Lauenstein, G., 'Bede: A Simple Sort of Saint', *Ligorian*, 65 (1977), pp. 44–8

Lemke, A., 'The Old English Translation of Bede's *Historia Ecclesiastica Gentis Anglorum* in Its Historical and Cultural Context', *Göttinger Schriften zur Englischen Philologie*, VIII (Göttingen, 2015)

Lozito, V., 'Le tradizioni celtische nella polemica antipelagiana de Beda', *Romanobarbarica*, 3 (1978), pp. 71–88

Lutterkort, K., 'Beda Hagiographicus: Meaning and Function of Miracle Stories in the Vita Cuthberti and the Historia ecclesiastica', in *Beda Venerabilis: Historian, Monk and Northumbrian*, ed. L. A. Houwen and A. A. MacDonald (Groningen, 1996), pp. 81–106

McCready, W. D., *Miracles and the Venerable Bede* (Toronto, 1994)

—, 'Bede, Isidore, and the Epistola Cuthberti', *Traditio*, L (1995), pp. 75–94

Mackay, T. W., 'Bede's Hagiographical Method', in *Famulus Christi*, ed. Bonner, pp. 77–92

—, ed., *A Critical Edition of Bede's 'Vita Felicis'* (Ann Arbor, MI, 1972)

Newlands, C. E., 'Bede and Images of Saint Cuthbert', *Traditio*, LII (1997), pp. 73–109

Renaud, G., and J. Dubois, *Édition practique des martyrologies de Bède, de l'Anonyme Lyonnaise et de Florus* (Paris, 1976)

Stacpoole, A., 'St Bede the Venerable, Monk of Jarrow', in *Benedict's Disciples*, ed. D. H. Farmer (London, 1980), pp. 86–104

Stancliffe, C., 'Cuthbert and the Polarity Between Pastor and Solitary', in *St Cuthbert, His Cult and His Community to AD 1200*, ed. G. Bonner, D. Rollason and C. Stancliffe (Woodbridge, 1989), pp. 21–44

Thacker, A., 'Lindisfarne and the Origins of the Cult of St Cuthbert', in *St Cuthbert, His Cult and His Community to AD 1200*, ed. G. Bonner, D. Rollason and C. Stancliffe (Woodbridge, 1989), pp. 103–22

Ward, B., *Bede and the Psalter*, Jarrow Lecture 1991 (Newcastle upon Tyne, 1991)

—, *High King of Heaven: Aspects of Early English Spirituality* (Kalamazoo, MI, 1999)

—, 'The Spirituality of St Cuthbert', in *St Cuthbert*, ed. Bonner, Rollason and Stancliffe, pp. 65–76

—, *The Venerable Bede* (London, 1990)

Weiss, J. P., 'Essai de datation du Commentaire sur les "Proverbes" (de Bède le Vénérable), attribué abusivement á Salonius', *Sacris Erudiri*, XIX (1970), pp. 77–114

West, P. J., 'Liturgical Style and Structure in Bede's Christmas Homilies', *American Benedictine Review*, XXIII/1 (1972), pp. 424–38

—, 'Liturgical Style and Structure in Bede's Homily for the Easter Vigil', *American Benedictine Review*, XXIII/4 (1972), pp. 1–8

Wilcock, P., trans., *Bede's Lives of the Abbots of Wearmouth and Jarrow* (Newcastle upon Tyne, 1973)

Wormald, P., *The Times of Bede: Studies in Early English Christian Society and Its Historian*, ed. S. Baxter (Malden, MA, 2008)

ACKNOWLEDGEMENTS

My grateful thanks to the following: Cecil Brown, Eric Cambridge, David Clifton, Rosemary Cramp, Julia Fernandez Cuesta, Michael Lloyd, Evelyn Nicholson, Rowan Williams.

PHOTO ACKNOWLEDGEMENTS

The author and publishers wish to express their thanks to the sources listed below for illustrative material and/or permission to reproduce it. Some locations of works are also given below, in the interest of brevity:

Photo Rev Peter Barham: 17; Biblioteca Medicea Laurenziana, Florence (MS Amiato 1), photos World Digital Library: 7 (f. 796v), 11 (ff. 2v–3r), 23 (f. 5r), 34 (f. IV), 35 (f. 11r), 36 (f. 221r), 37 (f. 67v), 38 (f. 218r), 39 (f. 219r), 45 (f. 7v), 46 (f. 7r); Bibliothèque municipale de Valenciennes (MS 99, f. 18r): 8; Birmingham Museum and Art Gallery (CC BY-SA 4.0): 33; © Bodleian Libraries, University of Oxford (CC BY-NC 4.0): 27 (Bodl. 819, f. 11r), 40 (MS Laud Gr. 35, f. 226v); British Library, London: 16 (Cotton MS Tiberius B V/1, f. 56v), 18 (Royal MS 13 A XI, f. 33v), 20 and 21 (Cotton MS Nero D IV, ff. 138v–139r), 25 (Cotton MS Nero D IV, f. 259r), 26 (Cotton MS Vespasian A I, ff. 30v–31r), 28 (Add. MS 89000), 29 (Add. MS 89000, f. 11r), 31 (Yates Thompson MS 26, f. 24r), 43 (Cotton MS Tiberius A XIV, f. 20v), 44 (Cotton MS Tiberius C II, f. 5v), 47 (Cotton MS Nero D IV, f. 25v), 49 (Yates Thompson MS 26, f. 62v); photos Michelle P. Brown: 3, 4, 5, 6, 9, 10, 13, 19; Cambridge University Library: 42 (MS KK.5.16, f. 128v); © Rosemary Cramp: 12; Alan Curtis/LGPL/Alamy Stock Photo: 2; Durham Cathedral Library: 14 (MS B.II.30, f. 172v), 30 (MS A.II.16, f. 37r); Everett Ferguson Photo Collection, Abilene Christian University, TX (CC BY-SA 4.0): 1, 32; Flickr: 15 (photo Michael Kooiman, CC BY-SA 2.0); Dave Head/Shutterstock.com: 24; National Library of Russia, St Petersburg: 41 (MS Lat. Q. V. I. 18, f. 26v); private collection: 50; photo © Zev Radovan/Bridgeman Images: 48; Trinity College Dublin: 22 (MS 58, f. 202v).

INDEX

Illustration numbers are indicated by *italics*